UNDERSTANDING
TRUMP

UNDERSTANDING TRUMP

NEWT GINGRICH

CENTER
STREET®

NEW YORK   NASHVILLE

Center Street
Hachette Book Group
1290 Avenue of the Americas, New York, NY 10104
centerstreet.com
twitter.com/centerstreet

First published in hardcover and ebook in June 2017
First Trade Paperback Edition: March 2018

Center Street is a division of Hachette Book Group, Inc. The Center Street name and logo are trademarks of Hachette Book Group, Inc.

The publisher is not responsible for websites (or their content) that are not owned by the publisher.

The Hachette Speakers Bureau provides a wide range of authors for speaking events. To find out more, go to www.HachetteSpeakersBureau.com or call (866) 376-6591.

Print book interior design by Timothy Shaner, NightandDayDesign.biz

Library of Congress Cataloging-in-Publication Data has been applied for.
ISBNs: 978-1-4789-2306-0 (trade paperback), 978-1-4789-2307-7 (ebook)

Printed in the United States of America

LSC-C

10 9 8 7 6 5 4 3 2 1

This book is dedicated to my wife, Callista, whose insight helped make this book possible, and whose support helped us get Donald J. Trump elected to the White House.

CONTENTS

UNDERSTANDING
TRUMP

FOREWORD

by Eric Trump

W hen my father called my family together to confirm that he would run for president, he said we would quickly learn who our real friends were. . . . He was right.

In a short time, it was clear that Newt Gingrich and his wife, Callista, were true friends of the Trump family.

When I met Newt, my first impression of him was that he was incredibly direct—a trait close to our own hearts, and a trait rarely found among the political elite. As we would soon find out, our family was about to face the toughest battle of our lives, and throughout the long, hard-fought Republican primary, and the general election, the Gingriches fought with us. Newt became more than just a surrogate; he became a friend who profoundly understood my father's tenacity and his passion for one singular goal: to Make America Great Again!

This understanding became vital. As the media and political pundits repeatedly failed to grasp my father's practical, commonsense approaches to trade, infrastructure, immigration, national security, the rebuilding of our great military, VA reform, manufacturing, jobs, taxes, health care, and so much more, Newt was able to accurately articulate my father's beliefs. His explanations were clear and compelling. At the same time, he understood how disconnected career politicians and the mainstream media had become for so many Americans seeking the American Dream—an ideal that seemed unattainable to many for the first time in history.

The opposition continued to be baffled, but that didn't matter. Newt was one of the very few who got it right, versus the tired rhetoric of the pundits, with their endless scripted lines and memorized sound bites. Newt knew the complexity of politics from the inside out, from the marble halls of Washington, DC, to the campaign trail in Middle America. He understood the soul of my father's message and the movement he created.

Understanding Trump is an inside look into possibly the greatest campaign of all time. My father gained the most primary votes of any GOP candidate in the history of the nation. He shattered voter registration records across the country. He turned traditional debates into "must-see TV." At a time when most would hold fast to a lifestyle that had become the epitome of the American Dream, my father chose to bring that dream back to those it had eluded for so long. Many books will be written by the very people who got it wrong and, quite frankly, who continue to get it wrong, but this book will stand apart because Newt was one of the very few who got it right—he is a friend and he was there from the beginning.

As to my father, there is no greater man. He is compassionate and caring. He is brilliant and strong. More than anything, he deeply loves our great country. He ran on one promise, to Make America Great Again and he is already well on his way!

WHY THIS BOOK?

t is astonishing to me, as a historian, how the elite media and much of the political establishment refuse to try to understand Donald Trump. They have been so rabidly opposed to him, so ideologically committed to left-wing values, and so terrified of the future that they haven't stopped and considered how extraordinary his success has been.

President Trump is one of the most remarkable individuals to ever occupy the White House. His set of practical business experiences—and his lack of traditional political-governmental experiences—make him a unique president.

President Trump is the first person to be elected president without first having served in public office or as a general in the military. He defeated more than a dozen other Republicans in the primary, many of whom were first-class candidates—governors, senators, business leaders, physicians, and so forth. He defeated a multibillion-dollar campaign machine for Hillary Clinton. He defeated the mainstream media, which opposed him at every turn. And he did this without an army of political consultants or spending hundreds of millions of dollars on TV ads.

The first few months of his presidency have been a whirlwind of activity, and he has already enacted enormous change. He has experienced victories as well as defeats. One thing I have learned about Donald Trump is that he learns very fast—and that the speed at which he operates optimizes his learning. So, one of the most fascinating aspects of his presidency will be how he overcomes the gaps in his knowledge of institutional government.

Trump's background could not be more different from my own. He is a very successful businessman with a knack for branding, marketing, and management. His abilities have made him both a billionaire and a household name.

I am an army brat who earned a PhD in history to learn how to help America solve its problems. I have a fair amount of political, legislative, and governmental experience that the president does not have.

President Trump and I met a few times casually before we really got to know one another—once in 1997 at a speech in New York, and in 2008 when he hosted the West Palm Beach Zoo Gala at Mar-a-Lago, his Palm Beach resort.

But we really became acquainted in 2009, after Callista and I joined Trump National Golf Club in Potomac Falls, Virginia. The club is a classic Trump success story. The bank had taken over the old Lowes Island course after it went broke. As usual, the bank was a bad manager, and the course had decayed and lost value. When the time was right, Trump stepped in and bought it at a fraction of what it was really worth. This smart business move earned Trump the only golf course on the Potomac River. It had a magnificent view from the clubhouse and enormous potential. It has been a great place for Callista and me to decompress and golf ever since.

In 2011, I was preparing to run for president, so I made a trip to Trump Tower. Donald was generous with his time, happy to discuss the campaign, and gave me several Trump ties—which he pointed out were longer than standard ties and had become the best-selling ties in America. We took a picture together and he encouraged a number of his friends to help my campaign. In the end, as a pretty good calculator of the odds, Trump endorsed Mitt Romney, but we remained friends and even campaigned together for Mitt.

By 2014, it was clear Trump was getting interested in running for president himself. We were together at a day-long conservative conference in New Hampshire sponsored by my good friend Dave Bossie of Citizens United. Trump had come up from New York in his helicopter. He made a speech, and before he left, he took Dave's kids up for a short flight. It occurred to me then that offering a helicopter ride was a method of building support that few candidates have.

Finally, in January 2015, Callista and I were in Des Moines, Iowa, for the Freedom Summit hosted by Dave Bossie and Representative Steve King of Iowa. Trump was staying at the downtown Marriott, and so were we. The night before the conference, Trump called Callista and me to ask if we could have breakfast the next day. Of course, we agreed.

It was classic Trump. He led the conversation with a couple of great real estate war stories in which he was successful. Then he got down to business. For forty-five minutes, he asked Callista and me questions about our experience running for president. Then, at the end, he asked me what I thought it would cost to run a campaign from start-up through the South Carolina primary.

I began to lay out what I thought. I told him he had to run a national campaign or the news media and voters would not take him seriously. I also told him he needed to plan to run in Iowa and New Hampshire, and I ran through various things we had learned in 2011 and 2012.

In a very Trump-the-businessman way, he said, "So, what's the bottom line?"

I thought for a minute and said he could be competitive for about $70 to $80 million.

His response was priceless. After a moment of thought, he said, "$70 to 80 million: that would be a yacht. This would be a lot more fun than a yacht!"

That's when Callista and I learned that a Trump candidacy was likely—and a Trump presidency was possible.

A few weeks after he won the South Carolina primary, I was talking to Trump on the phone. At the tail end of our conversation he jokingly said, "By the way, I know you said I needed to spend eighty million but I've only spent thirty million. I feel kind of bad."

Thus, I learned about Trump's frugality and his operating principle of "ahead of schedule and under budget."

Understanding Trump developed from all the things I have experienced since that meeting at the Des Moines Marriott as I have watched and worked with the Trump candidacy, transition, and presidency.

I hope this book will help people better understand that we may be at a watershed moment for our country. Trump represents the third—and hopefully final—great effort to break away from a half century of big-government liberalism dating back to the administration of Lyndon B. Johnson. The first big push came in 1981 when President Ronald Reagan took office. The second was in 1994, when we signed the Contract with America.

The Left and much of the media are horrified, because the age-old power structures on which they rely are specifically the ones President Trump is seeking to demolish and rebuild. Some in the establishment are confused, because Trump's campaign—and his first months in office—are totally opposite from business as usual in Washington.

His success calls into question their presumed expertise and collective worldview. But many Americans are happy. To them,

President Trump represents a force of change in Washington—the likes of which we've rarely seen in American history.

Trump's election is a tremendous opportunity to tear down the walls of big government, liberalism, and elitism and set the path for a bold new direction that is once again guided by the will of the people. His approach to politics and governing can be studied as a remarkable strategy for breaking out of the Left's intransigent power structure.

At the center of this phenomenon is President Trump, and as he learns and continues to evolve, this phenomenon will change with him. This book is a step toward understanding President Trump and his vision for the country, so we can achieve real and substantive change to make America great again for all Americans.

PART ONE

UNDERSTANDING TRUMP

It is impossible to understand President Donald J. Trump without first understanding where he came from. The knowledge he gained from decades of running a successful, world-spanning business shapes every decision he makes. The following chapters describe the most remarkable change agent to win the presidency. President Trump seems different because he is different. From building big buildings to running casinos, managing golf courses, creating the top-rated popular TV show The Apprentice, *and owning and running the Miss Universe contest, Trump has experiences and lessons from life and business no other president has had. To understand his presidency, you must understand his background.*

Anytime a meal was served when I flew with candidate Trump aboard his nicely outfitted 757, it was invariably McDonald's, Wendy's, or similar fast food. Here was this billionaire with a big plane and a professional crew, and his personal taste leaned toward main street American fast food. Friends who saw him in Palm Beach at the fancy Sunday brunch at his golf course reported the same pattern. Trump would wander through the line and get a cheeseburger and fries. It was a very practical reminder that in his heart Trump was raised as a middle-class guy from Queens—not a Manhattan socialite.

CHAPTER ONE

FROM QUEENS TO THE WHITE HOUSE

E ven today, months after Trump won the election and was sworn in as president, the news media still tries to cover him as if he were a normal politician, and his ideological opponents continue to be viciously dishonest. They are either clueless or lying. Ignore them.

America has never seen a candidate and a president like Trump. Many in the elite political class and the national media still simply do not—and cannot—grasp his methods.

Since he announced his bid for the presidency, Donald J. Trump has been misunderstood, underestimated, and misrepresented.

Think about the torrent of criticism Trump received for his announcement event at Trump Tower. In addition to the intense criticism he received for what he said about people who are in the country illegally, Trump was mocked for ad-libbing his speech, boasting about his wealth, and his theatrics.[1] The elites snubbed him, but his message resonated with normal Americans.

Trump understood that since he was running as an outsider, the more he sounded like a politician, the more it undercut his message. So he abandoned his prepared remarks and spoke extemporaneously. This choice to go without the security of written text at such a big moment was, in fact, an act of extraordinary message discipline. The pundits accused him of "rambling."

Trump also understood that most Americans believed that their voices were not being heard, that the only people whom politicians listened to were ones who could cut big checks. So Trump spent a lot of time boasting about his wealth and promising to self-finance his campaign. In the following days, much attention was paid to whether Trump was really worth $9 billion, as he claimed, or if he was worth "only" about $2 billion. The frustrated voters Trump was reaching out to heard only one word—billion. And they understood that they finally had a candidate who would not be bought.

The pundits also didn't realize that starring in and producing *The Apprentice* for over a decade had given Trump an ability to use television in ways they could not appreciate. Visuals matter more than words. Style matters more than convention. The overall impression matters more than the details.

Trump understood that he was being covered live and the cameras weren't going to turn away. So he forced the networks to cover him standing next to his supermodel wife, slowly descending the escalator into the ornate lobby of a building that had his name on it. Think about the image of success this visual conveyed to most Americans. He was communicating that the American Dream is not dead—it can be revived and made available for all once again. The pundits thought it bizarre.

Finally, Trump understood that a sizable bloc of voters was sick of the government not living up to its obligations—and the primary obligation of the federal government was to enforce the law and keep its citizens safe. These voters watched for decades as politicians promised to get serious about border security only to be bullied into inaction by the Left's accusations of racism. So, while Trump's remarks about drugs and criminals coming from Mexico was not fair to the vast majority of those here illegally who do not otherwise break the law, he sent a signal to all the voters sick of cowardice on this issue that he did not care about political correctness and could not be intimidated.

After weeks of nonstop media criticism and declarations that his announcement in mid-June had been a disaster, the first polls were released that included Trump. After one month of Trump campaigning, he was leading in an average of all the polls, and he lost the lead only for one three-day period for the rest of the primary election.[2]

You would think this would have been cause for the media and establishment voices to pause and reconsider their assumptions about Trump, but the coverage and analysis has only gotten worse from there.

If you want to understand President Trump, ignore what the political establishment and the mainstream media say about him. Instead, start with the key elements of his background that make him different from normal politicians and affect the way he operates.

QUEENS, NOT MANHATTAN

The first thing to understand about Donald Trump is even though he is associated with expensive tastes and luxury real estate, he is far more a product of Queens than of Manhattan. He grew up in a 2,000-square-foot stucco house, not Trump Tower. He also spent five years in a military prep school instead of some exclusive, private high school.

Trump's origin is important, because it explains how a billionaire could so successfully connect with the blue-collar workers who formed the foundation of his electoral victory. In *The*

Art of the Deal, he describes an upbringing that's similar to many working-class Americans:

> We had a very traditional family. My father was the power and the breadwinner, and my mother was the perfect housewife. That didn't mean she sat around playing bridge and talking on the phone. There were five children in all and besides taking care of us, she cooked and cleaned and darned socks and did charity work at the local hospital. We lived in a large house, but we never thought of ourselves as rich kids. We were brought up to know the value of a dollar and to appreciate the importance of hard work. Our family was always very close, and to this day they are my closest friends. My parents had no pretensions. My father still works out of a small, modest back office on Avenue Z in the Sheepshead Bay section of Brooklyn, in a building he put up in 1948. It's simply never occurred to him to move.

This background served him well in business before politics. It is easy to forget that while Trump's real estate and golf projects target the very wealthy, his retail and media products are aimed squarely at the middle class. Trump neckties, for instance, were at one time the best-selling ties in America. *The Art of the Deal* sold more than one million copies and, of course, *The Apprentice* was the top-rated show on television for several years.

This familiarity and comfortableness with everyday Americans also served Trump well as a builder. Trump spent hours on work sites talking to construction crews. There is no way he would be able to get useful information about how his projects were going if he came off as a stuffy elitist.

His daughter Ivanka spoke about Trump's connection with people when she introduced him at the Republican Convention.

"One of the reasons he has thrived as an entrepreneur is because he listens to everyone. Billionaire executives don't usually ask the people doing the work for their opinion of the work. My father is an exception," Ivanka said. "On every one of his projects, you'll see him talking to the super, the painter, the engineers, the electricians, he'll ask them for their feedback, if they think something should be done differently, or could be done better. When Donald Trump is in charge, all that counts is ability, effort, and excellence."

Trump also made it a habit to learn to perform every job in his hotel business. There is even a great video available online of Trump doing all the different jobs in one of his hotels, from cleaning rooms to delivering room service to walking the dog of a guest.

Donald Trump's lifetime familiarity and interest in working people—as friends, neighbors, customers, and as partners in his businesses—primed him for success as a candidate. He has a sixth sense about connecting with the American people.

For instance, Trump routinely spoke to crowds of ten to twenty thousand people, but if you watched his gestures and body language, you saw that he was connecting with audience members one by one. A thumbs up, a grin, a shout-out—all those small things let the audience know that he was genuinely engaged with them.

Trump is the same way one-on-one. Your conversation with him may be brief, but during that moment you have his undivided attention and interest. In this way, Trump reminds me of Bill Clinton—another president with a grounded middle-class background. When you are speaking with either of them, he is fully engaged in the conversation. At that moment, you are the only person who matters.

Trump's familiarity and comfortableness with working-class Americans also enables him to intuit what people care about and what they are looking for. Again, take his massive rallies as an example. The pundits routinely dismissed his crowds of ten to twenty thousand people as participants at some sort of carnival event, which wouldn't translate to people showing up to vote. They were wrong about this, obviously, but they were also wrong about why the rallies were so important.

The media coverage of Donald Trump was so unendingly negative that it could leave his supporters with the impression that they were all alone. Gathering tens of thousands of people together night after night, state by state, was proof that the movement to make America great again was the majority, and the negative, biased news media and political class were the minority.

In addition to giving strength and resolve to his supporters, I am sure the rallies were critical to maintaining Trump's spirit as well. He was able to stay in tune with, and be guided by, the will of the people during very tough moments on the 2016 presidential campaign.

I am glad to see that Donald Trump is continuing to hold rallies as president. It's important for him to see an arena full of people and be reminded that he speaks for them—that he has a moral authority that no one in the Washington bureaucracy or the elite class has.

AN ENTREPRENEUR, NOT AN ACADEMIC

Another key characteristic of Trump is that he is an entrepreneur, not an academic. He views knowledge as a tool to get something done, not as being valuable for its own sake.

There was a funny moment on the campaign when a radio host began quizzing Trump about whether he could name the leaders of different militant groups in the Middle East. Whereas a normal candidate would have tried to fudge an answer or change the topic, Trump replied bluntly, "Of course I don't know them. I've never met them. I haven't been . . . in a position to meet them. . . . If they're still there [when I become president], I will know them better than I know you."

The radio host pressed, "So the difference between Hezbollah and Hamas does not matter to you yet, but it will?"

Trump replied, "It will when it's appropriate. I will know more about it than you know, and believe me, it won't take me long."

Washington's collective elite gasped in horror. How could someone running for president be so unsophisticated? The highly educated lawyers, journalists, and bachelor of arts majors who compose the majority of Washington, DC, pride themselves on knowing lots of details about lots of things.

In Washington, if you can name the capitals of forty-two countries, you are thought of as a sophisticated person. (If you know the appropriate wine to drink in each of those countries, you are a superstar.) Whether that information is useful is of secondary concern to displaying that you know stuff, and therefore, you must belong in the club.

Trump is exactly the opposite. He makes certain he knows what he needs to know to be successful at the time he needs to know it. This is an entrepreneurial approach to knowledge rather than an academic one.

In fact, in stark contrast to the Washington intelligentsia, this is how most Americans learn—when they are motivated out of a need to accomplish something.

The type of blue-collar, practical Americans who make up Trump's base of support understand this, which is why Trump's apparent lack of knowledge about the finer details of public and foreign policy did not derail his campaign.

Roger Schank is a former professor of computer and cognitive sciences at Yale University, Stanford University, and Northwestern University. After thirty-two years of being a professor, he quit out of frustration and has been focused ever since on developing new learning systems based on delivering knowledge in an on-demand, need-to-know basis.

According to Schank, people learn by doing things that they want to do. In his study "What We Learn When We Learn by Doing," Schank says:

> To consider learning by doing from a psychological point of view, we must think more about learning in real life, which is, of course, the natural venue of learning by doing. There is, after all, something inherently artificial about school. Natural learning means learning on an "as needed" basis. In such a learning situation, motivation is never a problem, we learn because something has caused us to want to know. But school has no natural motivation associated with it. Students go there because they have no choice. The same is true of most training situations.

Schank aptly sums it up on his website: "Learning occurs when someone wants to learn, not when someone wants to teach."

Having spent much of the last two years working with Donald Trump to win the election and now succeed as president, I can personally attest that this rule applies to him.

Donald Trump can learn very quickly, but he will resist being taught anything. So, if you walk in and say, "OK, I have a thirty-minute briefing with sixteen PowerPoints," the meeting will immediately end.

Instead, if you want President Trump to know something, you have a casual chat. The times I spent on the campaign plane with him were a great illustration. Trump absorbs information all around him. He would be talking with Kellyanne Conway and me; she would be taking notes; he would be asking questions about one topic and suddenly make a connection and shift gears to a totally different idea.

In the course of those conversations, Trump would pick up all he needs to know. He then took the information, integrated it into his thinking, and began to test it. This is the point where Donald Trump learns—when he takes information and does something with it. He tries something, sees how it works, and either continues or switches to something else.

This approach has strengths and weaknesses, because he will eventually try things that don't immediately succeed or are poorly received. Our media will be rabid, because it has gotten used to slow-moving, bland, polished government that favors mediocrity over risk. Meanwhile, regular people will recognize normal human behavior. In fact, most people will consider this constant evolution and motion to be leadership.

A BUILDER, NOT A FINANCIER

After only a few days in office, President Trump was able to save American taxpayers a half-billion dollars on the disastrous F-35 Joint Strike Fighter. The fighter jet program began in 1996 and has become the country's most expensive weapons program in history. Lockheed Martin originally promised 1,013 fighters by 2016. Since then, the terms of the contract have changed several times. They've delivered fewer than 200, and the price has continued to increase. Only after Trump interceded did the company reduce the price tag. President Trump negotiated about $600 million off the most recent order for 90 jets, which brought that deal down to $8.2 billion. That brought the price per plane down to $91 million from more than $98 million, which represents about a 7 percent reduction.[3] Apply that reduction to the entire $400 billion program, and you would see a savings of $28 billion.

This practical ability to cut costs is related to another critical point of President Trump's personality. He is a builder, not a financier.

Financiers sit in offices and theorize about whether projects will be profitable. Good financiers end up with more money than they started with. Bad ones end up with less. But it's all second-order abstraction. This isn't too much different from sitting in a congressional office theorizing about whether your legislative plan is going to work.

Builders, meanwhile, must focus on more tangible metrics, ones that people in Washington have a hard time coming to grips with.

A builder, for instance, cannot claim success by writing a paper describing what the building will look like. You can't theoretically build a building, you must actually build it. If you have contracts with banks, loans in writing, and tenants ready to move in, not only do you have to have a building that stands, but you also must have it built when you say it will be built. Compare this practical, clear definition of success with that of the National Aeronautics and Space Administration (NASA), which has spent forty years studying how to get astronauts to Mars without having ever gotten us one inch closer to Mars.

Also, as a builder, you have to build something people are willing to pay for. In *The Art of the Deal*, Trump describes a situation at Trump Tower in which he had a new client who didn't like the building's entrance. The client offered to sign a long enough lease at a high enough rate that Trump agreed to redo the entrance, because it was a practical business decision.

This is opposed to typical Washington, which spends $1.7 billion a year to maintain more than 77,700 buildings that are either underutilized or completely vacant. And the 2017 budget proposed approximately $140 billion in funding for construction. Meanwhile, the Government Accountability Office reports about half of all federal offices are leased from the private sector.

I have discussed how bad federal real estate management is with the president and Jared Kushner, who is a senior adviser to and the son-in-law of President Trump. Kushner has his own very successful real estate company, and together he and the president could save billions on both construction and leasing by just applying their combined practical experience.

A PRAGMATIST, NOT AN IDEOLOGUE

Trump is also a pragmatist, not an ideologue. He is a person who gets up every day and wants to know what's really going on.

You saw this side of Trump when he accepted a phone call from the president of Taiwan in December, shortly after the election.

Those in the intelligence and foreign affairs communities protested about how damaging that call was, because decades of diplomatic tradition with China demanded that we pretend that Taiwan doesn't exist as a sovereign entity.

Trump's response—delivered, of course, with a tweet, perfectly punctured this convoluted nonsense: "Interesting how the U.S. sells Taiwan billions of dollars of military equipment but I should not accept a congratulatory call," he wrote.

In fact, the call had been planned for months. It was the perfect way for Trump to show China that he would not be bound by policies of the past. It sent Beijing a clear signal that US-China relations were going to change. Even our adherence to the One China policy, which was initiated under Richard Nixon and was officially adopted by Jimmy Carter in 1979, was on the table.

Trump's no-nonsense approach makes a lot of sense to everyone outside Washington. Trump wants to set aside the abstract establishment theories and get to what makes up the real world.

In a way, I would argue that Trump's way of thinking is a reversion to Tocqueville, Lincoln, and Washington. If you look at the original American system, it was extraordinarily fact based.

George Washington had to learn many practical things in his eight years commanding the Continental Army during the Revolutionary War. Historians have said Washington made many different mistakes once, but almost no single mistake twice. After winning the war, he was called on to preside over the Constitutional Convention to replace the failed Articles of Confederation. The delegates at Philadelphia were practical people who had managed businesses, won elections, written state constitutions, and helped win a war against the most powerful empire in the world. They brought enormous common sense to the task of developing a governing document. While they knew an enormous amount about political theory and history, they also understood the practical reality of writing a document that could be adopted and implemented. Their practical wisdom has worked now for almost 250 years. Washington then had to invent the presidency and its relation to Congress. His wise, practical steps created a framework we still use.

Similarly, Lincoln arrived as president on the eve of our deadliest war (more Americans were killed in the Civil War than in all our other wars through Vietnam combined). Lincoln's only military experience had been a few months as a volunteer in an Indian war in which he never fired a shot. Yet he checked every major book on war out of the Library of Congress and began educating himself. He tried a series of generals. He replaced them when they failed, and he promoted them when they succeeded. It was a painful, expensive, but effective way to build an army and win a war.

Tocqueville in his travels had noted this American pattern of approaching new challenges by gathering facts and then methodically trying out solutions until discovering what works. Theories based on European experiences and rules simply could not succeed in this new world.

Trump's approach is precisely the factual, trial-and-error, learn-by-doing, pragmatic model Tocqueville was describing. As a businessman, Trump is practical and willing to focus his energy and try unorthodox methods to find ways to accomplish his goals.

Take his election strategy, for instance. A normal candidate would have started by hiring a handful of consultants, raising money, and doing focus groups and polling. Trump didn't do that and relied on his instincts.

Yet you saw Trump's practical business sense overcome traditional campaign thinking during the general election. Remember, it was amateur Trump and not political veteran Hillary who figured out how to get 270 electoral votes. He stunned everyone by carrying Pennsylvania, Wisconsin, and Michigan—a feat that traditional politicos thought impossible.

His Wisconsin win alone illustrates Trump's acumen—although Reince Priebus's knowledge of the state and region was a great help. In the last week of the election, the Trump campaign decided to go to Minneapolis. The Democrats and the national media immediately thought this was a foolish, rookie mistake, because Trump had little hope of winning Minnesota. So, Hillary didn't follow him to Minneapolis.

What the Left—and apparently, the entire Washington press corps—didn't know is that Minneapolis television covers central Wisconsin. Trump got all the coverage of central Wisconsin without putting Wisconsin on the Democrats' radar. So it was the smaller, less expensive, practical Trump team that figured out how to get the keys to the American political system.

A FATHER FIRST

The best proof of Donald Trump's character and the best indicator of his many achievements can be found in the success of his children.

President Trump's children, all of whom are incredibly bright and accomplished, have a deep gratitude to their father for his attention, his guidance, his confidence in them, and the decisive role he played in educating them.

Every time I have seen President Trump with his children, I

have been impressed with how much he cares for them and how proud he is of their accomplishments.

Trump beamed with pride when he introduced his son Eric at the grand opening of his newly renovated Trump Turnberry golf resort in Scotland. It was clear this was Eric's project and achievement.

A few years ago, Callista and I talked with Trump about the great job he had done with the Trump Winery (the largest in Virginia) and Albemarle Estate, a luxury hotel at the winery outside Charlottesville. Trump promptly said, "That's Eric's job. He has been responsible for the entire project, and I think he has done really well!"

We were with the Trumps when they opened the new Trump International Hotel in Washington, DC. Donald Trump was glowing with pride about the job Ivanka had done. Anyone who's seen the Old Post Office knows that Ivanka developed a remarkably beautiful, world-class hotel.

Her father emphasized that not only did Ivanka design and implement a beautiful renovation of an old building, but she also brought it in ahead of schedule and under budget. Those are the two key characteristics that define the Trump family. They want to do things beautifully, but they also want to do them in a prudent way.

When I went out to Indianapolis to meet with then-candidate Trump about possibly becoming his vice president, he had Don Jr., Ivanka, and Eric in the room. We had an incredibly candid conversation, and it was interesting to me how much they were part of the discussion.

As I flew back home with the three of them, they generously allowed me to look at the drafts of their speeches for the GOP National Convention in Cleveland. Each was extremely personal and well done.

Don Jr., in particular, grew up working throughout the

Trump Organization, learning every level of the operation. Don Jr. and Eric have their father's complete trust and are now running a worldwide business empire on their own.

At the convention, Don Jr. said that his father has a profound ability to find the best in people and push them to excel:

> He's recognized the talent and the drive that all Americans have. He's promoted people based on their character, their street smarts, and their work ethic, not simply paper or credentials. To this day, many of the top executives in our company are individuals that started out in positions that were blue-collar, but he saw something in them and he pushed them to succeed. . . . I know he values those workers and those qualities in people because those are the individuals he had my siblings and me work under when we started out. That he would trust his own children's formative years to these men and women says all you need to know about Donald Trump.

Ivanka recalled making buildings with Legos on the floor of her father's office, while he "did the same with concrete steel and glass."

Like her eldest brother, Ivanka spoke of her father's uncanny ability to find potential in people and help them turn it into greatness. But she also shared how her father had imparted his values and willingness to dream big to his children:

> My father taught my siblings and me the importance of positive values and a strong ethical compass. He showed us how to be resilient, how to deal with challenges, and how to strive for excellence in all that we do. He taught us that there's nothing that we cannot accomplish, if we marry vision and passion with an enduring work ethic.

Eric, who spoke at the convention just before Callista and I did, highlighted philanthropy as the most profound virtue his father had bestowed on him:

> I want to thank my father over there for the life that he's provided me, for the life that he's provided my family, and the life that he's provided all of our employees around the world. I want to thank my father for the life that he's enabled me to provide for my future children as my beautiful wife, Lara, and I start thinking about that amazing chapter of our lives.
>
> To that end, I often think about the legacy I wish to leave my children, and to me, there are few things that I hold closer to my heart than charity. . . . Dad, you have once again taught us by example, you are my hero, you are my best friend, you are the next president of the United States.

Finally, his younger daughter, Tiffany, spoke in what was a heartfelt description of her father's impact on her life:

> For me, the measure of a parent is based on how they support and bolster you when you're down. A few years ago, someone very dear to me passed away, and the first call I got, as I knew I would, came from my father.
>
> Without his unwavering support and care for me during such a challenging time, I don't know how I would have made it through. As far too many know, it is the small, loving acts that help an enormous amount in times of grief.

In 2016 Barron was too young to give a speech, but I have a hunch we will hear from him during the 2020 convention.

So, if we look to his children as a barometer for the Trump presidency, we will find a president who will use the federal government to accomplish great things. President Trump will be guided by his morals and work ethic; he will promote success and charity in equal measure; and he will treat America with "unwavering support and care" during difficult times.

This is an impressive description of a father who loves his children and his country.

TRUMP DOESN'T JUST UNDERSTAND THE MEDIA, HE MASTERS IT

Trump got one of his first lessons in how the media could help him in 1980 when he was demolishing the Bonwit Teller building to construct Trump Tower at Fifty-Seventh Street and Fifth Avenue.

In *The Art of the Deal*, he describes the process of demolishing the building, which had two large Art Deco bas-relief friezes. He had told the Metropolitan Museum of Art that he would donate the friezes if they could be saved, but after his contractors told him removal would cost hundreds of thousands of dollars, he decided to break them up.

The next day, the *New York Times* ran a front-page photo of the sculptures being demolished. Trump wrote that he had immediately become "a symbol of everything evil about modern developers." More bad press followed, but Trump recognized something:

The stories that appeared about it invariably started with sentences like: 'In order to make way for one of the world's most luxurious buildings . . .' Even though the publicity was almost entirely negative, there was a great deal of it, and that drew a tremendous amount of attention to Trump Tower. Almost immediately we saw an upsurge in the sales of apartments. I'm not saying it's a good thing, and in truth it probably says something perverse about the culture we live in. But I'm a businessman, and I learned a lesson from that experience: good publicity is preferable to bad, but from a bottom-line perspective, bad publicity is sometimes better than no publicity at all. Controversy, in short, sells.

This background of wrestling in the New York media market primed him for politics.

The political media was flummoxed by Trump. They had no idea how to cover him—but he understood the media perfectly. He has used the media more effectively than any president in modern history—maybe since Abraham Lincoln.

He knew from more than a dozen years of producing *The Apprentice* that the media needs content. Papers must fill pages daily, cable news needs material hourly, Web-based news outlets need content by the minute.

So, what was a perfect day for Trump on the campaign? It was not meeting with consultants, raising money, or filming ads.

He would wake up and tweet—speaking directly to millions of his supporters. That would kick off the news day across the country. Then he would watch *Morning Joe* and call in and argue over what he tweeted. Then he would call in to *Fox & Friends* and calmly explain what he meant by the tweet. By the time he finished his 10:00 a.m. press conference—which was covered by the major media—he had saturated the news cycle all morning and set the tone for the day's news. Later that day, he would hold a twenty-thousand-person rally followed by an hour-long spot on Sean Hannity that evening.

It was routine for Trump to get millions of dollars' worth of free media attention without spending a penny. His primary opponents were drowning in his coverage. Most often, they only got attention by responding to something Trump said or did. This strategy worked through the general election—I've never seen anything like it in American politics. Hillary Clinton would speak at an event, and none of the major networks would go cover it, because they knew viewers would immediately switch over to see the next thing Trump did or said.

Meanwhile, the elite political press was reporting that Trump wasn't raising enough cash to be competitive.

AN UNSTOPPABLE WILL TO WIN

Even under intense opposition, and against apparently low odds, President Trump has an incredible will to win. I have seen it firsthand.

In mid-October 2016—just three weeks before election day—all the polls were bad. The decade-old *Inside Hollywood* tape with Trump using vulgar language had been exploited to the fullest by the elite media, and virtually everyone in the Trump campaign was jittery and frightened. I called Trump to discuss effective counterpunches, and he told me, "Just remember, I win. I always win. I am not quite sure how, but by election day we will be winning." It was a vivid reminder that this man had fought for every inch of his success in life, and he succeeded through seemingly impossible situations before.

Before he moved to Manhattan after college, he and his father had just made a $6 million profit on a large property they'd refurbished and sold in Cincinnati, Ohio. By all measures, the family business in Queens and Brooklyn was doing very well. But Trump still wanted more.

Despite Manhattan being much more expensive, Trump knew if he was going to find the type of success he craved, he would need to be where the action was.

In *The Art of the Deal*, Trump describes moving into a "dark, dingy little apartment" in Manhattan with a view of a water tank as being more exciting to him than moving into the top of Trump Tower with a view of Central Park fifteen years later.

"You have to understand; I was a kid from Queens who worked in Brooklyn, and suddenly I had an apartment on the Upper East Side," he wrote.

DREAM BIG, ACHIEVE BIG

The last main point to remember about Trump is that he believes in aiming high and accomplishing what others say is impossible.

Consider the vision he described during his first address to a joint session of Congress. President Trump set a high bar for America to meet by the time we celebrate our country's 250th anniversary in 2026:

> Think of the marvels we can achieve if we simply set free the dreams of our people. Cures to the illnesses that have always plagued us are not too much to hope. American footprints on distant worlds are not too big a dream. Millions lifted from welfare to work is not too much to expect. And streets where mothers are safe from fear, schools where children learn in peace, and jobs where Americans prosper and grow are not too much to ask.
>
> When we have all of this, we will have made America greater than ever before—for all Americans. This is our vision. This is our mission. But we can only get there together. We are one people, with one destiny. We all bleed the same blood. We all salute the same great American flag. And we all are made by the same God.
>
> When we fulfill this vision, when we celebrate our two hundred and fifty years of glorious freedom, we will look back on tonight as when this new chapter of American greatness began. The time for small thinking is over. The

time for trivial fights is behind us. We just need the courage to share the dreams that fill our hearts, the bravery to express the hopes that stir our souls, and the confidence to turn those hopes and those dreams into action.

Those who doubt that Americans can cure difficult diseases, put astronauts on other planets, or solve the problems in our welfare system in the next decade should remember that at one time, the Donald Trump presidency was regarded as impossible. In fact, from real estate to television to politics, Trump has been achieving impossible goals his entire adult life.

Given his track record, I am confident that America—with President Trump's leadership—can accomplish all those things and more.

I watched then-candidate Trump as he would shift with amazing speed. He could be flying to a rally with more than twenty thousand people, suddenly see a fact or a story and get Stephen Miller, an unsung hero of the Trump campaign, to add it to the speech as they moved toward the stadium. One of the keys to the campaign was Miller sitting at a table about ten feet behind Trump and banging away on the next speech or press release as they flew around the country. Understanding Trump requires understanding the principles by which he could shift so quickly from topic to topic.

CHAPTER TWO

THE FOUR-SIDED TABLE

One of the main reasons why the news media, pundits, and the political establishment fail to understand Donald Trump is that his philosophy does not fit into the normal conservative-liberal divide that has characterized American politics for the last twenty years.[1]

On issues like trade, foreign policy, Social Security, and Medicare, Trump has staked out positions that are at odds with decades of Republican Party establishment dogma.

One moment from the campaign sticks out to me as an example of just how different Trump is from the Republican Party of the last two decades. It was during the February 13, 2016, debate in South Carolina. Throughout the campaign, Trump had distinguished himself as a fierce critic of the Iraq War. This position may have helped him in New Hampshire, where he had just comfortably won the primary. But South Carolina is a much more conservative Republican state. There is a large military presence in the state, and George W. Bush is still very popular there. So, Trump's criticism of the former president could have been a liability. Nevertheless, during the debate, Trump criticized the Iraq War and former President Bush's leadership with as much force and clarity as he ever had before.

The next day, I called Trump and asked him why he would go out of his way to attack the former president in a state where George W. Bush was so popular. "The war was a mistake," Trump responded calmly. "Someone has to say it, and I don't care if I lose because of it."

I tell this story because Trump is often accused by the clueless news media of taking opportunistic positions. In fact, Donald J. Trump has a very clear set of guiding principles that informs the positions he takes and the way he governs as president.

These principles are best illustrated by imagining a four-sided table. One side of the table is anti-Left, one is anti-stupid, one is anti–political correctness, and the fourth is pro-American.

No matter what action Trump takes, you can be sure that it falls somewhere on the table.

ANTI-LEFT

Donald Trump is not a typical conservative. He does not approach governance through a matrix of smaller government versus bigger government or traditional values versus postmodernist values.

He is, however, emphatically anti-Left in his worldview, which naturally leads him to many conservative positions.

This outlook is not just political. Trump's entire life has been a pointed rejection of left-wing values.

The Left doesn't believe wealth is earned and views the existence of rich and poor people as evidence of America's moral failings. Trump, meanwhile, flaunts his wealth both as a measure of personal achievement and as a celebration of the greatness of America.

Trump made his money by developing real estate that caters to the ultrawealthy, and then moved into marketing books, clothing, and a television show based around his reputation for getting rich. His entire life has been dedicated to spreading an anti-Left worldview that being rich is good, success is earned, and that anyone who works hard enough can be wealthy.

This outlook toward life informs his politics and public policy.

Trump's "America First" approach to foreign policy is a rejection of the left-wing philosophy that assumes that because America is wealthy and powerful, it must be the villain.

Trump is for lower taxes because like most hard-working people, he viscerally rejects the American Left's anti-wealth, anti–individual achievement worldview.

And while Trump publicly embraced his Christianity late in life, he instinctually understands that he must fight against the Left's desire to destroy religion's vital role in American civic culture. That is why so many evangelical leaders embraced him early in the primaries, despite his history of divorce and more liberal social views. They saw him as an anti-Left warrior.

DRAIN THE SWAMP

Most vital to Trump's anti-Left positioning is his promise to "drain the swamp." A common trait of all left-wing movements throughout history has been the desire to empower an enlightened ruling class to make decisions on behalf of the people for their own good. It is believed by the Left that an educated, trained elite can make better decisions than the combined wisdom of the masses.

Trump's predilection for meritocracy—his belief that success should be earned and celebrated—is anathema to the crony capitalism and favoritism that is inevitable whenever a ruling class has too much power.

In fact, Trump has been arguing for decades that the members of the ruling class don't know what they're doing.

Here is an interview, for example, that Donald Trump did with Oprah Winfrey in 1988, where she asked him if he would ever run for president:

> I would say that I would have a hell of a chance of winning, because I think people, I don't know how your audience feels, but I think people are tired of seeing the United States ripped off.

Trump's campaign was a rejection of the ruling class of both parties, not just that of the Democrats. And because he was an outsider, he was automatically seen as the most anti–ruling class candidate in the race. This immediately made him, by definition, the most anti-Left candidate, which was precisely what Republican voters were looking for after eight years of the Obama administration's radicalism.

Trump's outsider status not only won him the primary but also enabled him to win the general election by breaking through the "blue wall" of states such as Wisconsin, Michigan, and Pennsylvania, which hadn't voted for a Republican presidential candidate since 1988. He united traditional Republican voters who believe in free markets, smaller government, and traditional morality with a newly energized group of blue-collar Democrats and disaffected rural voters who were just plain sick of the elites of both parties.

AN ANTI-LEFT PRESIDENT IN ACTION

Trump recognizes that it was voters' frustration with the ruling class that got him elected, which is why he has governed as the anti-Left president he promised to be.

Over vehement opposition from Democrats and the liberally aligned teachers' unions, Trump tapped Betsy DeVos to be his education secretary. This of course enraged the Left, because

DeVos has spent nearly her entire adult life—and millions of her own dollars—advocating against the status quo in education as a twenty-year proponent for school choice and other programs that offer children better opportunities to learn.

Trump has also vowed to eradicate the so-called Johnson Amendment, which prohibits tax-exempt religious institutions from endorsing political candidates. The Left hates the idea of repealing the amendment because its members want to silence the voice of as many Americans with traditional moral values as possible. Trump believes that the First Amendment's protections of freedom of speech and freedom of religion are not mutually exclusive.

Finally, the steps he has taken to clamp down on illegal immigration and move the United States toward a merit-based immigration system is a direct assault on the proglobalism worldview that urban elites, academia, and Hollywood have nurtured for the last two decades. Trump's belief that a nation without borders loses its authority to protect itself flies in the face of those who would like to see national identity diminished in favor of an international order based on centralized bureaucracy and a "World Court."

Trump also took a big first step at draining the swamp when he strengthened lobbying rules in his administration's ethics policy. Trump's ban bars political appointees from lobbying the departments they lead for five years after leaving their posts with the administration. Further, it bars any appointee from lobbying the Trump administration, and it disallows officials from ever lobbying on behalf of a foreign government. As he sat among many of his appointees before he signed the policy, Trump said, "Most of the people standing behind me will not be able to go to work" after leaving his administration.[2]

Hopefully, Donald Trump is just warming up. There is a lot of swamp to drain.

ANTI-STUPID

Trump's hostility to the left-wing ruling class is closely connected to the second side of the four-sided table illustration: anti-stupid.

The members of the ruling class justifies their power and station by claiming they are experts, that modern life is too complicated for ordinary citizens, and that a technocratic class operating bureaucratically needs to be given great power to manage the economy and almost every aspect of our lives.

Trump understands that the most effective way to attack the ruling class is to puncture its justification for power. So, one of his favorite tactics is to accuse the ruling class of stupidity. And the fact that Trump is an executive and has decades of experience finding and fixing instances of stupidity in large operations gives him the legitimacy to do so.

Here is Trump in his announcement speech discussing bad trade deals and economic policies:

> Right now, think of this: We owe China $1.3 trillion. We owe Japan more than that. So, they come in, they take our jobs, they take our money, and then they loan us back the money, and we pay them interest, and then the dollar goes up so their deal's even better.
>
> How stupid are our leaders? How stupid are these politicians to allow this to happen? How stupid are they?[3]

And later:

> Free trade can be wonderful if you have smart people, but we have people that are stupid. We have people that aren't smart. And we have people that are controlled by special interests. And it's just not going to work.

Here he is at a rally in Washington, DC, opposing the Iran

deal: "We are led by very, very stupid people. . . . We cannot let it continue."[4]

And here is how he described past US relations with Russia at a press conference in February 2017:

Hillary Clinton did a reset, remember? With the stupid plastic button that made us all look like a bunch of jerks. Here, take a look. [The Russian Foreign Minister] looked at her like, What the hell is she doing with that cheap plastic button?

In addition to using an anti-stupid posture on offense, he uses it on defense to parry attacks against him from the ruling class.

One of the strangest and most dishonest lines of attack against Trump during the election and his presidency has been accusations—supported only by circumstantial evidence and innuendo—that he is somehow unduly influenced by Russia. This was yet another attempt by the Left to delegitimize his election.

In January, before he took office, Trump was facing another barrage of criticism from his opponents in the establishment and mainstream media. They were desperately trying to create the impression that Trump's position that the United States should pursue better relations with Russia to fight ISIS was inappropriate.

The unspoken assumption behind those attacks was that the desire for better relations with Russia was so ridiculous or unwise that there had to be some nefarious reason for it.

In a series of tweets, Trump punctured this conventional wisdom of the ruling class:

Having a good relationship with Russia is a good thing, not a bad thing. Only "stupid" people, or fools, would think that it is bad! We have enough problems around the world without yet another one. When I am President, Russia will respect us far more than they do now and both countries will, perhaps, work together to solve some of the many great and pressing problems and issues of the WORLD!

REGULATIONS: THE PINNACLE OF STUPID IN DC

Trump's position as an outsider and an executive is also very effective when describing foolish and destructive regulations.

Here he is, a few weeks into his presidency, describing the legal barriers to letting patients who have exhausted approved treatment options from trying drugs not yet approved by the Food and Drug Administration (FDA):

> One thing that's always disturbed me, they come up with a new drug for a patient who is terminal, and the FDA says, "We can't have this drug used on the patient." But they say, "But the patient within four weeks will be dead." They [FDA] say, 'Well, we still can't approve the drug and we don't want to hurt the patient." But the patient is not going to live more than four weeks.[5]

Donald Trump was absolutely right to highlight the stupidity and cruelty of US drug policy with regard to terminally ill patients. Take the case of Abigail Borroughs.

Abigail was nineteen years old when a cancerous sore developed in her mouth. She did everything right, quickly sought treatment and had the sore removed. But despite a positive prognosis from her doctor, new tumors appeared, and things got worse. After finishing her first round of chemotherapy and radiation, the doctors found that the cancer had spread into her lungs and stomach. Her doctors had done all they could, so Abigail turned to cancer specialists at Johns Hopkins.

Doctors there knew about two drugs that could have potentially helped Abigail. They were her only real hope at defeating the cancer. The problem was, even though the drugs had cleared early trials that indicated they were safe for use, it would be years before the medicines were fully cleared by the FDA, which approves nearly every medical product in the United States for safety and effectiveness. Abigail did not have years. She was dying of cancer.

Abigail tried to enroll in clinical trials for the drug, but her condition didn't meet the exacting standards. Then she was turned down for "compassionate use"—a last-ditch effort in which the FDA allows a drug maker to give drugs to a patient who has no other options. In this case, the company denied the request, likely to protect the drug's track record as it lurched through the multimillion-dollar FDA approval process.

One of the drugs Abigail was requesting was called Erbitux. It was invented in 1983, when she was a toddler. The FDA didn't clear the drug for late-stage head and neck cancer like Abigail's until 2011, ten years after she died at age twenty-one. It took twenty-eight years to approve. How many Americans have died unnecessarily as a result of this one federal bureaucracy?

The FDA and the medical treatment bureaucracy denied medicine to a young woman who was dying because it might not be safe. This is what happens when health care decisions are dictated by distant number crunchers in Washington who have never met the patient and have no personal grounds for compassion, rather than by medical professionals who know and care passionately about their patients.

That is why President Trump called for streamlining the drug approval process at the FDA during his first address to a joint session of Congress. He told the story of his guest, Megan Crowley, who was diagnosed with Pompe disease, an illness that impairs muscle function, when she was only fifteen months old. Trump told the story of her father, who founded a company to look for a cure, which ultimately saved Megan's life.

"Megan's story is about the unbounded power of a father's love for a daughter," Trump said.

> But our slow and burdensome approval process at the Food and Drug Administration keeps too many advances, like the one that saved Megan's life, from reaching those in need. If we slash the restraints, not just at the FDA but across our government, then we will be blessed with far more miracles just like Megan. In fact, our children will grow up in a nation of miracles.

The world is currently experiencing an explosion of new scientific breakthroughs and technology that could dramatically improve people's lives. One of the biggest governing challenges we face is how to prevent bureaucracy and regulation from standing in the way of that progress. It is encouraging to see that President Trump understands this and we should expect more action is coming. In March, Trump tapped Jared Kushner to lead an "American Innovation" office at the White House, which will look at how to reorganize and streamline government for the twenty-first century.

Because he was a builder before becoming a candidate, President Trump is also very effective at describing how irrational and destructive environmental review and permitting regulations block construction—in particular commercial infrastructure projects. This is what he said in January:

> I have people that tell me they have more people working on regulations than they have doing product and it is out of control. It has gotten out of control. I'm a very

big person when it comes to the environment. I have received awards on the environment. But some of that stuff makes it impossible to get anything built.

During his first week in office, President Trump expedited unending environmental reviews for important government and commercial infrastructure projects, which allowed bridge and highway builders to hire workers sooner and complete projects more quickly for less money—a perfectly Trumpian concept that is completely the opposite of business as usual in Washington.

But Trump clearly plans to be much more aggressive. In April, at a town hall event with CEOs, President Trump pulled out a chart that was taller than he was, to explain the ten- to twenty-year process of interacting with the seventeen different federal agencies it requires to build a highway. He is setting the stage for his proposed $1 trillion infrastructure bill to have a major deregulation component.

ANTI–POLITICAL CORRECTNESS

Part of being anti-Left and anti-stupid means opposing political correctness—the third side of the Trump four-sided table illustration.

Certainly, it is important to be polite, and nobody should think that using racial or ethnic slurs is acceptable. But political correctness has morphed from a desire to avoid needlessly offending people to a tool of the Left to marginalize and vilify reasonable Americans who disagree with the elite liberal agenda.

No issue better illustrates the Left's bullying tactics than that of President Trump's effort to enact a pause in immigration from certain unstable, war-torn Muslim countries until a security review could be completed. This sensible policy, put in place after high-profile terrorist attacks in Europe had been carried out by recent immigrants from these areas, could not be debated on the merits by those on the Left, so they resorted to slander, and accused its supporters of bigotry.

Keep in mind that the Obama administration first said these nations were dangerous. But the propagandists in the media had already decided the order was a ban on Muslims. For days, the only stories you saw on TV or in print were about downtrodden refugees or travelers who were enormously inconvenienced because they had to stay at airports or cancel plans.

Here were the problems with the media's logic: First, given the choice of inconveniencing a noncitizen or endangering an American, Trump—and most Americans—would favor inconvenience every time.

Second, it simply was not a Muslim ban. This was a perfect example of the media not allowing the facts to get in the way of a good story. The largest Muslim population in the world is in Indonesia. Pakistan and India have the next-largest Muslim populations. So, the three largest Muslim-majority countries in the world are not on the list—nor are other Middle Eastern Muslim-majority countries.

Still, a federal court in Seattle put a hold on the ban while the Ninth Circuit Court of Appeals heard arguments from the Trump administration and opponents. Then, after the Trump administration revised the order, a judge in Hawaii again blocked the national security effort. It will be interesting to see how President Trump responds.

In this environment, it is easy to see why Donald Trump's rejection of political correctness is appealing to so many Americans. The backlash has been brewing for decades.

The term "political correctness" came into popular use in America in the late 1980s and early 1990s, as we realized the liberal academic elite at many of our colleges and universities were indoctrinating a generation of young adults with left-wing ideals.

The author and academic Allan Bloom discussed this in his 1987 book, *The Closing of the American Mind.*

Bloom explained that the education system once taught students the meaning of being American by focusing on accepting each person's natural rights—those inalienable human rights bestowed by God. In doing that, we "found a fundamental basis of unity and sameness" because race, class, religion, and other cultural differences "dim when bathed in the light of natural rights, which give men common interests and make them truly brothers."

Bloom warned that this natural rights–focused education was being replaced by a doctrine of openness, which abandons the idea that natural rights unify communities. The openness doctrine dictates everyone must accept all cultures, and "there is no enemy other than the man who is not open to everything."

Of course, learning about other cultures and ideas is an important hallmark of education, but as George H. W. Bush said to students at the University of Michigan in 1991, "although the movement arises from the laudable desire to sweep away the debris of racism and sexism and hatred, it replaces old prejudices with new ones. It declared certain topics off-limits, certain expression off-limits, even certain gestures off-limits."

Americans don't like being told what they are allowed to say, think, and do. Frustration with political correctness was part of the political environment in 1994, which led to the first Republican majority in the House of Representatives in forty years, and my becoming Speaker of the House.

I would argue that a similar event has just happened with the election of Donald Trump. The Left, the media, and the political establishment were horrified by the results of the 1994 and 2016 elections. They should examine their role in creating a politically correct bullying culture that helped lead to those results.

PC AND CONVENTIONAL WISDOM

There is also another form of political correctness that is just as insidious, and that is adhering to groupthink and never bucking the conventional wisdom.

As an outsider in politics, Donald Trump is especially effective at busting up conventional wisdom. The most obvious example is how he ran his campaign. Despite having enormous resources to bring to bear, Trump never went the typical consultant-dominated route of hiring a huge staff and buying lots of television time. Instead, Trump kept a very lean staff and relied on earned media to drown out all the television attack ads aimed at him. Trump believed that seeing him personally and unedited on television would wipe out most of the damage from negative attack ads. He turned out to be right.

This ability to puncture conventional wisdom is important because much of the conventional wisdom in Washington is dumb. The way things are done are a product of habit rather than utility, and sustained by an echo chamber of establishment talking heads spouting nonsense on television, radio, and other sources.

A perfect example was the ridiculous uproar when it came out that Trump had decided to stop receiving daily intelligence briefings, opting instead for briefings two to three times per week. Washington was beside itself from this break from tradition. Didn't Trump care about national security?

Trump broke up this nonsense quickly, explaining that the briefing was so repetitive that it was a waste of time. His instructions were to brief him only on new developments. Of course, this model makes more sense than the most powerful person in the world spending an hour a day being told the same things he was told yesterday.

The problem of the commander in chief and senior military leaders drowning in detail affects far more than just intelligence briefings.

The way we have handled ISIS is a perfect example. The National Command—which includes the highest-ranking members of our military and the president—has focused far too much on ISIS without dealing with the larger issue of radical Islamic terrorism. We've done this for years. First we fought Al-Qaeda, then the Iraqi insurgency, and now we are focusing on ISIS. We have been fighting terrorists one front at a time, and the result is a game of Whac-A-Mole that has done nothing to end global radical Islamic terrorism or stabilize the Middle East.

By way of comparison, imagine if we had treated the invasion of Guadalcanal in 1942 the way we have dealt with ISIS. We never would have won World War II. In World War II, we thought globally. The invasion of Guadalcanal was handled by forces and commanders on the ground in communication with the top brass, but the National Command was worried about bigger-picture problems. For example, the number of oil tankers and freight ships available in 1942 was absolutely critical. That was worth the National Command focusing on. And when it was solved, the National Command moved on to tackling the next global problem. We didn't try to micromanage ground operations from Washington, DC. Fortunately, the highest levels of our military then thought globally about all fronts of the war and let commanders on the ground deal with day-to-day conditions.

President Trump must resist the news media's and the political establishment's demand that he drown himself in unnecessary details. Failure to do so will paralyze his presidency.

This was a principle I first learned by observing President Reagan. I eventually developed a metaphor called the "antelope and chipmunk" theory of leading to describe his approach, and it is one that I have shared with President Trump and his team.

It goes like this: The president must be a lion. Lions cannot hunt chipmunks, because even if they catch them the lions will starve to death. Instead, lions must hunt antelopes—big animals—to survive.

President Reagan was a lion. He was focused on three things: defeating the Soviet Union, growing the American economy, and reviving the American spirit. Those were his antelopes, and he refused to get bogged down in chipmunks.

Every time a chipmunk ran into his office, President Reagan would listen patiently, and then say, "Have you met my chief of staff?" That's how Jim Baker amassed the largest chipmunk collection in the world.

I have been encouraged to see that President Trump, as commander in chief, is focused on the antelope and is not getting drowned by chipmunks. One of his first actions as president was to give more authority to military commanders to conduct strikes against terrorist targets in certain areas. He knows that terrorists move around constantly, so speed is of the essence. He doesn't need to add an extra layer of decision making. Instead, President Trump set a clear strategic directive to be more aggressive in hunting down targets and is letting his military commanders handle the tactics.

Meanwhile, when President Trump uses his voice to discuss national security, he has mostly kept the focus on the big picture—defeating radical Islamic terrorism, as well as standing up for American values. We can expect to see a much faster, operationally flexible and strategically focused national security apparatus under President Trump.

PRO-AMERICAN

Donald Trump is anti-Left, anti-stupid, and anti-PC. This allows him to be aggressively pro-American, the final part of the four-sided table that explains Donald Trump's philosophy.

The clearest expression of Trump's pro-American stance is his America-first approach to foreign policy and trade.

As soon as he took office, President Trump began work securing our border and returning the rule of law to our immigration system.

It was baffling. Even if we set the threat of terrorism aside, heroin and opioid abuse is devastating communities across the nation. And the US Drug Enforcement Administration has said most of the drugs in the United States have entered the country by being smuggled across the southern border. What reasonable person would say signing an executive order to hire up to ten thousand more US Immigration and Customs Enforcement officers and up to five thousand more US Border Patrol agents was a bad idea?

President Trump also signed orders to cut federal funding to so-called sanctuary cities like Chicago and Los Angeles, where instead of immediately turning criminal aliens who are released from police custody over to immigration officials, the crooks are let back out onto the streets.

Leaders in cities granting asylum to such criminals immediately doubled-down on protecting criminal aliens from law enforcement.

"We're very clear about our values and very clear about our priorities," said Chicago's mayor, Rahm Emanuel, according to a *Chicago Sun-Times* article on March 28.

Chicago had over seven hundred murders and over four thousand shootings in 2016. Given the carnage, I am curious what the people of Chicago think about Mayor Emanuel prioritizing the imagined rights of criminal noncitizens over public safety.

PRO-AMERICAN SPIRIT

The most important part of Trump's pro-American principle—which has received almost no media coverage—is his desire to make America great again for all people and heal racial divides here at home.

You can see Trump's desire to unify the country in a speech he gave as a candidate in October 2016 in Charlotte, North Carolina, entitled "A New Deal for African Americans."

African American citizens have sacrificed so much for this nation. They have fought and died in every war since the Revolution, and from the pews and the picket lines they have lifted up the conscience of our country in the long march for Civil Rights. . . . I have heard and have listened to the concerns raised by African American citizens about our justice system, and I promise that under a Trump administration the law will be applied fairly, equally and without prejudice. There will only be one set of rules—not a two-tiered system of justice.

This is just the beginning. Because I will never, ever take the African American community for granted. It will be my mission to prove to this country that yesterday does not have to be tomorrow. The cycle of poverty can be broken, and great new things can happen for our people.

Trump's final message in Charlotte perfectly framed his pledge: "Together, we will have a government of, by and for the people. And we will make America great again for all Americans."

He gave a similar speech a month earlier in Detroit, Michigan.

These speeches were part of a pattern in which Trump actively met and communicated with members of African American communities. The elite media largely ignored these two speeches, because they had been convinced by past polls that Trump would not make great gains with black voters.

But what the media missed was the clear message Trump sent to all Americans: that he wanted to unify the country by directly appealing to African Americans. By speaking so openly and candidly with black voters about their concerns and the issues that impact their communities, Trump also blunted most of the left-wing fear tactics Democrats have used for decades with African American voters. These two speeches made it much more difficult for the Left to demonize Trump to turn black voters against him in states where he was competing with smaller margins.

He carried on his message of unity in his inaugural address, saying, "It is time to remember that old wisdom our soldiers will never forget: that whether we are black or brown or white, we all bleed the same red blood of patriots, we all enjoy the same glorious freedoms, and we all salute the same great American flag."

With these words, he flipped the Left's narrative that patriotism and nationalism are akin to racism. To Trump, it is impossible to be both patriotic and racist, because of our shared love of America. He continued this line of thought:

> And whether a child is born in the urban sprawl of Detroit or the windswept plains of Nebraska, they look up at the same night sky, they fill their heart with the same dreams, and they are infused with the breath of life by the same almighty Creator. So, to all Americans, in every city near and far, small and large, from mountain to mountain, and from ocean to ocean, hear these words: You will never be ignored again.

These are clear messages that seek to uplift and bring together everyone in America. It doesn't get more pro-America than that.

My wife, Callista, and I belong to Trump National Golf Club in Virginia. It is a beautiful property along the Potomac River. Before he was a candidate, every once in a while, Trump would helicopter in from New York, play a round, and then have dinner. He would often be alone and invite us to join him. He would ask how the club felt to us as members. What did we think of the new layout? How was the kitchen? Were the staff friendly and responsive? He was very proud of Trump National, and he would discuss his vision to create a challenging course that would attract PGA competitions. He invested millions in redoing the entire golf course to make its holes more competitive and to ensure great views for television coverage. The course now has the PGA Senior Championship for 2017. Every time we saw Trump at the club, he wanted it to be a great club. He loves it. Making America great again is a natural outgrowth of how Trump thinks of everything he does.

CHAPTER THREE

WINNING, BIG LEAGUE

Understanding Trump's philosophy will get you only so far. To really grasp Trump, you must understand his doctrine and his psychology—the collection of attitudes and methods he uses to achieve success. That doctrine is fast, aggressive, disruptive, and confounding to the unwary.

He places a greater emphasis on speed than mistake avoidance, sets big goals and remains flexible. He capitalizes on his opponents' weaknesses and works relentlessly to diminish or avoid their strengths. From the outside, it appears chaotic, but by all measure—Trump's success in the real estate, hotel, television, and golf course businesses, and his winning the presidency—the Trump Doctrine is effective.

Trump does not believe it is possible to plan so much that you completely avoid mistakes, and to him it's a waste of time to try. This is the total opposite of the way bureaucratic Washington works. Look at NASA as an organization. They've become so good at planning to get to Mars that by the time its astronauts are ready to fly there, it will probably be easier just to stack all their plans and climb.

Part of NASA's problem is that it has lost the ability to make mistakes. The Wright Brothers failed five hundred times over five years before they flew. NASA would have cut them off around the third failure. It's a fundamentally different model. The Trump model is to move very rapidly, and if you make a mistake, figure it out and respond so quickly that it doesn't hurt very much.

During Trump's first address to a joint session of Congress, he laid out a vision to put "American footprints on distant worlds." That won't happen without big changes at NASA, and I predict President Trump will make them.

When he first took office, Washington, DC, was not ready for his Manhattan pace. The media and the establishment wailed that he had brought too much chaos and disorder to the White House. What he really brought was a long-overdue disruption and the start of clear progress.

What no one in the elite class seems to understand is that Trump's fast-paced style is an important part of his strategy to break up decades-old power structures in Washington and get things done. During the campaign, we would discuss the importance of the first few days of his presidency. Trump knew from taking over properties and projects that setting the pace and the intensity from the very beginning was vital. Six months before the election, he was already thinking about a series of executive orders for the first few days. He also knew from the reaction of his crowds that his supporters wanted immediate action.

Trump must keep going at breakneck speed to keep his opponents on the Left and in the media off balance. If he slows down to let the elites catch up, he will lose some of his advantage. That must not happen, because only by moving faster than the entrenched system will Trump be able to make America great again—especially for the millions of American Trump supporters the Left and the establishment had happily forgotten.

OODA—LOOP: BRINGING JET FIGHTER TACTICS TO WASHINGTON

Trump operates more like an entrepreneur launching a start-up than a traditional executive. This means he is constantly looking for the next opportunity, acting quickly, and continually assessing results. His model reinforces success, starves failure, and requires very fast feedback. This is similar to what the military calls an OODA loop, which stands for observe, orient, decide, act, and then loop back to observe again. The theory was developed by US Air Force Col. John Boyd, a celebrated military strategist who studied fighter jet combat, specifically how the American F-86 Sabre fought Soviet-made MiG-15s in Korea.

The first step is to observe what's going on, then quickly orient yourself to the situation, make a decision about what to do, act faster than your opponent, and then pivot back to observing. By doing this repeatedly, you will inevitably build up a momentum that your opponent can't cope with. Since Boyd developed it for the military, the strategy has been applied to business, litigation, law enforcement—and now Trump has applied it to politics. I don't know if Trump learned this method during the five years he was in the New York Military Academy or if he just picked it up after years of sparring over New York real estate, but he clearly applies it.

You saw this on the campaign, when he was constantly outmaneuvering his opponents and setting the tone of the entire race. He would go to rallies, see what topics evoked the most reaction from the crowds, orient his focus to those issues, decide what his best message was based on those reactions, and then act on them. Most often, that action would be in the form of a tweet designed to capture the news media's attention. Then he would immediately switch back to observing to see how his tweets or comments were perceived by his supporters.

He could never have been this nimble if he had had an army of consultants and policy advisers attempting to direct his every move. Normally, a candidate may have a good idea about a reaction to some event, so he will tell one of his consultants, and that person will take it to the team to ponder. Each member of the team has to make his or her own edits—because that's what consultants are paid for. By the time the team-approved response is ready, the moment is gone—and it looks nothing like what the candidate originally wanted to say. Trump bypassed all that with his lean staff. He was his own primary consultant.

This method also helped him decide not to use paid TV advertising. Consultants love TV advertising because they often get a percentage of the placement. Jeb Bush's consultants made substantial money placing ads that didn't work. Hillary's consultants must have made tens of millions of dollars. There is no penalty for incompetence or malpractice among political consultants.

Since Trump was his own consultant and he was paying for a substantial part of his own campaign, he had no reason to be stuck with obsolete, ineffective techniques. He decided paid television ads were expensive and inauthentic. He concluded that his personal appearances were far more effective than paid ads. He saw Facebook and Twitter working. So, he decided to use Facebook and Twitter as his main vehicles for media outreach. He then trained the media to cover all his tweets, and suddenly he was getting millions in earned coverage at no cost.

The OODA loop also enabled Trump to identify and avoid his opponents' strengths and exploit their weaknesses. In the early days of the campaign, when he was learning how to be a candidate and learning how to debate, you could see him doing all this instinctively. He would watch each of his opponents in the debates and measure them. He was very quiet most of the time. He watched all the candidates on the stage, and also the media. The whole time, he was observing each of his competitors and thinking, "How do I avoid the thing you're really good at? What's your weakness? How do I go after it?"

As president, he has been following the same order of operations. As soon as he took office, he took action by signing a slew of executive orders. These were based on what he had observed over the course of his campaign. Now, as president, he is running many different OODA loops at the same time for each of his orders and legislative efforts—border protection, ending sanctuary cities, tax reform, and so forth.

He observes, orients, makes a decision, and acts. And he has also combined this effective military strategy with another talent from his business expertise—branding.

BRANDING, NOT ATTACKING

Branding is different from attacking. Branding is about establishing an identity. It can be an incredibly effective tool politically. The Left has maintained the support of minorities—despite its being utterly incompetent and doing nothing to help them— simply because it has worked so hard at branding Republicans and conservatives as racists.

Being a businessman, Trump understands branding better than most people in the world—and definitely better than his sixteen Republican primary opponents did. Trump's first big success was taking out Jeb Bush, and he did it entirely by giving him a brand. Jeb had huge amounts of money. He had all of his father's and brother's network. He had the natural bias of the elite media. He was considered the de facto Republican nominee before the primaries even started.

So how did Trump take out Jeb Bush? He called him "low energy." Jeb is a good friend of mine, and he was a very accomplished governor who enacted real reform. But thanks to Jeb's laid-back manner, the description stuck to him like glue. (Remember how closely Trump observed all his primary opponents.)

Trump kept it up over the course of the primary. It became a fact by repetition.

It got to a point where Trump got inside Jeb's head and Jeb was literally running around in New Hampshire, so people could see he was not low energy. But by that time, Trump had so completely dominated media coverage of the race, and had so constantly repeated the "low energy" brand he'd made for Jeb, that there was nothing Jeb could do. Once Jeb was no longer a direct threat, Trump moved on to his other opponents—Little Marco and Lyin' Ted. He used the same strategy, and it worked. Trump feeds success, so by the time the general election came, Hillary Clinton became Crooked Hillary.

But Trump didn't use branding only against his opponents, he used it to sell his message and his candidacy. Think about the red hats. *Dilbert*'s creator, Scott Adams, pointed this out in his blog—which I read regularly. Any conventional politician running a campaign would have put his or her name on the hats. Trump didn't. He knew people already knew his name. Trump was associated with high-end hotels and expensive real estate. He knew that was not the brand he needed to win the trust and support of middle-class Americans. He also knew that patriotism was the core American value that unites us as a people. So his hats said "Make America Great Again." That phrase took hold, striking a chord with a huge swath of the country, and expressed the core of Trump's campaign perfectly. It wasn't about Donald J. Trump, it was about making America great. That's what effective brands do.

But part of Trump's challenge is protecting his own brand.

The Left, the establishment, and the media don't, can't, or won't understand Trump, so they spread fictions. One of the most dishonest has been the repeated accusations that Trump, even now that he has removed himself from his business, is profiting from being president.

After spending a significant amount of time with Trump before and during the election, I can see clearly that Trump is doing this only for the good of the American people. He's a multibillionaire. His life would have been much easier, much less stressful, and much more lucrative had he stayed in business and out of the political arena.

This being said, Trump and his team will need to combat this narrative from the Left very aggressively, because it could significantly undercut his appeal to the millions of Americans sick of crony capitalism and insider deals who elected him.

ALWAYS ON OFFENSE

Trump's military-like doctrine of maneuvering and constant assessment also means Trump is always on the offensive. No matter what happened in the campaign, you never saw Trump making excuses or explaining himself. If he got into a tough spot, he immediately started attacking in another direction.

I explained it this way in a speech at the National Defense University after the election: If you look at the Army of Northern Virginia, which was the main Confederate battle force in the American Civil War, and the Israeli army, you'll see that they have the same doctrine. If you are surprised, one-third of your forces go into defense, two-thirds go on counterattack. You never give up the initiative. That's perfectly Trumpian. Trump's core model is, you hit me, I hit back, and I hit harder than you hit me. He learned this tactic as a businessman battling with the New York media. If one of the New York media outlets wrote a critical story, Trump responded bluntly and immediately to ensure he was in the next edition. He was always attacking, always involved, always at the center of attention.

He applied the same principle to politics. When one of his primary opponents or a pundit attacked him in a news article or a TV interview, Trump let no slight go unanswered. And his opponents learned quickly that if they decided to take on Trump, they would need to be ready to go twelve rounds. None of them were, and that's part of the reason Trump won.

During the heat of the primary season, Bill O'Reilly asked me one night why the other Republican candidates weren't attacking Trump. Bill rightly pointed out that Trump was clearly the front-runner, and the other candidates needed to attack him if they had any chance of winning. I explained to him that they were all afraid. Donald Trump is the grizzly bear in *The Revenant*. If you get his attention, he will wake up, walk over, bite your face off, and sit on you. The other candidates watched him do that to their competition and decided they'd rather let the bear eat someone else.

Trump's military-like "always on offense" doctrine may explain why the men and women of the armed forces supported him three to one over Hillary Clinton.[1] They recognized that he would make a strong commander in chief—especially against the particularly brutal forces that threaten the United States.

Now, Trump's practice of always being on the offense and always pushing the system to accommodate him does have its downsides. Look at the way Trump announced the ninety-day travel ban from certain countries during his first month in office. Without giving the media—or even many people in his administration—much lead time, Trump held a press conference and signed an executive order implementing the ban over a weekend. I think if he had waited four to five days, thought it through, talked with staff, and fully explained it to the press and the public, the announcement and the ban would have been more understood and better received. This is exactly the approach he took for the revised travel ban, which drew much less public criticism, even if it is still encountering legal challenges.

But Trump has an enormous agenda—trade, border security, defeating radical Islam, deregulation, and more. If he takes the conventional, cautious Washington approach to everything he is trying to do, he'll complete about 10 percent of his goals.

That's not how Trump does anything. So, he's rushing the system every day. He's trying to hit Washington in five, six, seven different directions. He signed the travel ban, then his order to end sanctuary cities, then his order to speed up EPA reviews on important infrastructure projects, then his order to approve the Keystone XL and Dakota Access pipelines. This caused all the various parts of the Left to run in different directions. Sure, the travel bans have been stopped by the courts—for now—but few of his other orders have been halted.

I tell everybody who works for me that I much prefer errors of commission rather than errors of omission. When in doubt, do something. But keep moving. Trump has a similar bias. He criticizes mistakes but he very seldom fires people over them.

The great challenge of those in the Trump-Pence administration is to get up every morning and remember that they are not here to accommodate Washington, they are here to kick over the table. They will need to continue to push the system until it changes to fit their goals.

AHEAD OF SCHEDULE, UNDER BUDGET

Another part of Trump's doctrine, which is in some ways driven by his desire to move quickly, is to set a goal of being "ahead of schedule, under budget." This was critical to his business as a real estate developer, because delays cost money.

One of the best illustrations of Trump's ability to keep productivity high and costs low is a story from his book, *The Art of the Deal*.

New York City has a skating rink in Central Park called Wollman Rink, and it had a problem in 1980—it was no longer making ice. The City of New York undertook a project to fix the skating rink. After six years and $13 million in wasted taxpayer money, the rink was still not making ice.

Trump had a town house that had a view of the Wollman Rink, and he got sick of looking at the iceless skating rink. So he got into a print war with then-mayor Ed Koch. Trump started writing letters to the editors of various newspapers in New York calling out Koch and the city for failing to fix Wollman Rink. Trump had a keen insight for how to get the city's attention, as he wrote in *The Art of the Deal*:

If there's one thing I've learned from dealing with politicians over the years, it's that the only thing guaranteed to force them into action is the press–or more specifically, fear of the press. You can apply all kinds of pressure, make all sorts of pleas and threats, contribute large sums of money to their campaigns, and generally it gets you nothing. But raise the possibility of bad press, even in an obscure publication, and most politicians will jump. Bad press translates into potential lost votes, and if a politician loses enough votes, he won't get reelected. If that happens, he might have to go out and take a nine to five job. That's the last thing most politicians want to do.

Mayor Koch got so tired of Trump's attacks in the news media he finally challenged Trump to fix the rink himself. The mayor turned the rink over to him, and gave him six months and $3 million to fix it.

Trump knew he had to deliver, because he had made such a fuss in the paper. He wrote about having to pack his bags and move to Argentina if he ended up one dollar over budget or one day late, because Koch and the rest of the city would never let him live down the failure to fix the rink after all he had said.

The next thing Trump wrote in the book is one of the key things that made me fascinated with him and motivated me to write this book. He acknowledged that he didn't know anything about building skating rinks—despite having been fully engaged in a public haranguing of the mayor over Wollman Rink.

So Trump decided he needed to talk with someone who was an expert at building skating rinks, which naturally made him think of Canada. In his book he wrote, "Ice skating is to Canadians what baseball is to Americans, the national pastime. The top builders I figured were probably the companies that built rinks for Canada's professional hockey teams."

Ultimately, he got in touch with a Toronto-based company that had built the rink for the Montreal Canadiens hockey team. Trump got a crash course in what it takes to build a quality skating rink, then he had some people from the company fly down to look at Wollman Rink with him. It must have been the first time anyone who actually knew how to build an ice rink had looked at Wollman Rink. Within three months, at a cost of $2.25 million, the rink was open for business. It's still there and still making ice—and it is now called the Trump Wollman Rink in Central Park.

I love this story because it shows that Trump is a pragmatic, sensible conservative who knows how to finish difficult projects under immense pressure. And there are other examples. I was told by Rudy Giuliani that an even better example is the Ferry Point Golf Course in the Bronx, which neither Giuliani nor former mayor Michael Bloomberg could get built.

They turned the Ferry Point project over to Trump and he finished the course in eighteen months. There's now an eighteen-hole golf course in the Bronx. Giuliani said it was an even greater achievement, because it was technically more complicated than Wollman Rink.

Trump has a great opportunity to bring his tremendous, practical business expertise to Washington. However, one of the biggest obstacles he will run into is the mind-set of the bureaucrats at the Congressional Budget Office (CBO) and the Office of Management and Budget (OMB).

The CBO's mission is to provide Congress with objective, nonpartisan, realistic analysis of projects or pieces of legislation, and specifically to calculate how much projects or legislation will cost taxpayers. They call this process "scoring." Unfortunately, the agency is a left-wing, bureaucratic defender of big government and liberalism.

Every CBO estimate is high, because the CBO assumes complete mediocrity at every phase of every project. We fought with the CBO on a daily basis when I was Speaker of the House. We never gave up ground, and this proved critical to balancing the budget.

Furthermore, it is an incompetent, corrupt institution. When CBO first scored Obamacare, it invited Obama aid Jonathan Gruber, the law's architect, to come be an academic advisor. Not only that, but the CBO used a near identical model to score the bill as Gruber used to write it. So CBO let the person who wrote the abysmal law influence whether or not it would fair well in a supposedly objective analysis. And Gruber is the same advisor who later, in 2013, pointed to "lack of transparency" in the creation of the law and the "the stupidity of the American voter" as critical to getting it passed. At the same panel, he said the law was written "in a tortured way" specifically to fool the CBO into considering the law's central pillar—the individual mandate—was not a tax, which he acknowledged would have killed the bill.

The result of CBO letting the fox in the henhouse was Obamacare's original scoring, which was so wrong it was totally indefensible. A year later the CBO produced a new score that was so much more expensive that it was clear Obamacare would have been defeated if it had been the original score.

Imagine Trumpian military contracts. Imagine an infrastructure plan based on Trumpian terms. The CBO will not be able to score anything entrepreneurially, so it will totally screw up what Trump's trying to do. If the House and the Senate let the CBO survive, they are not going to be able to do anything Trump wants to do, because the bureaucrats won't score it intelligently.

Keep that in mind when we see the CBO estimate for the border wall with Mexico. If President Trump and Congress can cut through the bureaucracy and the red tape, the wall will end up costing much less than the CBO will claim.

The Office of Management and Budget is the executive branch parallel to the CBO. It is filled with sincere, intense, very smart experts at scoring the bureaucratic world Trump is dedicated to dismantling. It will find it very hard to score Trump's management style and his aggressive cost cutting and application of common sense.

President Trump's entrepreneurial management will save tens and ultimately hundreds of billions of dollars in federal funds, but it will be very hard in the early days to get the CBO and OMB to correctly score it.

BUILDING RELATIONSHIPS

Despite his aggressive approach to business and politics, Trump knows that without relationships he never would have built a multibillion-dollar business or won the presidency. If no one in New York was willing to sit down and talk with Trump, he wouldn't have been able to buy or sell anything. So, a part of his doctrine has to do with building and maintaining strong relationships with potential allies.

In *The Art of the Deal*, Trump tells this story about the importance of strong relationships:

> The Penn Central trustees had hired a company headed by a man named Victor Palmieri. . . . I had never heard of Victor Palmieri, but I realized immediately he was someone I wanted to know. . . . By building a close relationship with Victor from the start, I was able, in effect, to work for him rather than to be just another buyer. That was terrific for me. For example, we drew up agreements giving me an exclusive option to purchase the 60th street and 30th street yards. . . . The Penn Central even agreed to pay my development costs. . . . Palmieri, in turn, helped give me credibility with the press.

As I've already mentioned, Trump has a talent with people that is similar to that of former president Bill Clinton. When you are talking to Trump, you are the center of his focus. He is fully engaged. This will undoubtedly serve him well as he builds relations in Congress and abroad.

Already, Trump has had productive meetings with leaders from some of our country's closest allied nations, such as British prime minister Theresa May, Canadian prime minister Justin Trudeau, and Japanese prime minister Shinzo Abe. He also hosted Chinese president Xi Jinping for a multiday summit on trade and national security.

These early meetings are important. Trump is pursuing significant changes in our international agreements that could cause tension, and it will be important to have strong personal relationships with those leaders to serve as a foundation for trust.

President Trump has also started rebuilding bridges from the White House to the Capitol, which were all but demolished under the previous administration. President Obama rarely met with anyone who was not a Democrat—and even more rarely with any member who was not in leadership. Since arriving in office, President Trump has met with hundreds of members of Congress—including those who are not in leadership and those who are not in his party.

As the president builds more of these relationships in Congress, he will learn how he needs to tweak his policies and make the right deals to bring more of his legislative goals to fruition.

THE ART OF THE DEAL

Finally, the most central, defining asset of Donald Trump's doctrine—and perhaps his greatest skill—is his ability to negotiate. He lives for the deal. He expresses this in the opening line of *The Art of the Deal*:

> I don't do it for the money. I've got enough, much more than I'll ever need. I do it to do it. Deals are my art form. Other people paint beautifully on canvas or write wonderful poetry. I like making deals, preferably big deals. That's how I get my kicks.

As soon as he was elected, Trump got to work negotiating on behalf of the American people.

In December, Trump negotiated with Carrier, the air conditioner maker, and the state of Indiana to keep a majority of its 1,100-employee workforce at a plant in Indiana. The company had said it would move many of the workers to a facility in Mexico. In exchange for $7 million in tax incentives from the state, Carrier would make $16 million in capital improvements at its Indiana plant.

In January, Trump merely criticized Ford Motor Company for its plan to build a $1.6 billion plant in Mexico. Once Trump put public pressure on the automaker, Ford announced it would instead invest $700 million in Detroit, where it would create seven hundred jobs.

In February, after Trump convinced Lockheed Martin to lower its latest bill for ninety F-35 fighter jets by $600 million the month before, he shaved $1 billion off the cost of two new Air Force One planes after one hour of discussions with Boeing.

Because he loves to wheel and deal so much, he has become incredibly good at it. He knows that every yes is preceded by several rejections.

He was turned down at nearly every turn when he first set out to develop Trump Tower.

In *The Art of the Deal*, Trump describes how when he first approached Bonwit Teller to tell them he wanted to buy the store and building, a man named Franklin Jarman politely told him, "You've got to be crazy if you think there's any way we'd ever sell this incredible site."

But Trump persisted. He wrote letters month after month to Jarman and was ignored, until he saw that Genesco, the company that owned the building, was in financial trouble and had hired a new chief executive named John Hanigan. Trump called Hanigan, and they met within a half hour. A few weeks later, Trump had a deal signed for the building and the remainder of the land lease for $25 million.

Then Trump overcame several other "no" situations while he was acquiring the land under the building, securing financing for construction, and getting a commonly applied development tax incentive from the city of New York. He overcame all of them.

He talks about the tax incentive in chapter 2, "Elements of the Deal":

> When the city unfairly denied me, on Trump Tower, the standard tax break every developer had been getting, I fought them in six different courts. It cost me a lot of money, I was considered highly likely to lose, and people told me it was a no-win situation politically. I would have considered it worth the effort regardless of the outcome. In this case, I won—which made it even better.

In the business world, no is the standard first answer, and Trump understands that. It's going to give him enormous ability to get his policies through Congress, because he will always look for ways to get to yes.

As of the date I am writing this, Trump and congressional Republicans have not been able to reach a deal on the repeal and replacement of Obamacare. But given Trump's success in the past, I'm betting he'll get to yes on health care too.

PART TWO

UNDERSTANDING THE RISE OF TRUMP

The election of President Trump could be a watershed moment for America's future. For decades, members of America's elite—in government, academia, and the media—have steered the country in a direction counter to the will of the American people. Trump fully understood this. He was in tune with normal Americans and ran as their champion against the elites. That is why Trump beat more than a dozen well-qualified Republican opponents and defeated the multibillion-dollar Hillary Clinton campaign. But because he is the champion of the people against the elites, Trump will have to continue fighting for his entire presidency. The following section describes the battlefield and provides insight into how Trump can continue to win.

When I read Nassim Nicholas Taleb's short essay on the "IYI"—Intellectual Yet Idiot—it was as though a bright light had entered the room. For years, I had dealt with people who were credentialed, glib, smugly arrogant, and just plain wrong. They refused to listen to facts or to the lessons of the real world learned through studying history. They firmly believed things that simply weren't true. To make things worse, they refused to learn from their mistakes and kept repeating the same failed approaches. Suddenly, the concept of IYI explained the phenomenon of well-educated but really stupid people. Watching Trump, I realized he had learned through years of business to distinguish competence from idiocy.

To better understand how powerful this insight is, let's turn to Taleb's work.

CHAPTER FOUR

THE RISE OF THE IYI

There is a growing disconnect between the governing elite and normal working people. The author Nassim Nicholas Taleb, who wrote *The Black Swan: The Impact of the Highly Improbable*, crystalized this disconnect with an amazing term—Intellectual Yet Idiot (IYI).

In an essay Taleb wrote in September 2016, called "Intellectual Yet Idiot," he described the IYI as a rising group of people who are quietly filling roles in government, politics, journalism, and academia. Taleb said members of this group are characterized by being highly qualified on paper but bereft of real practical intelligence. The essay is part of a larger upcoming book by Taleb called *Skin in the Game*. The essay is included in an appendix of this book.

"Idiot" is a harsh word, but Taleb's piece is one of the most useful essays I have read.

The concept of IYIs succinctly describes the global pattern of normal people rejecting the rule of the incompetent elite. We've seen it in Brexit, the rise of populist parties in the West, and of course, with the election of Donald Trump.

Taleb is talking about people who are naturally gifted at writing essays and taking tests. This natural ability helps them breeze through primary education and gets them to elite colleges and universities. There, they are taught by professors (many of whom are the kind of people good at writing essays and taking tests). The professors are so impressed by their students' test-taking and essay-writing abilities that they write glowing letters of recommendation on behalf of the students, so the students can get jobs working in government, politics, the media, or academia.

The only problem with these people is they don't know how to do anything. Virtually their entire lives have been spent in classrooms. These people could write brilliant essays on how to change a tire, but should their own car get a flat, they would have to call AAA to fix it. They are intellectuals, yet idiots.

Taleb's essay perfectly explains the problems I see with the federal bureaucracy. Our government is filled with highly educated, intelligent career bureaucrats who have never manufactured a car or built a building, never grown their own food or operated a farm, never practiced medicine or performed surgery, and yet they are empowered to write regulations governing all those industries based on their understanding of academic works describing them.

And the same holds true for many political consultants who give advice on those industries, along with journalists who cover them and college professors who lecture on them. This of course leads to regulations, political analysis, news stories, and major academic studies that turn out to be destructive and fail in the real world.

Trump could not be more different. He has always made it a point to rely on people who actually know what they are doing. Throughout his career as a builder, he would regularly get advice from painters, carpenters, and other craftsmen on the designs of his buildings. When he set about fixing Wollman Rink, he sought out and found people who made a living building ice rinks. Trump favors people with practical knowledge over those with academic knowledge. And he has a tremendous amount of practical knowledge himself.

When Trump and I were at the Trump Hotel in Las Vegas to help Mitt Romney in October 2012, we had some extra time to walk around and look at his new property. Trump emphasized the practical knowledge it took to build something as opposed to just financing it. At one point, he said to me, "I could estimate the amount of cement needed for virtually any building. I have done it so often, it is just second nature. In fact, there are a hundred practical skills that let me produce a better hotel at lower cost than my competitors."

And when we would chat at Trump National about the amazing renovation he was doing, it was clear he talked with the golf architect and personally supervised the quality of the work.

THE MARK OF THE INTELLECTUALLY IDIOTIC

There is near-endless evidence that our bureaucracies are bloated with highly educated people who provide almost no real value to the American government. One great example is the so-called Waters of the United States rule, which was enacted by the Environmental Protection Agency (EPA) in 2015 and defines the criteria for rivers, lakes, and streams over which the EPA and the Army Corps of Engineers have jurisdiction.

In a supposed effort to bring clarity to the law, the intellectual yet idiots who wrote the regulations made the criteria for waterways so broad that, as US senator Lamar Alexander of Tennessee points out, they give federal agencies jurisdiction to regulate mud puddles in farmers' pastures.

In February, President Trump ordered new officials at the EPA and the Corps of Engineers to review the rule.

It is also ludicrous that the EPA regulates dust under the Clean Air Act. The EPA treats dust that blows off dry riverbeds, gravel roads, and parched fields as a particulate matter pollutant.

That means farm dust falls under the same regulatory category as soot from coal-fired power plants.

In 2011, Republicans caught wind that the EPA was considering tightening federal regulations on dust after an EPA panel looked at rules in Arizona and California, where the states have required that about 7,800 farms implement dust-control measures.

After House and Senate Republicans raised this issue, and the public was made aware the federal government was interested in regulating a completely natural phenomenon, EPA administrator Lisa P. Jackson told the *Washington Post* that the EPA would not likely implement a new rule. However, Jackson said the EPA would still need to spend several more months formally reviewing the dust issue. So, the intellectual yet idiots at the EPA acknowledged they weren't going to try to prevent dust from forming—but they still needed to study it to be sure.

This election clearly pointed out disconnected intellectual-yet-idiot members of the beltway political intelligentsia——on the left and the right.

Throughout the GOP primaries, the Republican elites in Washington held on to a completely out-of-touch theory that Trump was "a factional candidate with a 'hard ceiling' of support limited to one-third of the party," according to *Bloomberg Politics* on February 22, 2016. These Trump opponents believed that as the crowded GOP field winnowed, most Republican voters would rally to Trump's remaining opponent and "soundly defeat the blustery billionaire for the nomination," the news outlet reported. Consultants for Senators Marco Rubio and Ted Cruz both said Trump had roughly a 30 percent ceiling and could be beaten in a two- or three-man race.

Despite *Bloomberg* reporter Sahil Kapur citing several polls and enlightened consultants to the contrary, this theory was carried by some Republicans right up until the day of the convention. Trump won 44.9 percent of delegates in a four-person race with Cruz, Rubio, and Governor John Kasich.

After Trump's victory in the primaries, Democrats developed their own "ceiling theory." In June 2016, Jon Wiener wrote a piece titled "Relax, Donald Trump Can't Win" for the left-wing publication *The Nation*. In the column, Wiener applies the same flawed logic many Republicans used during the primary. A summary of that logic looks like this: things in the past happened this way, therefore they will happen this way in the future.

Wiener—like so many others on the left—sought to compare Trump's candidacy to those of Mitt Romney, John McCain, and George W. Bush. This was the same mistake made by all members of the elite in this election. They failed to realize that Trump and the movement around him were unique—and that support for Trump was led by the American people, not big donors or beltway kingmakers.

Intellectual yet idiots are also easy to find in our lawmaking bodies and media. For example, read the arguments almost anytime you see the term "gun control" in the newspaper or on TV.

Intellectual proponents of most gun control measures will be able to recite pages of statistics about gun violence, but when it comes to talking about firearms, they shoot blanks.

Take Representative Diana DeGette, a Democrat who represents the 1st District of Colorado. DeGette has led support through Congress for legislation to ban the sale of high-capacity magazines. Now, as most people who actually own firearms know, a magazine is the device that holds ammunition and feeds rounds into a weapon.

According to an April 3, 2013, blog post by *Denver Post* writer Allison Sherry, when DeGette was asked a straightforward question about "how a ban on magazines holding more than 15 rounds would be effective in reducing gun violence" at a *Denver Post* forum, DeGette responded with the following:

I will tell you these are ammunition, they're bullets, so the people who have those know they're going to shoot them, so if you ban them in the future, the number of these high-capacity magazines is going to decrease dramatically over time because the bullets will have been shot and there won't be any more available.

The congresswoman has decided the federal government needs to ban the sale of high-capacity magazines—and clearly has no idea what they are.

In the same vein, many reporters are woefully ignorant when it comes to firearms and the laws that regulate them. This is particularly distressing, since virtually every major news agency employs at least one person to report on crime. Take the now famous August 17, 2014, tweet by the *Huffington Post*'s justice reporter Ryan J. Reilly: While covering the riots that broke out after the shooting of Michael Brown in Ferguson, Missouri—which was later declared by the Department of Justice to be a justified shooting by police—Reilly tweeted out a picture with the following caption: "I believe these are rubber bullets, can anyone confirm? #Ferguson."

The accompanying photograph showed four bright orange foam earplugs.

The groupthink of the elite media is notorious. Once the mental lemmings have decided on a theme, they use group beliefs to avoid thought. There was a theme in 2016 that Trump would be very dangerous in foreign policy. Reporters were not quite sure how he would be dangerous, but they were sure he would be. In a two-week period, they moved wildly from "Trump will lead to a war with Russia" to "Trump will be too weak and soft on Russia." The reporters knew they were supposed to be afraid of Trump overseas, they were just confused about on which pattern they should focus.

Intellectuals yet idiots of course abound in academe. The

modern intellectual Left rests on the ability to reject reality in favor of theory. A perfect IYI moment occurred at my alma mater, Emory University, when some supposedly ruthless, vicious person used chalk to write "Trump 2016" on the sidewalk. This traumatized the IYI students on the left, who wrote a letter to the university's president protesting this invasion of their "safe place" on campus. Worse, the president wrote back apologizing and offering group therapy for anyone who was psychologically stressed by the chalk on the sidewalk. It is not surprising that some students are IYIs, but it is troubling when a university president validates their idiocy. After Trump's victory over Clinton, some campuses offered aromatherapy and grief counseling for those whose psyches were shattered. You can't make this stuff up.

But college campuses rejecting the election is no great surprise. Academia has long favored having the American people ruled by the elite. A good example of that is Georgetown professor Jason Brennan's book *Against Democracy*—published by Princeton University Press—wherein he declares democracy a failed experiment and argues instead for "epistocracy." He defines this system as "the rule of the knowledgeable." This is from the book's own description:

> Just as defendants have a right to a fair trial, citizens have a right to competent government. But democracy is the rule of the ignorant and the irrational, and it all too often falls short. Furthermore, no one has a fundamental right to any share of political power, and exercising political power does most of us little good. On the contrary, a wide range of social science research shows that political participation and democratic deliberation actually tend to make people worse—more irrational, biased, and mean. Given this grim picture, Brennan argues that a new system of government—epistocracy, the rule of

the knowledgeable—may be better than democracy, and that it's time to experiment and find out.

Here we have a liberal member of academia, who has more degrees than accomplishments, essentially arguing for literacy tests at the polls because he says the American people are too uneducated to make their own decisions about their government. Not surprisingly, the *Washington Post* reviewer and fellow academic Ilya Somin wrote that Brennan's ideas could be feasible at the state and local level, because he found that "[Brennan's] analysis of epistocratic alternatives to democracy is worth serious consideration—even if most of these ideas are nowhere near ready for large-scale implementation."

The biggest problem with having intellectual yet idiots running our government, political organizations, media, and universities is that these institutions become echo chambers that only promote their brand of groupthink. New ideas that are different or counter to the accepted worldview are labeled aberrant, extreme, or dangerous, which smothers the basic principle that a healthy democracy requires free and full debate of differing opinions. This is how Taleb describes it in his essay:

> The IYI pathologizes others for doing things he doesn't understand without ever realizing it is *his* understanding that may be limited. He thinks people should act according to their best interests *and* he knows their interests, particularly if they are "red necks" or English noncrisp-vowel class who voted for Brexit. When plebeians do something that makes sense to them, but not to him, the IYI uses the term "uneducated." What we generally call participation in the political process, he calls by two distinct designations: "democracy" when it fits the IYI, and "populism" when the plebeians dare voting in

a way that contradicts his preferences. While rich people believe in *one tax dollar one vote*, more humanistic ones in *one man one vote*, Monsanto in *one lobbyist one vote*, the IYI believes in *one Ivy League degree one vote*, with some equivalence for foreign elite schools and PhDs as these are needed in the club.

Keep in mind: Taleb wrote this before the 2016 election—but this is exactly what has happened in America. The vast difference between those four pillars of our society—government, politics, media, and academia—and the American people was perfectly expressed in President Trump's election.

WHERE THE IYI LIVE

Another author, Charles Murray, who is a brilliant scholar with the American Enterprise Institute, touched on a related issue in his book *Coming Apart: The State of White America*. In the book, Murray talks about the forming of what he calls "super zip codes." This is another observation about how the elite are stratifying themselves away from the rest of society. The basic premise of Murray's idea is that people who go to Princeton, Harvard, or Yale marry people from those schools. Then they move to neighborhoods with other people who went to Princeton, Harvard, or Yale. They send their children to prep schools, so they, too, can grow up to go to Princeton, Harvard, or Yale, and the cycle continues. The result is that you end up with relatively large neighborhoods made up of people who are in the top 5 percent economically, and the top 5 percent in educational attainment.

These people end up doing the same things, consuming the same media, and ultimately thinking the same way—which is to say completely differently from the other 95 percent of Americans. When the rise of Trump began, people in the super zip codes—many of whom consequently are major political donors—wrote him off. They didn't understand how anyone in America could support him or recognize that he connected with and related to normal working people. They didn't understand the great reach of Trump's TV show *The Apprentice*. They didn't watch it, so in their closed minds no one did. If only Trump had been on PBS, immediately following *Downton Abbey*, the elites would have understood how good he was on television.

The *Washington Post* took Murray's work and created an interactive map of the super zip codes. The paper reported in November 2013 that on average, median income for households in these zip codes is $120,000 a year, and 70 percent of adults in these areas graduated from college.[1] US census data shows that the median income for all US households was $51,939 in 2013. Not surprisingly, the highest concentrations of these zip codes are in the coastal Northeast—especially around Washington, DC—and around Silicon Valley and Los Angeles.

But the *Washington Post* said Washington, DC, was a special case. More than one-third of the zip codes in the district's metropolitan area are in the top 5 percent of income and higher education. These zip codes are also contiguous, according to the report—meaning there is a 717-square-mile wall of out-of-touch affluence almost surrounding our nation's capital. In the paper's reporting, William H. Frey, a demographer at the Brookings Institution, described it as "a megalopolis of eggheads." And he's right. This population makes up a significant portion of the intellectual yet idiots Taleb is talking about. And they govern us on a day-to-day basis.

Now, this relates to President Trump, because he understood in the campaign that he needed to make sure he was communicating with all Americans—not just the ones who live in super zip codes. Trump's campaign speeches were written in the language of normal Americans. Because he connected with all these regular people, the media and liberal elites dubbed him a populist—

their way of discrediting the views of the Americans who elected Trump. Hillary Clinton, on the other hand, spoke to Americans in the language of the elite. This guaranteed that whatever she was saying did not resonate with most of the American people, although people in the "megalopolis of eggheads" ate it up.

Despite now living in the White House, Trump is not an IYI citizen of this megalopolis. Trump is a builder. He couldn't get away with writing a nice essay about Trump Tower to get tenants to move in—he had to actually build Trump Tower and build it well.

And Trump doesn't hire IYIs. He doesn't have any use for them. Anyone who has run for office knows that conventional wisdom says the higher up you go, the more consultants there are, and the more they tell you that your main goal is to raise money to pay more consultants. Trump immediately recognized this for the scam that it is. At one point in the spring of 2016, when the Trump movement was growing, someone suggested that because the campaign was getting bigger, it should hire someone to lead communications across the country. Trump was incredulous. He reminded that person that he *was* the campaign's lead communicator.

And Trump's skepticism about consultants was proved correct. Jeb Bush raised $110 million, had a legion of political consultants, and commanded a huge political network—and earned only one delegate. Trump had a small team of people who could get results, and he defeated all his rivals. This was so hard for the intellectual yet idiots to understand. During the general campaign, a reporter asked me if I was concerned that Hillary Clinton had spent $22 million at the time, and Trump had only spent $300,000. I directed the reporter to ask Jeb's $110 million delegate.

Jeb Bush is a dear friend and was an excellent governor. And I mention this anecdote only to show that Trump values people who have gained practical knowledge—knowledge that must be learned by doing rather than by hearing a lecture or reading a book. Trump himself learned the bulk of the real estate trade by working with his father—not while he was attending the University of Pennsylvania's Wharton School.

He talks about his experience at Wharton, and his realization that knowledge gained working in the real world was more useful than abstract education, in *The Art of the Deal*:

> Perhaps the most important thing I learned at Wharton was not to be overly impressed by academic credentials. It didn't take me long to realize that there was nothing particularly awesome or exceptional about my class-mates, and that I could compete with them just fine. The other important thing I got from Wharton was a Wharton degree. In my opinion that degree doesn't prove very much, but a lot of people I do business with take it very seriously, and it's considered very prestigious. So all things considered, I'm glad I went to Wharton.

And I've seen how President Trump gains this knowledge. During the first two months of his presidency, I watched the same pattern. He would start with something he had never done, and he would learn by doing it.

For example, he entered the postelection transition period with limited knowledge of world leaders. But he did not sit through long briefings. He simply scheduled call after call to chat with different leaders. People were astonished how long some of the calls were and how many questions the president asked.

Similarly, President Trump entered office with limited knowl-edge of the Congress, but he began talking to and seeing mem-bers—and not just the leadership. It was typical for Trump to invite dozens of senators with their spouses for a reception. It was also typical for him to shrewdly observe that a number of Democrats and Republicans would end up chatting with each other in that social setting. I suspect you will see a lot more social gatherings at the White House. With President Trump's enormous energy, his remarkable memory, and his lifetime of being a good host, Trump will learn every obscure detail about Congress very rapidly.

Having a president who favors practical knowledge over formal knowledge creates a huge opportunity for us to shrink government by replacing many of the intellectual yet idiots that Taleb discusses with a smaller number of people who can solve our country's problems rather than write about them.

One good example of an institution in need of right-sizing is the Pentagon. When the Pentagon was built, it was designed to house 31,000 employees, so that what was then the US Department of War could defeat the Axis powers from half the world away. At that time, those 31,000 staff members wrote reports on carbon paper, with manual typewriters and filed the reports in triplicate in large filing cabinets. Beetle Smith, who was secretary to Chief of Staff George Marshall, would run drills to train the staff so they could find and retrieve files for Marshall at a moment's notice.

I'm certain they were incredibly fast, but can you imagine how much faster it is to send an email over the Pentagon's secure network? Can you imagine how much less time and fewer people it takes now to send that email than it did to type, file, and later retrieve a report at the Pentagon in 1943? At least 40 percent of the Department of Defense's bureaucracy must be superfluous or duplicative. Trump has a great opportunity to get the IYI out of the Pentagon and cut it down to a triangle. This could transform our national security apparatus from a typical slow-moving bureaucracy into an efficient engine for keeping our country safe and protecting our interests abroad.

There is a terrific small book by Col. David Johnson called *Fast Tanks and Heavy Bombers: Innovation in the US Army, 1917–1945* that relates a story about how Marshall worked to rid the military of intellectual yet idiots. Johnson describes a scene that played out in the summer of 1940. The Germans had swept through Poland

and France, and Marshall called in the American army chief of the cavalry to find out how he planned to respond to the German blitz.

The cavalry chief told Marshall he had analyzed the German attack, understood why the Polish cavalry had failed against the German tanks, and knew what they needed to do better. He suggested to Marshall that the allies should develop trucks that could carry the cavalry up to the battlefield, so the horses would be fresh. Marshall thanked him, concluded the meeting, and immediately called in Beetle Smith to have the commandant retired as of noon and have the post of cavalry chief abolished. In large part, we won the war because Marshall was decisive and willing to make the military leaner and better performing, by getting rid of high-ranking intellectual yet idiots who planned to fight tanks on horseback. I'm certain Trump and Secretary of Defense James Mattis will be able to find some similar "chiefs of cavalry" in the Pentagon.

THE IMPORTANCE OF REAL INTELLIGENCE

I usually relate the chief of cavalry story with a half grin, but it highlights why having a rising class of people in important positions in America who are educated beyond their experience can be dangerous.

Dennis M. Gormley, an international security scholar who teaches intelligence, military strategy, arms control, and nonproliferation policy at the University of Pittsburgh, wrote an article titled "Missile Contagion, Survival" in 2008. He later developed a book by a similar name. But in the article, Gormley discusses the same concept that's raised in "Intellectual Yet Idiot" in different terms.

In his article, which is about the threat of proliferation and development of land-attack cruise missiles abroad, Gormley talks about the difference between explicit knowledge and tacit knowledge. Explicit knowledge, he says, is "information or engineering formulations that can be recorded and easily passed from one place to another." Tacit knowledge, he explains, "is the product of a uniquely fertile social and intellectual environment composed of mentors and protégés."

In other words, explicit knowledge is what you would learn from a traditional education and tacit knowledge is what you learn by actually doing something.

In the context of Gormley, he said as early as 2002 that Iraq had significant *explicit* knowledge about how to extend the effective range of first-generation Chinese cruise missiles from 150 kilometers to 1,000 kilometers. These are missiles capable of carrying nuclear, biological, or chemical payloads. Thankfully, Iraq lacked engineers who had *tacit* knowledge of actually converting these missiles, so they "achieved only modest progress in most cases, over as much as seven years of development work."

Gormley suggests that tacit knowledge is so much more important than explicit knowledge to this process that controlling the spread of tacit knowledge is a good way to control the spread of cruise-missile proliferation itself.

"Thus, while a flow of technology is necessary, it is not sufficient to enable cruise-missile proliferation without the critical support of a small and exceptionally skilled group of engineers in an equally small number of industrial countries. This is the good news. If states can more effectively control the spread of these 'black arts,' there is hope that the worst features of the contagion can be checked," Gormley wrote.

Gormley is concerned about a very specific issue related to arms control, but I think his theory works across disciplines, and it relates closely to the concerns Taleb raises.

In the United States, we have a surplus of explicit knowledge in our bureaucracy, political establishment, media, and institutions of higher learning. President Trump is leading a movement to bring tacit knowledge to the forefront of our federal system, so that it can return to being a practical government that effectively works for its people.

During the 2016 campaign, and now in the presidency, one of the continuing surprises to President Trump has been the willingness of the elite media to lie. Initially, he would be shocked and uncertain how to respond. Despite all his experience in fighting with the New York City media (arguably the most aggressive and confrontational in the country), he was simply unprepared for the brutality and depth of dishonesty of our national media. To this day, he is surprised when reporters repeat various stories—even when it is clear how false they are.

CHAPTER FIVE

THE PROPAGANDA MEDIA

Trump is the first candidate in modern history who has been able to sustain and succeed against a full assault by the news media. This is one reason the media elite are so hostile to him. They don't like losing.

In part, Trump simply outfoxed the media on the campaign trail. He knew they were constantly criticizing what he said and how he said it—while at the same time digging through his past to find anything else to criticize. But he also recognized that media outlets were trapped in their mania, and he could always gain and use their attention.

With a strongly worded tweet, he could raise the hackles of the news organizations. Then he could call a press conference and be sure that every camera available would be present and rolling. That provided him a free, effective opportunity to make his case to the American people despite the media din.

What Trump intuitively understood, and which completely eluded reporters, was that the constant hostility was hurting their cause. Each time Trump was attacked for saying American interests were more important than global concerns, or that American jobs were more valuable than cheap products from other countries, or that rights of Americans should be protected over those of immigrants, normal Americans felt attacked themselves.

And to those same Americans, the assault on Trump for expressing rational self-interest on behalf of our country was a breaking point. The growing liberal bias and animosity toward dissenting opinion that had developed over the Obama era had become too great to endure.

When Trump sensed the pressure valve about to release just days after he announced his candidacy, he launched his own offensive through his Twitter account and TV appearances. This open defiance of the established media elite cemented him as the standard-bearer for middle Americans, who had been left behind by the country's cultural elite.

I tapped into this during my 2012 presidential campaign, but it apparently took another four years of propaganda on behalf of the Obama administration before the public reached its boiling point.

THE AUDACITY OF BIAS

And make no mistake, the media was totally smitten with President Obama.

Set aside the blatant examples—like when MSNBC's Chris Matthews said in December 2008 that hearing Obama speak sent a thrill up his leg. One needs only look to a 2008 Pew Research Center report that found that nearly 37 percent of people asked said coverage of the Democratic primary race that year favored Obama, while only 4 percent reported seeing a bias toward Hillary Clinton.[1]

What's remarkable about this perceived bias is that many of the same people polled also were aware of several scandals that might have sunk less favored, unanointed candidates. According to Pew, 62 percent of the people surveyed had heard a great deal about Obama's connection to the Reverend Jeremiah

Wright, the militant pastor who made headlines for asking God to damn America and saying the United States was at fault for the September 11, 2001, terrorist attacks.

It's no surprise the people heard about it. The remarks made headlines for weeks. But as I told Bob Schieffer on *Face the Nation* in 2015 when the media was trying to destroy Representative Steve Scalise over controversy surrounding a speech he had given twelve years earlier, Obama got a pass on the Reverend Wright controversy.

Obama gave an eloquent speech distancing himself from Wright's church and claiming he hadn't heard Wright's hateful remarks. The media collectively shrugged and said "Oh, OK." Coverage completely ignored that Obama had attended Wright's church on the south side of Chicago for twenty years. Critical media coverage of this issue had virtually ended by April 30, 2008.

Citing a Project for Excellence in Journalism campaign coverage index, Pew also reported that Obama had "received more press coverage than either [Mrs.] Clinton or John McCain in 11 of the past 17 weeks [January through May 2008]. Clinton has dominated the campaign coverage in 4 of the last 17 weeks. McCain has not led the two Democratic candidates in terms of news coverage since the week of Feb. 4–10, when he became the presumptive Republican nominee following his victories in the GOP Super Tuesday primaries."

And this was just the beginning. For the entirety of his first term, Obama was treated with kid gloves by the media. Major news organizations largely avoided asking tough questions about the death of US ambassador Christopher Stevens and three other Americans in the September 11, 2012, attack on two US installations in Benghazi, Libya. They abdicated their duty to hold the president accountable to the Congress, and later devoted more energy toward attacking the legitimacy of the House Select Committee on Benghazi. After the media was forced to question the erroneous claim that the attack was a result of reaction to a film and not radical Islamic terrorism, they quickly accepted Obama's next excuse—that the botched protection of the ambassador and other Americans was due to mistakes by lower-level State Department employees.

As the veteran journalist and *Weekly Standard* editor Fred Barnes wrote in January 2013:

My drift here ought to be obvious. I'm referring to the way the media treat Obama. It's not always adoring. It's intermittently fair and even-handed. But overall, what's distinctive about the press coverage of Obama is the absence of fault-finding, criticism, and dogged questioning. And when Obama makes excuses, as he often does, the media tend to echo them.

No president in my lifetime has been covered so favorably and so gingerly. Never has the press corps been so unwilling to pursue stories that might cast the president in an unflattering light. As a group, the media pride themselves on taking an adversarial approach to politicians and government officials. But in Obama's case, the press acts like a helpmate.[2]

Barnes further points out that Obama's treatment by the press is even more pronounced when compared with coverage of George W. Bush. Barnes notes that Bush was constantly criticized for tactics he used while fighting terrorism, the use of Guantanamo Bay detention facility, and his use of surveillance provisions under the Patriot Act. Meanwhile, when Obama used similar tactics, failed to close Guantanamo as he promised, and specifically when he signed legislation to continue warrantless wiretapping in the United States for intelligence gathering,

"Bush was harshly criticized by the media on this very issue. Obama got a pass," Barnes wrote.

It wasn't until the end of Obama's eight years in office that the press started to realize he was not the champion they had hoped for. Once the media awoke from a nearly decade-long Obama groupthink, journalists were almost surprised to realize he had been one of the most secretive, opaque politicians to sit in the Oval Office. After Obama's lecturing journalists in a March 2016 speech, and tweaking reporters for giving what he called "false equivalence" to coverage of Donald Trump's candidacy, *Politico Magazine* writer Jack Shafer had enough. He wrote on March 29, 2016:

> How do we hate Obama's treatment of the press? Let me count the ways. Under his administration, the U.S. government has set a new record for withholding Freedom of Information Act requests, according to a recent Associated Press investigation. FOIA gives the public and press an irreplaceable view into the workings of the executive branch. Without timely release of government documents and data, vital questions can't be answered and stories can't be written.

Shafer went on to express frustration over Obama's "insider threat program" which was a concentrated effort to find and punish government whistleblowers in the administration. Indeed, CNN's Jake Tapper reported that "the Obama administration has used the Espionage Act to go after whistleblowers who leaked to journalists . . . more than all previous administrations combined." The online fact-checking publication PolitiFact rated Tapper's assessment as true.[3]

And the *New York Times* reporter James Risen—whom the Obama administration threatened to jail for refusing to reveal his sources in a leak investigation—called the Obama White House on CNN "the most antipress administration since the Nixon administration" and described it as having tried to "criminalize investigative reporting."

But the frustrations of Schafer, Tapper, and Risen didn't seem to catch on with the rest of their media colleagues under Obama. And at the same time, news organizations' contentment with Obama's barriers to media access didn't transfer when they started covering Donald Trump.

When Trump denied access to the *Washington Post*, the *Des Moines Register*, and several other publications during the campaign—and later when Press Secretary Sean Spicer didn't invite several mainstream media outlets to a small, off-camera press meeting in February—news agencies went nuts. The Associated Press even boycotted the Spicer gaggle—deciding that the status of its fellow elite media outlets was more important than informing the public. Meanwhile, in 2008, when Obama kicked the *Dallas Morning News*, the *New York Post* and the *Washington Times* off his campaign plane, the media once again gave him a pass and accepted his assertion that there were no more seats. *Glamour* kept its spot on the aircraft.

THE MEDIA VERSUS TRUMP

Not only is the press calling foul on Trump when it let Obama skate for similar actions, reporters are actively skewing their coverage of Trump.

As the website *RedState* reported on February 28, 2017, the *New York Times* deliberately mischaracterized a speech that President Trump gave at the Conservative Political Action Conference.

During the speech, Trump said, "We are also going to save countless American lives. As we speak today, immigration officers are finding the gang members, the drug dealers, and the criminal aliens and throwing them the hell out of our country."

In the story by Glenn Thrush, the quote was presented as: "His speech also included a promise to *throw undocumented immigrants 'the hell out of the country'* [italics mine] and a recitation of his law-and-order campaign promises."

And the media has vociferously pushed false narratives about Donald Trump throughout his candidacy. The *New York Times* printed a supposed exposé on Trump in May 2016 alleging that he treated former girlfriends poorly.[4] The Monday after the weekend article ran, Rowanne Brewer Lane—the paper's lead source for the story—appeared on *Fox & Friends* and spoke to several other media outlets because she felt she needed to tell the American people that the *New York Times* had misrepresented her story.

Brewer Lane said to *Fox & Friends* that Trump "never made me feel like I was being demeaned in any way. He never offended me in any way. He was very gracious. I saw him around all types of people, all types of women. He was very kind, thoughtful, generous, you know. He was a gentleman."

It was clear to Brewer Lane that the *Times* reporters had set out with their own narrative—which is that Trump is some sort of abusive monster—and had planned to malign her comments from the start. Not only did they seek to lie to their readers, but they were brazenly dishonest with Brewer Lane.

"They promised several times that they would do it accurately. They told me several times and my manager several times that it would not be a hit piece and that my story would come across the way that I was telling it and honestly, and it absolutely was not," she told *Fox & Friends*.[5]

This was the moment when I realized something profound was breaking in the old order, and the old order in its desperation was getting clumsy and stupid.

Just consider the *Time* writer, who was serving as a pool reporter in the White House the day Trump took office. Now, to explain, there are times when it's unreasonable or impossible to let reporters from all the media outlets cover an event. Most of the time that's because the space is too small or there are issues with security—as with the Oval Office. So, at times when everyone can't have a reporter at an event, there are pool reporters whose job it is to represent all the media.

The day Trump was inaugurated, after noting that a bust of Winston Churchill had been moved into the Oval Office, *Time* magazine writer Zeke Miller told his colleagues in the pool that a bust of Martin Luther King Jr. had been removed. This report of course caused furor throughout the country, as reporters across the nation picked up this juicy tidbit from Trump's first day. It was a serious charge because it reinforced the Left's assertion that Trump and Republicans were racist. If true, it would drive a real wedge between African Americans and the new President. There was only one problem: The bust of King was never removed from the Oval Office. It's still there today. The report was entirely false.

The reporter later claimed in a tweet that the erroneous story was an honest mistake. He said he looked twice for the bust, but it had been obscured by a door or a Secret Service agent. OK, sure. Reporters are people, and people make mistakes. But the trouble with that excuse is it doesn't explain why the reporter didn't ask White House Press Secretary Sean Spicer about the bust, or even take a few extra moments to get a better look around the room.

Instead, the reporter saw what he thought was an opportunity to show President Trump in a bad light, and he took it without giving a thought to accuracy or fairness. Counselor to the president Kellyanne Conway later said the lie had been repeated by more than three thousand media outlets.

This situation tipped the media's hand and laid bare the false narrative they were trying to promote, that Trump brought in the bust of Churchill and had gotten rid of the bust of King, proving how much of a white, imperialistic, racist, "alt-right" president that Trump was going to be. Keep in mind, all this reporting happened immediately after Trump had given an inaugural speech that was completely antidiscriminatory and reaffirmed Trump's position that to be racist is to be unpatriotic and un-American. Here's one of the most powerful passages from Trump's inaugural that illustrates this message:

It is time to remember that old wisdom our soldiers will never forget: that whether we are black or brown or white, we all bleed the same red blood of patriots, we all enjoy the same glorious freedoms, and we all salute the same great American flag.

And whether a child is born in the urban sprawl of Detroit or the windswept plains of Nebraska, they look up at the same night sky, they fill their heart with the same dreams, and they are infused with the breath of life by the same almighty Creator.

So to all Americans, in every city near and far, small and large, from mountain to mountain, and from ocean to ocean, hear these words: You will never be ignored again.

But these words—which came out of the president's mouth in front of the entire nation—did not fit the media's narrative of who this president is, so they ignored them.

And the intentional ignorance didn't stop. In February, a White House correspondent for the American Urban Radio Networks claimed that while on the campaign trail, Trump said that white people built America.

He never said this, or anything like it.

After a day of confusion among White House officials, and rabid excitement from the media, the reporter told the *Washington Examiner* she was talking about a speech Trump gave on March 12, 2016 in Vandalia, Ohio. Trump was speaking to the entire crowd of people there at the rally, and said:

> We cannot let our First Amendment rights be taken away from us, folks. We can't let it happen. We can't let it happen. We have a right to speak. I mean, we are law-abiding people. We are people that work very hard. We are people that have built this country and made this country great.

Trump was talking to his supporters after he had to cancel an event in Chicago due to lawless actions by left-wing fascist protestors.

Only a reporter who had a predetermined narrative could construe this statement as being exclusive to white people.

Another perfect example of the media tossing traditional standards aside in order to attack Trump is when *BuzzFeed*, CNN, and several other news organizations reported on a completely unverified, unsubstantiated report allegedly made by a former British intelligence officer that claimed President Trump and several of his associates were vulnerable to *kompromat*— which is the Russian term for compromising material used to blackmail, extort, or otherwise influence public officials. The report had been floating around Washington for months, and no official agency had confirmed any of it.

Despite having no way to verify the information, and ignoring the fact that the source of the report had been hired by Hillary Clinton to do opposition research on Trump, the media ran with the story—bypassing even the most basic principles of journalism. Supposedly smart, trained journalists just threw spaghetti on the wall to see if it would stick. To the media, the allegations about Trump must have just been too good to fact-check. In their voracious pursuit of damning news about the president, the media reported that Trump's lawyer, Michael Cohen, had met with Russians in Prague—which was somehow proof that Trump had a nefarious relationship with the Russian government.

There was one problem: at no point did anyone involved, in either the intelligence community or the press, stop to ask Cohen about the allegation—or consider that there could be more than one person in the world named Michael Cohen. As it turned out, the Cohen who works for Trump had never been to the Czech Republic, much less Prague. Still, the press saw the shot and took it.

This kind of propaganda is what Trump is going to have to face every day of his presidency. And it will be endlessly frustrating to not only Trump—but also for the same Americans who have had their faith in the media eroded.

THE PEOPLE VERSUS THE MEDIA

I was told a story several years ago by Mark Bowden, who wrote *Black Hawk Down*, that really helps explain the Washington media.

Mark used to work for the *Philadelphia Inquirer*, and at one point he decided to write a book, *Bringing the Heat*, about the Philadelphia Eagles football team. The Eagles knew his work and knew that he was a genuinely curious person who wanted to learn about what it was like to be on a team trying to win a championship. Mark told me most of the players were nice to him, but he learned very quickly they despised sports journalists. For the players, the idea of some fifty-year-old overweight guy who couldn't run twenty yards without passing out, sitting up in the air-conditioned press box bloviating over whether they should have run their touchdown route better just infuriated them.

In fact, you see the same thing in the Washington press and political academia. These people are voyeurs. They don't do anything.

In the White House press corps, you might have somebody representing the *New York Times* or *Time* magazine, who has covered the White House for maybe five years and is therefore empowered to render judgment on the president. The first thing to realize is: This person couldn't be the president if his or her life depended on it. This person has no clue about how difficult and complex it is to be the president. Yet the media refuse to reassess, continue to be wrong, and will apparently stop at nothing to force their narrative.

And Americans are starting to get sick of it.

According to a Gallup poll published September 14, 2016, public trust in the media has dropped to the lowest level Gallup has ever recorded.

Every year since 1997, the pollster has asked Americans, "In general, how much trust and confidence do you have in the mass media—such as newspapers, TV, and radio—when it comes to reporting the news fully, accurately and fairly?" The available answers are "a great deal," "a fair amount," "not very much," or "none at all."

In 1997, 55 percent of those polled responded either "a fair amount" or "a great deal." In 2016, that figure was 32 percent—a 23 point drop over nineteen years. And Gallup's polling data shows this year was not aberrant, it was right on trend. Trust in media remained between 50 percent and 55 percent from 1997 to 2005, with the exception of a 10-point dip in 2004 that rebounded the following year. But since 2005, through the last part of George W. Bush's second term and the entirety of President Barack Obama's two terms in office, trust in media has steadily waned.

I suggest that this might be a good marker for when the media's left-wing tendencies began to define its coverage on a regular basis. Gallup's data shows 2005 marked an extreme high for the Left's trust in the media. While only 31 percent of Republicans and 49 percent of independents found the media trustworthy in 2005, a whopping 70 percent of Democrats thought the nation's news outlets were doing a good job—likely because at the time they were relentlessly criticizing President Bush. In fact, it has largely been the opinions of independents and Republicans that have driven down the results of Gallup's media-trust poll.

Over the eight years of Obama's term, the Left's approval of the media ranged from 60 percent in 2008 to 55 percent in 2015—only recently dropping to 51 percent in 2016 with Trump's election. At the same time, distrust of media grew for the rest of the nation. Independents ranged from 41 percent in 2008 to 30 percent in 2016 while Republicans went from 27 percent to 14 percent over the same period.

I expect this trend will continue until the so-called journalists stop being propagandists, rediscover objectivity, and reearn the respect of the American people.

So far, it doesn't appear that any of them have learned anything. These are the same people at the *New York Times*, the *Washington Post*, CNN, MSNBC, and the rest who failed to understand that Trump would win the Republican primary, were flabbergasted when he won the general election, and have still not stopped to look inward and assess the level to which they were out of touch with most Americans.

Here are a few quick reminders.

Shortly after Trump entered the race, the famed political analyst Nate Silver dismissed him as "the world's greatest troll."

"In the long run—as our experience with past trolls shows—Trump's support will probably fade. Or at least, given his high unfavorable ratings, it will plateau, and other candidates will surpass him as the rest of the field consolidates," Silver wrote on July 20, 2015.

After Trump beat sixteen other highly qualified candidates in the Republican primary, the *Washington Post*'s senior political reporter Aaron Blake explained on August 9, 2016, that Trump won by simply going further right than his primary opponents were willing to go, and Trump didn't understand the nuances of general election campaigning.

"Trump was focused like a laser on the win, and he wasn't politically experienced or humble enough to grasp that how you claim that win can be just as important come summer and fall," Blake wrote, later writing that Trump "lost the general election to win the primary. And he clearly still doesn't understand that."

And even after Trump became our nation's 45th president, those in the elite media couldn't reconcile that the narrative they had painstakingly built over the election didn't stick with the American people. In response, they immediately focused their effort trying to reenforce that narrative and explain the mistake the voters had clearly made.

Just look at the following MSNBC headlines after the election: "Trump Slams the Author of a Report He Hasn't Read, Doesn't Understand"; "Does Donald Trump Understand His Own Executive Orders?"; "Even Now, Trump Struggles to Understand the Basics of Unemployment." These are all from the month of January.

Perhaps the only self-aware political assessment made by the elite during the 2016 cycle came from Larry J. Sabato, the director of the University of Virginia's Center for Politics.

"If Trump is nominated, then everything we think we know about presidential nominations is wrong," Sabato wrote on August 13, 2015, on the Center for Politics *Sabato's Crystal Ball* website.

So far, we are seeing the same elite propagandists who were wrong about the primary, wrong about the election, and wrong about the president's cabinet picks, trying to paint Trump's presidency as chaotic. Think about this: if a sports analyst consistently misreported games he or she observed, he or she would not be a sports analyst anymore. Yet news reporters face no consequences for consistently misreporting politics.

SUBJECT BIAS

Clearly, not every journalist is a liberal propagandist seeking to push his or her own narrative. I have great respect for real journalists, who genuinely want to inform the public about the actions of their government. But some reporters create traps for themselves, and their editors are letting them fall in. Just look at the way news organizations large and small have approached stories about illegal immigration. Virtually every news agency in the country has written at least one story about what it's like to be an illegal immigrant in its community.

These stories are formulaic. First, reporters introduce the local person here illegally as the main character. Then they detail the hardships he or she endured to get to our country and highlight how hard it is to find safe work and housing without proper documentation. The reporters then explain how terrible it would be for the main character to return to his or her own country, and they finish by talking to lawmakers about how and if this person's life should be made easier or worse through legislation.

Not surprisingly, the *New York Times* has mastered the model. Here's an example from June 8, 2014, by Damien Cave. The story is dramatically titled "An American Life, Lived in Shadows":

> Ignacio, a father of four, bounces along in his pickup truck, driving at exactly the speed limit through an aging suburb. The clock says 6:44 a.m. Religious pen-

dants hang off the mirror. His teenage son sits beside him, chatty if half-awake, as they approach an apartment building for a day of roofing in dire heat.

A police cruiser suddenly appears to the right. Ignacio stays quiet, hands on the wheel, but in his mind he repeats the prayer that covers his 12 years living here illegally: "No me pare, no me pare"—"Don't stop me, don't stop me."

"We used to have such a comfortable life, money to pay for our house, the car, to go wherever we wanted," Ignacio says, referring to a time before Oklahoma's 2007 law against illegal immigrants forced him to close his successful hair salon. "Now we are biting our nails, trying to make enough money every month."[6]

In many cases, these stories are remarkable, interesting, and compelling. They are full of conflict, determination, and great struggle. As a community, reporters then pat each other's backs for telling the stories of the downtrodden. So, journalists get awards for writing personal stories about people here illegally. Other journalists then see the praise their peers get and think, "I bet I can write a story about an undocumented immigrant in my community," and the cycle continues.

Meanwhile, people in middle America who are constantly reading, watching, and listening to these stories sit and think, "What about me? I haven't had a job in months. I'm having trouble paying for housing. I'm a legal American. I'm following all the laws, and I'm still struggling."

The inherent bias betrayed by these "day in the life" stories are clear as day to the American people. So some news organizations drop the premise altogether.

Just look at the first three paragraphs of this story on the website for PBS Kids titled "Immigration: Living Undocumented."[7]

I'm not entirely certain which aspect of this "news" story is most alarming: that it was paid for with tax dollars or that it's a clear effort to indoctrinate children with liberal immigration policy.

> You may have heard the term 'illegal immigrants' in the news or mentioned by adults. What does that mean, exactly? How can a person be illegal?
>
> It's kind of a weird thing to call someone, so we choose to use the term "undocumented immigrants," meaning they don't have the official paperwork that allows them to live in a new country. When immigration through legal channels is too expensive, complicated, or slow, or when the situation is too desperate, people are often left with this option.
>
> Do you picture undocumented immigrants sneaking across national borders in the dark of night or hidden in a truck? This does happen. But just as often, families will enter a new nation as visitors and then choose to stay for good. For many, this new life is better than where they lived before, but it usually has serious challenges and dangers too.

This narrative is designed to build sympathy for people here illegally while ignoring border patrol agents whom we pay to keep them out, taxpayers who pay for their health care through hospital funding, legal immigrants who are inappropriately stigmatized by the actions of rule breakers, and a host of other Americans negatively affected. And, of course, doing sympathetic in-depth stories about people robbed, raped, or killed by criminal aliens would be shunned by most reporters and their editors. In Germany, this led to the suppression of stories about 2,500 assaults on New Year's Eve 2015. Only when social media boiled over with anger about victims and eyewitnesses did the media and the government reluctantly admit it had happened.

It was this deep cultural bias in the media that Trump had to overcome with his campaign.

TRUMP'S MEDIA WORK-AROUND

Media organizations are quickly learning that Trump doesn't need them to communicate with Americans.

As of February, Donald Trump had 25.4 million followers on his personal Twitter account and 15 million on his @POTUS account. He had 21 million people who liked his personal page on Facebook. During the campaign, he was able to leverage that network of people to bypass cable news media (and avoid paying for publicity). He would tweet out plans to hold a rally somewhere, and thirty thousand people would show up—all with smartphones. Those people would then post pictures and status updates about the rally, showing their enthusiasm for Trump, and influencing their personal networks.

When you start examining the number of people Trump was reaching through those networks, it is truly breathtaking. Pew Research Center said in its *Social Media Update 2016*, which was published three days after the election, that 86 percent of Americans used the Internet, and 79 percent of those people use Facebook.[8] The survey of 1,520 adults living in the United States found that 32 percent of adults who used the Internet have Instagram accounts, and 24 percent use Twitter.

Brandwatch, a social media–focused marketing company, reported that as of March 2016, the average Facebook user had 338 friends. The median Facebook friend figure was 200, and at the same time, the company reported the average Twitter user had 208 followers.[9]

So, based on those statistics, we can estimate that 25,800 people at a 30,000-person Trump rally used the Internet. Of those

Internet users, 20,382—or 79 percent—used Facebook and had approximately four million friends combined (using Brandwatch's median figure to adjust for friend-heavy outliers like Trump).

That's a bigger potential audience than any of the cable news channels—all from one rally.

If the media continues to present a false vision of the president, Trump should be prepared to break up the liberal media's monopoly on White House coverage.

If members of the media don't step back and reconsider how they plan to cover President Trump, they will be locked in a war with the administration for as long as he is in office.

You've seen already that Trump is not backing down. During a speech at the Conservative Political Action Conference, he told the crowd the media was "the enemy of normal Americans."

In February, he informed the press he would not be joining them for the annual White House Correspondents Dinner. The dinner is traditionally a roast of the president, but that's now everyday programming in today's propaganda media.

Sean Spicer may have the most difficult job in Washington. He has to contend all day with people who deeply oppose President Trump, are hostile to the Trump agenda, and constantly look for opportunities to attack or belittle the president and his team.

The Trump team should redefine the entire process of communicating with the country. There is no reason the White House press corps should be dominated by elite media hostile to the president. Membership can be dramatically broadened to include local media organizations from across the country and alternative conservative media. Skype and FaceTime could be used to allow one or two citizens to ask questions at each press briefing.

A lot can be done to open up the process.

Candidate Trump had consistently underestimated the depth of genuine hostility from the Left. He still had a childhood sense that if you ran a hard race, then everyone would rally around the winner. Again and again, some bad story would come up that accused him of racism or bigotry, or some good story would be ignored, or some totally phony charge of him treating past female employees badly would dominate the news for several days. He would express surprise and frustration. Every time, I would say to him, "These people are your mortal enemies. You represent the end of their world. They will never give up as long as you are in office." While what I was saying was accurate, it so conflicted with Trump's childhood civic lessons he still can't completely accept it.

CHAPTER SIX

TOXIC IDENTITY POLITICS

There has been a fundamental shift in the way that liberals approach civil rights.

This shift has twisted a unifying movement that favors equal rights for all people into a brand of toxic identity politics, which is dividing the nation along racial, religious, sexual and gender lines.

No moment in the 2016 campaign captured the divisive nature of identity liberalism better than Hillary Clinton's description of half of Donald Trump's supporters as "deplorables" who were "racist, sexist, homophobic, xenophobic, Islamophobic—you name it" and who were "irredeemable."

The election of Donald Trump was due in part to a national rejection of this identity-based liberalism.

Liberalism did not always take this approach. The civil rights movement of an earlier generation attracted a broad-based coalition of Americans. It succeeded in passing the landmark Civil Rights Act of 1964, which outlawed discrimination by race, sex, color, religion, or national origin. The law attracted overwhelming bipartisan support. Sixty-three percent of Democrats and 80 percent of Republicans supported the legislation in the House of Representatives, while 69 percent of Democrats and 82 percent of Republicans supported it in the Senate.

That generation of civil rights leaders also succeeded in passing the overwhelmingly bipartisan Equal Pay Act of 1963, which outlawed paying women less than men for the same work. It was passed by voice vote in both the House and Senate. (An earlier version of the bill attracted support from 79 percent of Democrats and 90 percent of Republicans in the House.)

This civil rights movement succeeded because it was firmly rooted in America's founding principles. It was a direct call to the Declaration of Independence's affirmation of the "self-evident" truth that "all men are created equal." It was dedicated to a vision of a color-blind society in which, as Dr. Martin Luther King Jr. put it, his children "will not be judged by the color of their skin, but by the content of their character."

That vision of a color-blind society with equal rights for all has now been abandoned by the Left in favor of a race- and gender-obsessed insurrection against American ideals.

Today, the Left says that statements expressing the desire for Dr. King's color-blind society are racist.

The University of California's guide titled "Recognizing Microaggressions and the Message They Send," for example, says that statements such as "When I look at you, I don't see color" denies "the individual as a racial/cultural being." The Left has shifted from judging people by the content of their character to believing that we are defined by our race.

Psychology Today published an article in 2011 titled "Color-blind Ideology Is a Form of Racism."[1]

Identity liberalism also rejects the idea of America as a "melting pot"—a phrase coined by a Jewish immigrant from England in 1908 to describe the idea that all immigrants can learn to become Americans by adopting key national values while at the same time strengthening the American character by bringing the best of their native culture to their new home.

Instead, the Left opposes assimilation and instead aspires for a country in which all subgroups of Americans—defined by their race, nationality, religion, sexuality, and so forth—never shed their differences to become one people. It is a recipe for the balkanization of America—for conflict, not unity.

I was born in Harrisburg, Pennsylvania, and grew up as an army brat. The army was integrated, and I routinely went to school with African Americans. It was a real shock to transfer in 1960 as a junior from Stuttgart, Germany, to Fort Benning, Georgia. The army base was integrated, but the state of Georgia was legally enforcing segregation. There were white and black bathrooms, water fountains, schools, and so forth. It did not make for a united community.

Over the last twenty years, the Left has shifted from being antisegregation and prointegration to championing a new desire for racial identity and the new segregation. Black students at the University of Michigan demand a racially segregated space for blacks only. On campus after campus, courses are being offered that are explicitly antiwhite.

The toxic nature of identity liberalism is why most Americans view race relations as worse now than in decades past.[2] This is tragic, because as the nation's first African American president, Barack Obama had the opportunity to help heal the nation of its racial divides.

Unfortunately, this didn't happen, because the Left learned the wrong lessons from his election.

LEARNING THE WRONG LESSONS FROM THE OBAMA VICTORY

Barack Obama's overwhelming victory in 2008 was a cultural watershed that inspired hope for millions of Americans.

I attended his January 2009 inaugural and remember looking out at the vast crowd. Seeing that level of support from Americans looking for change, I told Callista as we left the Capitol that if Obama governed from the center, he could split Republicans in the House and Senate and build an enduring Democratic governing majority for decades.

As president, Obama did anything but govern from the center. Instead of enacting mainstream policies to solidify his broad-based support, he pursued what I described in an earlier book as a "secular-socialist" agenda that alienated key segments of the people who had voted for him in 2008.

But it wasn't just Obama and the Left's policies that alienated Americans, it was their politics. The Left, and the Democratic Party apparatus that is its vehicle, decided a permanent Democratic majority could be built mainly on the strength of blacks, Hispanics, college-educated women, sexual identity politics, and young liberal voters—leaving out the rest of the broad coalition Obama had built in 2008.

This conclusion was tempting to draw because it was precisely what two liberal writers predicted in a 2002 book called *The Emerging Democratic Majority*. The authors argued that demographic trends would guarantee Democratic Party dominance as the country became less white over time. The election of an African American president by a coalition of young liberals and minorities seemed to prove their thesis.

But as Nate Cohn wrote for the *New York Times* in December 2016, the "core of the Obama coalition" was not a massive voting bloc of minority voters. It was "an alliance between black voters and Northern white voters." Specifically, Cohn pointed to non–college educated working-class white voters in the upper Midwest.

The Left overlooked this fact and pursued a strategy of base mobilization by doubling down on explicitly identity-oriented politics. Rather than finding unifying fights that attracted broad-based support based on mutual self-interest and common values, the Left obsessed over race and gender issues. The Democrats embraced Black Lives Matter, put gay marriage and transgender issues front and center, and painted those who disagreed with them as haters.

By focusing so much of its rhetoric on explicitly identity-based appeals, the Left forgot to study the actual message that Obama had used to build his winning coalition.

The truth is that as a candidate in 2008, Obama was very careful to avoid explicitly identity-oriented politics. His approach on matters of race was usually framed within universal American values and tried to avoid divisiveness.

Ta-Nehisi Coates is a very left-wing black activist and author. He wrote an article in January 2017 reflecting on what it meant, as a black man, to have an African American president. I suspect I don't agree with Coates on very much, but his observations about Obama's approach to issues involving race are very astute.

In the article, Coates calls Obama "the most agile interpreter and navigator of the color line I had ever seen. He had an ability to emote a deep and sincere connection to the hearts of black people, while never doubting the hearts of white people."[3]

Coates had an opportunity to interview the former president for the article. When discussing how his early work as a community organizer in Chicago affected him, Obama told Coates:

> When I started doing that work, my story merges with a larger story. . . . How do I pull all these different strains together: Kenya and Hawaii and Kansas, and white and black and Asian—how does that fit? And through action, through work, I suddenly see myself as part of the bigger process for, yes, delivering justice for the [African American community] and specifically the South Side community, the low-income people—justice on behalf

of the African American community. But also thereby promoting my ideas of justice and equality and empathy that my mother taught me were universal. So I'm in a position to understand those essential parts of me not as separate and apart from any particular community but connected to every community. And I can fit the African American struggle for freedom and justice in the context of the universal aspiration for freedom and justice.[4]

It is also worth noting that the most significant obstacle Obama faced in the 2008 election was when tapes of his pastor spouting anti-American rhetoric surfaced. Obama responded with a speech on race framed within universalist, pro-American values to reassure voters that he did not share his pastor's divisive outlook.

Compare this universalist, pro-American-values approach to the antagonistic rhetoric you hear from Democratic Party leaders and the Left today.

In July 2016, the highest-ranking Democrat in the House of Representatives, Minority Leader Nancy Pelosi asserted that "non–college educated white males" vote Republican "because of guns, because of gays, and because of God—the three Gs—God being the woman's right to choose."

A Democratic congressman representing Ferguson, Missouri, hung a painting depicting police officers as pigs in the US Capitol.

Speaking before an African American audience, Vice President Joe Biden said that Republicans wanted to "put y'all back in chains."

Even Obama, once he took office, started to veer from his universalist approach from the 2008 election into explicit identity liberalism.

He began weighing in on highly publicized law enforcement matters in a totally inappropriate manner. For instance, in the early days of his presidency, Obama remarked that police had acted "stupidly" in the case of an African American Harvard professor arrested for breaking into his own home because his door was jammed. Obama automatically assumed the officer was racially motivated. He made a huge mistake by ramping up the racial rhetoric during the Trayvon Martin shooting incident in Florida by saying, "If I had a son, he would look like Trayvon."

The Democrats and the Obama administration also made the decision to put gay, lesbian, and transgender issues in the front and center of the Democratic Party. Public opinion on gay marriage has changed radically in the past few decades, and one could argue that fully embracing it made sense for Democrats. But identity liberalism demands that the full gamut of concerns for the community, no matter how niche, be given the spotlight.

Peter Thiel, a gay Republican, summed it up well when he said at the Republican Convention, "I don't pretend to agree with every plank in our party's platform. But fake culture wars only distract us from our economic decline.

"When I was a kid, the great debate was about how to defeat the Soviet Union. And we won. Now we are told that the great debate is about who gets to use which bathroom. This is a distraction from our real problems. Who cares?" he said.

The Left's focus on identity politics served only to alienate working Americans living paycheck to paycheck and wondering when their concerns were going to be met. This is in part what paved the way for Trump to break through the "blue wall" of Rust Belt states during the election.

Finally, and most destructively, Democrats adopted a conscious strategy of delegitimizing the concerns of Americans who rejected Obamacare and other policies of the Obama administration as evidence of racism against a black president.

In a hearing of the Senate Commerce Committee in May 2014, then-chairman Senator Jay Rockefeller, a Democrat from West Virginia, fed this insidious narrative:

It's very important to take a long view at what's going on here. And I'll be able to dig up some emails that make part of the Affordable Care Act that doesn't look good, especially from people who have made up their mind that they don't want it to work. Because they don't like the president, maybe he's of the wrong color. Something of that sort. . . . I've seen a lot of that and I know a lot of that to be true. It's not something you're meant to talk about in public, but it's something I'm talking about in public because that is very true.

And Democratic US representative Steve Cohen of Tennessee told Bridget Johnson with *PJ Media* in June 2015 that "we need people to forget about being against Affordable Care Act. A lot of the reason they're against it is because it's President Obama, who's African-American, and because it helps a lot of people that are poor and lower income."

This is the same Representative Cohen who, according to *Politico*, in January 2011 compared Republicans to Nazis for opposing the law on the House floor.

"They say it's a government takeover of health care, a big lie just like Goebbels," Cohen said, referring to a Nazi propagandist. "You say it enough, you repeat the lie, you repeat the lie, and eventually, people believe it. Like blood libel. That's the same kind of thing."

The result of this obsession with identity liberalism is that a potentially unifying presidency became a divisive one. The hope for a better, more unified America—the 2008 Obama brand—faded into a cacophony of race, gender, and sexual orientation-based antagonism.

As a writer for the *New York Times* put it in a 2015 article called "The Year We Obsessed Over Identity," "We had never really had a white president until we had a black one."[5]

INTERSECTIONALITY: THE FAULTY THEORY BEHIND THE LEFT'S IDENTITY LIBERALISM

The faulty theory behind the Left's attempt at coalition building through identity liberalism is called "intersectionality."

If you have ever heard the term "white privilege" or been told to "check your privilege" by a Leftist, this is where the idea comes from.

Intersectionality was coined and developed as a concept in 1989 by Kimberlé Crenshaw, a law professor seeking to explain why the interests of black women were left out of traditional feminist concerns.

"Intersectionality . . . was my attempt to make feminism, anti-racist activism, and anti-discrimination law do what I thought they should—highlight the multiple avenues through which racial and gender oppression were experienced so that the problems would be easier to discuss and understand," she wrote in a 2015 opinion piece.[6]

> Originally articulated on behalf of black women, the term brought to light the invisibility of many constituents within groups that claim them as members, but often fail to represent them. . . . Intersectionality has given many advocates a way to frame their circumstances and to fight for their visibility and inclusion.[7]

In theory, intersectionality builds coalitions by getting different minority groups to recognize that their griefs all have common, intersecting causes. In practice, it breeds division and resentment among the coalition it is trying to build.

Rather than leveling an alleged racial- and gender-based hierarchy of power, it inverts it, putting the supposedly least privileged persons at the top. The result is a self-narrowing bullying culture of privilege checking, because each group is trying to one-up the others in the rankings of who is most oppressed so that their niche concerns receive the most attention. Intersectionality replaces the call to recognize our shared humanity and the common goal of equal rights with a compulsion to divide us into smaller and smaller groups.

A January 2017 story in the *New York Times* perfectly captured the toxic nature of intersectionality in practice.

It was the week before President Trump's inauguration, and the Left was mobilizing for a counterdemonstration the day after his inauguration in Washington, DC, and other major cities.

Jennifer Willis, a white woman from South Carolina, was planning to attend with her daughters. But then she read a Facebook post by a march volunteer that made it seem as if white voices were not wanted.

The volunteer, who was a black activist from Brooklyn, advised "white allies" to "listen more and talk less," according to the *New York Times*. She even went so far as to suggest that those who were not activists before the election shouldn't show up. "You don't get to join because now you're scared too. I was born scared."

Taken aback by this exclusionist attitude, Ms. Willis decided not to attend. "This is a women's march," she said to the *New York Times*. "We're supposed to be allies in equal pay, marriage, adoption. Why is it now about, 'White women don't understand black women'?"[8]

It turns out that lecturing strangers based solely on their gender and color of their skin is not an effective way to build bridges.

In case you think the attitude displayed by this march organizer is an aberration, take a look at these headlines from popular articles posted on liberal websites over the past few years.

"Let's Hope the Boston Marathon Bomber Is a White American"[9]

Top: A young Donald J. Trump with his siblings. *Above left*: Donald Trump stands with his parents, Fred and Mary Anne Trump, at his graduation from New York Military Academy. *Above right*: Donald Trump with his father following his graduation from The Wharton School. (*Photos from the Trump family collection*)

Top: Donald Trump and his father, Fred Trump, survey the city skyline. (*Courtesy of the Trump family collection*) *Above*: President Ronald Reagan shakes hands with Donald Trump at a reception for members of the Foundation for Art and Preservation in Embassies in the Blue Room on November 3, 1987. (*Courtesy of the Ronald Reagan Library*)

Top: I was honored to join Trump at a campaign rally in Cincinnati, Ohio in July 2016. (*Getty Images*) *Above left*: I enjoyed talking with Eric Trump in the green room at the same Cincinnati rally. (*Courtesy of Eric Trump*) *Above right*: Donald Trump points to a supporter in the crowd at a campaign rally in Greensboro, North Carolina. (*Courtesy of the Trump Presidential Campaign*)

Top: Donald Trump interacts with supporters at a campaign event in Charlotte, North Carolina. *Above*: Donald Trump is greeted by vice presidential nominee Mike Pence, family, and friends as he arrives on his helicopter at the Republican National Convention in Cleveland, Ohio. (*Photos courtesy of the Trump Presidential Campaign*)

Top: The Trump family takes the stage at the Republican National Convention in Cleveland, Ohio on July 21, 2016. (*Getty Images*) *Above left*: Donald Trump shakes hands with vice presidential nominee Mike Pence. (*Courtesy of the Trump Presidential Campaign*) *Above right*: Callista and I were honored to be greeted by Candidate Trump in the green room prior to our remarks at the Republican National Convention. (*Courtesy of Callista Gingrich*)

Above: President Trump takes the oath of office on January 20, 2017 with First Lady Melania Trump and their son, Barron, by his side. (*Getty Images*)

Top: Following his election in November 2016, Callista and I were honored to join President-Elect Trump at Trump Tower in New York City. (*Courtesy of Jared Kushner*) *Above left*: President Trump greets Israeli Prime Minister Benjamin Netanyahu at a joint press conference at the White House on February 15, 2017. (*Official White House Photo*) *Above right*: President Trump shakes hands with Canadian Prime Minister Justin Trudeau on February 13, 2017. (*Official White House Photo*)

Top: President Donald Trump addresses a joint session of Congress on February 28, 2017. *Above*: I had the privilege of meeting with President Trump in the Oval Office in March 2017. (*Official White House Photos*)

"White Guys Are Killing Us: Toxic, Cowardly Masculinity,
   Our Unhealable National Illness"[10]
"Yes, Diversity Is about Getting Rid of White People (And
   That's a Good Thing)"[11]
"White Men Must Be Stopped: The Very Future of
   Mankind Depends on It"[12]
"The Plague of Angry White Men: How Racism, Gun
   Culture and Toxic Masculinity Are Poisoning America"[13]
"29 Things White People Ruined"[14]

Within this mentality, it is easy to understand why so many
Democrats responded to any opposition to the secular-socialist
Obama agenda with accusations of racism. If the prism through
which you view the world is one defined by race, gender, and
sexual orientation, then everything must be motivated by either
acceptance or hostility to those aspects of identity.

Again, this is a fundamentally different approach from
that of the civil rights leaders of decades past. For example, Dr.
King actually warned civil rights advocates against viewing all
issues through the prism of race. In his final book, *Where Do
We Go From Here: Chaos or Community*, King wrote specifically about the importance of addressing poverty as a universal issue as opposed to addressing only how it affected the black
community.

In the treatment of poverty nationally, one fact stands out:
There are twice as many white poor as Negro poor in the
United States. Therefore I will not dwell on the experiences
of poverty that derive from racial discrimination, but will
discuss the poverty that affects white and Negro alike.[15]

It was also telling to see what issues animated the Left during
the Obama presidency.

A writer at the liberal website *Vox* wrote a very prescient article in the summer of 2016 called "The Smug Style in American Liberalism." In it, he points out that the Left managed to organize massive boycotts of states that passed bills deemed hostile to the gay and transgender agenda, enlisting corporate entities to pull their assets in an attempt to bully the states' leaders to back down. Meanwhile, the decision by many of these same states to refuse Medicaid expansion under Obamacare—an issue that affects vastly more people—barely inspired a peep from these same activists.[16]

The Left also poured enormous energy into protesting—sometimes with violent results—the shootings of black men by police and others. Some of those shootings were unjustified, and the offenders were eventually tried and found guilty. Many others, however, turned out to have been much more complicated situations than the initial media reports suggested. That didn't matter to the Left and its newly formed identity politics front group, Black Lives Matter. This is why the phrase "hands up, don't shoot" is still used as a rallying cry on the Left to protest the police, even though it came from protests against the shooting of Michael Brown, who never surrendered to the Ferguson police officer in question.[17]

It is also worth noting that intersectionality began to gain popularity on the Left right around the time it was becoming clear that the Great Society programs of Lyndon Johnson, which promised to lift up the poor and eliminate racial disparities, had been proved to be a failure.

Since the legal barriers limiting the rights of African Americans and women had been removed decades earlier, persistent inequality required that the Left develop new theories for why African Americans and women had not made the gains that were promised.

They began to focus on invisible obstacles—they call them institutional barriers and unconscious biases—baked into the structure of society that discriminate against minority groups.

This was easier for those on the Left to do than to accept that the big government liberal programs they cherish were failing to deliver the education and job prospects that they promised.

TRUMPING IDENTITY LIBERALISM

The problems with the Democrats' identity liberalism quickly began to manifest itself during the Obama presidency. The Democrats began to hemorrhage white, working-class voters who felt excluded from identity politics and wanted their economic concerns met and their dignity as Americans respected.

Democrats lost the House of Representatives and the majority of governorships in 2010 due to a rejection of Obamacare and the administration's failure to adequately address the economic downturn. During that election, the Republicans' share of white voters without college degrees increased to 62 percent, from 54 percent in 2008. The House slogan of then–minority leader John Boehner, "Where are the jobs?" proved to be very powerful.

Democrats also lost the House because minority populations are clustered in a small number of congressional districts. This makes identity liberalism particularly ineffective at generating the turnout necessary to succeed in the House in midterm elections.

Obama's reelection in 2012 allowed the Democrats to ignore their growing weakness with working-class whites. He managed to use Mitt Romney's history at Bain Capital restructuring companies to paint him as exactly the sort of rich CEO who had been moving factory jobs overseas. Obama also successfully made the case that the country's continuing economic weakness was the fault of President Bush, and that Mitt Romney would take us back to Bush's policies.

Obama's skill at campaigning brought the Democrats a temporary reprieve, but they made notably little progress in the House of Representatives and at the state level despite Obama's comfortable victory over Romney.

The 2014 election is when the weakness of identity liberalism really became visible. Republicans gained nine seats in the Senate, thirteen seats in the House, two governorships (including heavily Democratic Maryland), and the control of eleven additional statehouses.

Alarm bells should have gone off among Democratic leaders that identity liberalism was failing to pull together the sort of dominant coalition predicted in the aforementioned *Emerging Democratic Majority*. In fact, one of the coauthors of the book, John Juids, wrote an article warning that Republican gains with the middle class, in particular non–college educated whites, was creating an "emerging Republican advantage."[18]

The party, however, couldn't break away from its obsession with identity liberalism.

Hillary Clinton's campaign in 2016, in stark contrast of that of Barack Obama in 2008, was a veritable smorgasbord of identity liberalism.

First, she explicitly ran as the first woman president. Her campaign slogan was "I'm with her." Her campaign accused her primary opponent, Bernie Sanders, of sexism and his supporters of being "Bernie bros" (sexist frat boys). This was just the warm-up round for the general election, when her campaign and the mainstream media spent enormous energy defining Trump as a sexist misogynist.

And as the *Huffington Post* reported, Clinton made history in two ways during her first presidential debate with Trump. She was the first woman to participate in one, but she was also the first candidate in American history to call her opponent racist during a debate. Clinton said Trump "has a long record of engaging in racist behavior."

Citing a University of Virginia professor, the *Huffington Post*, a liberal website, reported, "The word 'racist' has never been used in a televised presidential debate."

Clinton wasn't done, however. She went on to accuse all Americans of harboring "implicit bias" toward other groups and suggested that police needed retraining to deal with their unconscious racism.

These claims sent the same message to Trump's supporters that her "basket of deplorables" comment delivered.

Throughout the campaign, there were warning signs that this approach was backfiring.

Trump was drawing massive crowds with an anti-PC message that was an explicit rejection of identity liberalism and a laser focus on the economic concerns of the working class that Clinton and the Democrats were ignoring.

While most polling showed Clinton with a comfortable lead, a deeper dive into the numbers showed her weaknesses. After the Democratic convention, the *Atlantic* editor Ronald Brownstein warned that the party's message was alienating more people than it was attracting. "Reduced reliance on working-class whites since the 1990s has freed Democrats to pursue a more consistently liberal cultural agenda," he wrote. "But anyone watching this convention's first nights might easily view social inclusion, not economic opportunity, as the party's core priority. 'One of the challenges for Democrats is talking about diversity, talking about gender in a way that doesn't put people on the defensive, [and] make them feel like they are being . . . accused of being bigoted,' says Democratic pollster Margie Omero."[19]

In addition, union leaders who supported Clinton reportedly tried to warn her campaign that she was not addressing their members' concerns, but they were also ignored.[20]

Of course, the results of the election were shocking at the time, but in hindsight, they were consistent with the trends of previous elections. Trump continued to build on Republican advantages with the middle class and non–college educated whites. Meanwhile, the power of identity liberalism to boost turnout among the minority community proved to be a mirage. African American turnout was down significantly from 2008 and 2012 without the nation's first black president on the ticket. And Trump actually increased the share of the vote received from African Americans and Hispanics over Mitt Romney. It turns out that identity liberalism even alienates members of minority groups more concerned about economic issues than niche social justice fights.

Furthermore, Donald Trump was making an appeal based on identity as well—that of being an American. His patriotic call to make America great again overwhelmed explicit appeals to race, gender, and sexual orientation. This universal appeal based on broad issues and common culture trumped identity liberalism.

REFUSING TO LEARN THE LESSON OF THE TRUMP VICTORY

Immediately after the election, there was a lot of recrimination on the Left about what happened. In that environment, after such a shocking loss, there was an opportunity for the Left and the Democrats to reassess the usefulness of identity liberalism in building a stable governing coalition.

Mark Lilla, a college professor, wrote a widely shared piece in the *New York Times* called "The End of Identity Liberalism." In it, he argued that the Left's fixation on identity politics alienated the working class whose chief concern was economic anxiety. He called for a "post-identity liberalism" that would, like earlier successful liberal movements, appeal "to Americans as Americans and emphasize the issues that affect a vast majority of them."[21]

In other words: do what Trump just did, only do it as Democrats.

One of the candidates for the role of DNC chairman in 2017 was more blunt, remarking that all Democrats offered in 2016 was a message of "How offensive!" and that the party needed to "grow up." The candidate, Raymond Buckley, ultimately dropped out of the race.

Even President Obama, despite the fact that the party's embrace of identity politics occurred during his presidency, offered this warning: "One message I do have for Democrats is that a strategy that's just microtargeting particular, discrete groups in a Democratic coalition sometimes will win you elections, but it's not going to win you the broad mandate that you need."[22]

But within a few weeks of Obama's warning, the Left reverted to form, insisting that identity liberalism was still the key to political success, and viciously attacking those who suggested otherwise. The fact is that identity liberalism is where all the energy is in their party, and any attempt to moderate this approach is met with fierce hostility.

Sally Boynton Brown, one of the candidates for chair of the Democratic National Committee, for example, said during a debate that the party must provide "training" for Americans on "how to shut their mouths if they are white." She continued, saying that her job as a white woman was to "listen and be a voice and shut other white people down when they want to interrupt."[23]

Steve Philips, a senior fellow at the liberal Center for American Progress, responded to Lilla, insisting that the party must not make the mistake of pursuing the votes of the "wrong white people"—by which he meant those who don't subscribe to identity liberalism.

Even liberal darlings like Bernie Sanders are not spared the wrath of the liberal identity police.

Sanders's surprising challenge to Hillary Clinton during the Democratic primary was partially due to his strength with white working-class voters.[24] Sanders warned Democrats during his outsider primary campaign against Clinton that their party was losing touch with this key Democratic constituency. Ultimately,

Clinton's identity-politics-fueled campaign won the battle with Democrats and lost the war with everyone else.

After Donald Trump won the election by dominating among the working class in Midwestern states, you would think that the Democratic Party's leaders might be open to taking Sanders's warnings more seriously. "It is not good enough for someone to say, 'I'm a woman! Vote for me!' No, that's not good enough," Sanders said a few weeks after the election. "What we need is a woman who has the guts to stand up to Wall Street, to the insurance companies, to the drug companies."

In response, a former Clinton operative responsible for minority outreach said, "I like US Senator Bernie Sanders but his comments regarding identity politics suggest he may be a white supremacist, too."[25]

That's right. Sanders, a Jewish socialist from liberal Vermont who spent his college years protesting discriminatory housing policy at the University of Chicago, is a white supremacist, according to the identity-obsessed Left.

These sorts of unhinged accusations are par for the course from advocates of identity politics. It's not enough that you believe in equal rights for all people—you cannot acknowledge any other issues or suggest anything else is important.

It is clear that on the Left, broad-based economic liberalism has taken a back seat, and the universalist vision of the original civil rights movement based on American ideals has been repudiated.

The Democratic Party's full-scale transformation into a cult of identity liberalism has changed the political discourse in America from a battle over ideas into a battle among identity groups. In this identity-obsessed environment, your political opponents aren't just attacking your policy positions or theories, they are delegitimizing you as a person. No wonder so many college students demand safe spaces free from opposing viewpoints.

They actually feel personally attacked because they see no difference between their political positions and their self-identity.

USA Today reported on November 15, 2016, that institutions of higher learning across the country were treating the results of the election the same way they typically treat tragedy.

Colleges and universities sponsored postelection recovery meetings, self-care events—and in the case of the University of Kansas, made therapy dogs available to students.

One of the more alarming reactions came from Boston University, where the dean of students sent an email telling students upset about the election to disengage. According to the newspaper, the email advised students:

> "If you feel distressed by what is in the media, for the moment, limit your consumption of Facebook, Twitter and other social media sources that are likely to be full of distressing material," reads one tip, curated by Boston University's Dean of Students. "This also includes watching and reading the news. There are apps and websites such as LeechBlock, or SelfControl that can help you by temporarily blocking access to social media or certain websites."

Universities are supposed to be preparing students for reality—not advising them to hide from it.

For younger Democratic activists, it will be very difficult for them to unlearn identity liberalism. The truth is, it is very seductive. People love talking about themselves, and identity liberalism's focus on narrow subgroups of personal identity and niche issues allows its practitioners to turn inward to obsess over their own uniqueness and how they are personally affected by racism, classism, sexism, or whatever. And if you are constantly talking about yourself, you never bother to listen to anyone else.

Year after year, the American people have grown more and more alienated from the arrogance of the bureaucracies, the bullying of the elites, and the failure of the current system to work for them. Everywhere I went before Trump's campaign, people were angry at Washington and frightened for their futures, their children's futures, and their country's future. Yet members of official Washington from both parties seemed wedded to business as usual. Then along came Trump. When Trump and I would talk about America's leadership, with regard to trade in particular, Trump would repeat over and over, "They are just terrible negotiators. We got taken to the cleaners every time." He was confident he could turn it around very quickly. After seeing him in action over the campaign, I was, too.

CHAPTER SEVEN

THE GREAT TRANSITION

P art of the reason Trump and his message were so successful in the 2016 election is that America is undergoing a Great Transition, and Trump was the only candidate who seemed aware of it.

Trump candidly expressed to the American people something politicians have willfully ignored for decades: most of our policy decisions—both in trade and defense—are based on a world that no longer exists. The era of the post–World War II, ultrarich America that faced little economic competition on the world stage is over.

Immediately following World War II, the United States had to help rebuild our trading partners in Europe. This initiative was called the Marshall Plan, and it provided roughly $12 billion to aid the recovery of Western Europe. For context, when you adjust for inflation, that's about $162 billion in today's currency[1]—four times the amount we currently spend on foreign aid. It was critical that we did so, because a war-torn, weakened Europe was a prime target for communism. Indeed, the Soviet

Union rejected any aid under the Marshall Plan for the Eastern Bloc nations, because Stalin knew aid money from the United States would weaken Soviet influence in the region.

So, we helped rebuild Western Europe, and we separately sent millions of dollars in aid (which would be billions in today's dollars) to a host of Asian countries, including Japan, China, and India, as well as Israel and several others. We could afford to do this because we had virtually no competition on the world stage. No other major developed country could compete with the United States economically, because their factories, their communities, their people—all their economic engines—had been bombed into oblivion.

Since then, the United States has framed its foreign aid and trade policies around the world I just described—the world as it was immediately after World War II. We have approached nearly all our foreign relations as the benevolent, wealthy, endlessly generous United States that can freely provide for the less fortunate of the world without a meaningful return. That was OK for the thirty-five years that followed the war. Our national debt stayed relatively flat until 1980, our production more than doubled in that time, and our debt as a percentage of our gross domestic product (GDP) had lowered from 118 percent in 1946 to about 32 percent. We were by an enormous margin the strongest economic power on the planet.

That started to change toward the end of the last century. The rebuilt world was waking up. Europe and Japan had recovered, China had seen decades of sustained growth and was on track to become the economic power it is today, and much of the rest of the world had prospered during the postwar recovery.

We made some adjustments to become more competitive. President Reagan's agenda of lower taxes and less regulation succeeded in giving the US economy a boost, sparking a broad-based economic boom.

On trade, however, the United States continued to act as if it had no real competition—and by the end of the twentieth century, middle-class Americans began to be hit hard.

For decades, median household income tracked pretty closely with real GDP in the United States, according to economic data from the Federal Reserve Bank of Saint Louis. This meant that our country's economic growth was benefiting everyone. That began to change in the late 1990s. Household income has essentially stayed flat since 1999 while GDP has increased by 20 percent. The economy is growing, but middle-class Americans do not benefit.

MAKE FREE TRADE FAIR AGAIN

The idea behind free trade is straightforward: if two or more countries that each specialize in making products the others can't agree to trade those specific products without tariffs or taxes, then all the countries can benefit economically by exporting large amounts of their specialty products.

In theory, this is a good idea. What's missing from the pro–free trade mantra is that all countries almost never benefit equally. The country that benefits the most in any trade agreement is the country that produces the most products that are highly desired by a majority of countries in the agreement.

For decades, that country was the United States. However, as globalization took hold, companies began opening factories in countries with much lower standards of living. If you only have to pay foreign workers a fraction of what you pay Americans, it becomes impossible to produce many types of goods in the United States at prices that are competitive.

It also only makes sense to enter agreements when we are buying products we actually need. It's not a good deal for us if we are importing something we can already make at American facilities, with American workers.

IGNORED BY BOTH PARTIES

The impact of America's Great Transition from being the world's undisputed power and patron to being one of several self-interested nations competing on a global scale has largely been ignored by the elites in our government. This is partly due to mental inertia and partly due to the influence of entrenched special interests.

On the Left and Right, our politicians and bureaucrats have ignored the anxieties that have manifested themselves in the issues of trade and immigration, because raising alarms would divide their bases.

Large multinational companies with headquarters in America—which are active campaign donors to both sides— apply pressure on politicians because the companies benefit from free trade agreements.

President Trump has been crystal clear that his priority is seeing that American workers have jobs. The special interests of giant multinational corporations that benefit from open trade borders will no longer steer our trade policies from the shadows.

The industries argue that cheap labor and material costs available in other countries allow companies to produce and sell their products to Americans at lower prices, which means more money in American wallets.

This narrative ignores that when American companies outsource their labor or look for cheaper materials elsewhere, Americans lose jobs. What good is a cheaper widget if you don't have the paycheck to buy it?

The "more in the wallet" argument also ignores something that Arthur C. Brooks, the president of the American Enterprise Institute, frequently writes about: long-term happiness comes from earned success, not handouts, deals, or even more money.

In op-eds Brooks wrote for the *New York Times* in 2013

and the *Philadelphia Inquirer* in 2014, he pointed out that studies show employment has a greater effect on happiness than income.

Citing the General Social Survey, a project of the independent research organization NORC at the University of Chicago that's mainly funded by the National Science Foundation, Brooks says people who feel like their work is successful are two times more likely to say they are happy.

While income greatly affects the results of the survey for those who live in poverty, Brooks said that impact diminishes for people who make at least middle-class incomes.

"This is not about money. The secret to happiness through work is earned success—the belief you are creating value with your life and value in the lives of others," Brooks writes.

While Brooks argued for policies that promote entrepreneurship in America—an important effort in its own right—the data also speak to the importance of prioritizing good-paying American jobs over getting lower prices at the cash register.

NAFTA: HINDSIGHT IS 20/20

A good example of the disconnect between the priorities of the American people and the large corporations who influence Washington is the North American Free Trade Agreement (NAFTA), which Trump early on called "single worst trade deal ever approved in this country."

NAFTA was a free trade agreement the United States entered with Mexico and Canada. It was originally negotiated by President George H. W. Bush in 1992, but it wasn't implemented until President Bill Clinton took office. Clinton added labor and environmental provisions before he brought it to Congress in 1993, but it was still widely supported by Republicans—including myself. In some ways, it represented the last gasp of that post–World War II America, and we in Congress either didn't realize it or didn't want to accept it.

I was the Republican whip during the NAFTA vote, and Republicans delivered more yes votes than Clinton and Gore could get on the Democratic side. Little did we realize back then that the time had come to shift from the post–World War II model of generosity to a more pro-American attitude.

We thought the cost to the United States would be minimal, and Mexico would gain jobs by exporting goods to the United States that we would otherwise buy from China. In fact, Mexico ended up taking jobs from us instead of China, and the difference in Mexican and American salaries was so great we were creating a flood of jobs out of the United States.

In 1994, when NAFTA was implemented, the US per capita GDP was $27,776 in 1994 dollars, according to the World Bank. Canada's GDP at the time was $19,859 per capita, so this wasn't a huge difference. But Mexico's 1994 per capita GDP was $5,690.[2] Added to that, the main US industries affected by the removal of tariffs on Mexican and Canadian products in NAFTA were auto manufacturing, textiles, and agriculture—all things the United States does very well.

According to the US Bureau of Labor Statistics, the overall number of manufacturing jobs in the U.S. has declined from 17.7 million in 1993 to 12.2 million today. Automotive jobs dropped from 1.1 million to 944,600 and textile jobs went from 836,500 to a mere 128,900 today.[3] NAFTA isn't solely responsible for that. Automation caused many of the job losses in the automotive industry—but NAFTA didn't help.

At the same time, thanks to NAFTA, the automotive industry in Mexico has exploded. According to a 2014 paper by the Wharton School—Trump's alma mater—Mexican automotive exports to the United States have substantially increased.[4]

As recently as 2008, Japan exported almost twice as many cars to the United States as did Mexico. This year, however, Mexico will export 1.69 million vehicles to the U.S., surpassing the 1.51 million vehicles exported by Japan to the same market. By 2015, Mexico will export 1.9 million vehicles to the U.S., surpassing Canada as the largest exporter to the U.S.

Overall, Mexico's output of vehicles reached 2.93 million units in 2013. By 2020, almost 25 percent of all North American vehicle production will take place in Mexico, compared with only 10 percent in Canada and 65 percent in the United States. For both the U.S. and Canada, those numbers will represent a considerable decline in their share of the North American production pie.

The arrangement with Canada appears to be a more mutually beneficial situation—which makes sense, since our per capita GDP figures are similar. In 2015, Canada imported $11.9 billion more than it exported to the United States. And meanwhile, Canada's overall trade and GDP have grown since NAFTA was implemented—as has US investment in Canada, according to a February article by David Floyd for *Investopedia*.[5] However, Canada's automaker unions have complained the country has also seen auto jobs flee to Mexico.

AMERICA FIRST

President Trump has opposed NAFTA since the beginning of his campaign, calling the agreement the "worst trade deal in history." And in the first months of his presidency he told Congress that he would be renegotiating the agreement with our northern and southern neighbors. He's not completely against trade agreements of any kind. As he said during his joint address to

Congress, he "believe[s] strongly in free trade but it also has to be fair trade."

President Trump also prevented a replay of NAFTA by canceling US participation in the Trans-Pacific Partnership—a twelve-nation trade deal negotiated by the Obama administration—just three days after taking office. As the *New York Times* reported, Trump canceled the plan, which was based on outdated agreements going back to the Cold War:

> "We're going to stop the ridiculous trade deals that have taken everybody out of our country and taken companies out of our country, and it's going to be reversed," Mr. Trump told them, saying that from now on, the United States would sign trade deals only with individual allies. "I think you're going to have a lot of companies come back to our country."

The United States can no longer afford to be the world's benefactor. It is time to fight for every advantage we can.

OBEYING THE RULES

But for Donald Trump to bring jobs back to the United States and reinvigorate the middle class, renegotiating NAFTA with Mexico and forming more favorable trade agreements with other countries will be only part of the puzzle. He will also need to deal with China—our largest trading partner.

According to the Office of the US Trade Representative, the United States bought $497.8 billion worth of goods and services from China in 2015 and sold the country only $161.6 billion in goods and services. That means Chinese companies made $336.2 billion off of trade with the US last year.

China achieves this lopsided trade ratio through a deliberate strategy of cheating and stealing.

As an illustration of China's shenanigans, just look at the aluminum trade. China is the world's largest producer of aluminum.

The *Wall Street Journal* reported in September 2016 that one of China's largest aluminum producers was avoiding a US tariff by rerouting its product through several other companies to Mexico. The United States put the steep tariff on Chinese aluminum imports in 2010 after China flooded the US market with the metal a year earlier. China's market surge in 2009 drove the price of aluminum down by 30 percent, which helped force eighteen of the twenty-three US aluminum smelters out of business.

After this, a US aluminum trade representative from California suspected a major Chinese aluminum producer, Zhongwang Holdings, was dodging the tariff. The newspaper reported that the representative chartered a plane to fly over one of the company's factories in Mexico—where he found a stockpile of aluminum that amounted to 6 percent of the world's supply. The owner of the company, Liu Zhongtian, is a member of China's ruling Communist Party.

The Chinese chicanery that President Trump most often rails against is the country's proclivity to devalue its currency. The Chinese government artificially lowers the value of its own currency, the yuan, to cause Chinese goods to be less expensive—and therefore more desirable—in the world market. Doing so naturally grows China's economy at the expense of American companies, which can't compete with unfairly lowered prices. This causes the United States–China trade balance—the $336.2 billion figure I mentioned earlier—to swell to even greater amounts.

Now, the International Monetary Fund said in 2015 that China is no longer manipulating its currency inappropriately. Fine. But that doesn't undo the damage wrought by years of devaluation that cost the United States and other countries millions of jobs and trade. You can't cheat at seventeen holes of golf, then claim a clean win because you marked the eighteenth hole correctly.

Another, more blatantly illegal, way that China is cheating at trade—and getting away with it—is by stealing business secrets from the United States and other countries.

The National Bureau for Asian Research found in its 2013 *Commission on the Theft of American Intellectual Property* report that China is stealing hundreds of billions of dollars of business and trade secrets from Americans every year. The exact amount is difficult to pin down, because no one can record all the pirated movies and software, stolen business practices, and counterfeit products China is fencing. This is, after all, a black market. But the authors of the intellectual property report found "annual losses are likely to be comparable to the current annual level of U.S. exports to Asia—over $300 billion." The report cites Gen. Keith Alexander, who led both the US Cyber Command and the National Security Agency. He described what China is doing to the United States as "the greatest transfer of wealth in history."

And William Evanina, who was the director of the National Counterintelligence and Security Center under US National Intelligence Director James Clapper, told *Bloomberg Technology* in November 2015 that cyberattacks are costing the United States economy $400 billion a year—and China was responsible for about 90 percent of those attacks. That would account for $360 billion.

The authors found this massive, systematic theft was costing the United States millions of jobs, hindering US innovation, and hurting economic growth in America.

But China is not the only bad player in world trade. The entire global trading system is rife with corruption that has festered over decades of inattention. The world stage has changed for trade, and our country has been stuck in the first act.

This is exactly why President Trump is taking an America-first approach to new trade deals and applying that principle when he renegotiates old ones. He told a group of Pennsylvania steel workers back in June 2016 that America "lost our way when we stopped believing in our country."

"We allowed foreign countries to subsidize their goods, devalue their currencies, violate their agreements and cheat in every way imaginable, and our politicians did nothing about it," he said. "Trillions of our dollars and millions of our jobs flowed overseas as a result."

In April 2017, Trump met with Chinese president Xi Jinping, and they agreed to a framework that would open up China to more American exports. There is still a lot of work to be done, but by insisting on America first, President Trump has begun to reset American trade policy for the realities of the twenty-first century. America can no longer afford to be the world's most generous patsy.

Callista and I were excited to be at the inauguration of President Trump. We had attended both of President Obama's inaugurations as loyal citizens, but this was different. We knew president-elect Trump, and we liked him. It was fun watching his family come out. His speech was inspirational. We left with a feeling of hope that America had turned a corner. I had talked with the president-elect a number of times since the election about the vital importance of this key moment. He clearly had stopped and focused on what he wanted to say. I was impressed with how much the inaugural was his personal message to all Americans.

CHAPTER EIGHT

THE INAUGURAL

Americans in 2016 were intensely frustrated with the status quo and angry at the so-called leaders who were unable or unwilling to change things. Americans were tired of being told how to think by the IYI and the propaganda media, sick of toxic identity politics, rejecting fake news and fake education, and feeling the burden of the Great Transition. As a genuine outsider, Donald Trump was in tune with the American people instead of the elites in the media, academia, and government. That's why Trump won.

Now that he is president, it is critically important that Trump maintains that connection with the American people. He must keep focusing on the issues that got him elected, and resist becoming captive to the priorities of the Washington elite.

As Trump's first act as president, the inaugural address he delivered after he took the oath of office on January 20, 2017, was a good indication that he intends to deliver real solutions for the American people on the issues they care about.

It is worth taking some time to review this remarkable speech for two reasons.

First, it is a powerful distillation of the underlying issues we have discussed in the past few chapters that led to the rise of Donald Trump. Second, because it sets the stage for the focus of the rest of this book—how Trump and the Republican Congress must govern if they hope to succeed.

THE END OF THE RULE OF THE IYI

President Trump's inaugural address spoke directly to the millions of frustrated Americans who have watched their communities decay while the intellectual yet idiots in our government and media claimed the economy was improving, unemployment was down, and America was leading in the world.

Just as Trump did throughout his campaign, the president assured those Americans that they would no longer have to listen to or be led by out-of-touch elites in the nation's capital. The intellectual yet idiots will no longer chart the course of our country.

This was his specific condemnation of the old order in both parties. This should have been a very serious focus in the national media, because Trump was making a specific statement. It's very powerful:

> Today's ceremony, however, has very special meaning. Because today we are not merely transferring power from one administration to another, or from one party to another—but we are transferring power from Washington, DC, and giving it back to you, the American people.
>
> For too long, a small group in our nation's capital has reaped the rewards of government while the people have borne the cost. Washington flourished—but the people did not share in its wealth. Politicians prospered—but the jobs left, and the factories closed.

The establishment protected itself, but not the citizens of our country. Their victories have not been your victories; their triumphs have not been your triumphs; and while they celebrated in our nation's capital, there was little to celebrate for struggling families all across our land.

This comment reminded every appointee, civil servant, and member of the House and Senate what the Trump Revolution is about. It is about the American people joining together to reclaim the future of our country.

President Trump went on to say:

That all changes starting right here and right now because this moment is your moment, it belongs to you. . . . What truly matters is not which party controls our government, but whether our government is controlled by the people. January 20, 2017, will be remembered as the day the people became the rulers of this nation again.

President Trump made it clear that his administration would be about the people. This reliance on the sovereignty of the people is at the heart of both American populism and of the whole sense of what makes Trump so different.

He knows he will fail if he makes his presidency about Donald Trump. He will succeed only if he reorients the federal government toward serving the needs of all Americans, instead of catering to the priorities of the elite.

ENDING FAKE EDUCATION AND REJECTING TOXIC IDENTITY POLITICS

President Trump also pledged that American communities would soon again have "great schools for their children." Great schools would be places where students in the United States gained true knowledge instead of reinvented history. And parents would not have to worry about their children being indoctrinated with liberalism—or any political perspective except the belief that America is the freest and greatest nation on earth.

Perhaps most important, President Trump addressed the problem of identity politics that has been dividing and sowing strife in our country for decades. He called for all Americans to celebrate their differences but to never forget we are one people under God.

> At the bedrock of our politics will be a total allegiance to the United States of America, and through our loyalty to our country, we will rediscover our loyalty to each other. When you open your heart to patriotism, there is no room for prejudice.
>
> The Bible tells us, 'How good and pleasant it is when God's people live together in unity.' We must speak our minds openly, debate our disagreements honestly, but always pursue solidarity. When America is united, America is totally unstoppable.

This passage is important, because it expresses an aspect of President Trump's personality that is completely overlooked by the media. To Trump, bigotry cannot exist within a patriotic heart. To be racist—to hold any other American in low regard based on their gender, religion, race or heritage—is to be completely unpatriotic.

RECOGNIZING THE GREAT TRANSITION

Looking at President Trump's inaugural address, and the events surrounding it, you can see that he was keenly aware of all the social and economic forces that were obvious to ordinary Americans but seemingly ignored by our leaders. His recognition of the Great Transition was crystal clear. Other politicians on both sides of the aisle have for years touted America's generous—in other words, disadvantageous—position on trade and foreign aid. A foundation of President Trump's campaign was his willingness to say out loud what normal Americans were thinking: that our leaders have been making bad deals and spending our tax dollars to benefit other countries while getting little if anything in return.

Trump perfectly articulated this idea in his inaugural address:

For many decades, we've enriched foreign industry at the expense of American industry; subsidized the armies of other countries while allowing for the very sad depletion of our military; we've defended other nations' borders while refusing to defend our own; and spent trillions of dollars overseas while America's infrastructure has fallen into disrepair and decay.

We've made other countries rich while the wealth, strength, and confidence of our country has disappeared over the horizon. One by one, the factories shuttered and left our shores, with not even a thought about the millions upon millions of American workers left behind.

The wealth of our middle class has been ripped from their homes and then redistributed across the entire world. But that is the past. And now we are looking only to the future. . . . From this day forward, a new vision will govern our land. From this moment on, it's going to be America first. Every decision on trade, on taxes, on immigration, on foreign affairs, will be made to benefit American workers and American families. . . .

We will seek friendship and goodwill with the nations of the world—but we do so with the understanding that it is the right of all nations to put their own interests first.

We do not seek to impose our way of life on anyone, but rather to let it shine as an example for everyone to follow.

President Trump expressed one simple fact in his inaugural address that has eluded so many of America's recent presidents: his primary job is to lead the United States. Trump doesn't want to be the president of the international order, or president of some collective group of nations. He is—and only wants to be—the president of one country.

President Trump has spent a lifetime negotiating deals. He understands that when he negotiates with other countries, the leaders of those countries are going to be rationally self-interested. It only makes sense for the United States to approach negotiations the same way.

With regard to foreign aid to other nations, Trump showed in his speech that we are in a new era. While aggressive foreign aid programs made sense after World War II to rebuild and sustain our allies to defend them against Soviet influence, its usefulness has faded. The Soviet Union disappeared, and other countries have become wealthier. President Trump recognizes that we now need to fundamentally adjust our foreign policy. Instead of subsidizing the planet, we need to represent our own interests.

MOVING FORWARD WITH OPTIMISM, RESOLVE, AND CONFIDENCE

The media largely reported his inaugural address as "dark" since Trump expressed a realistic view of crime in America. Specifically, TV anchors jumped on Trump's use of the words "American carnage." The media was so obsessed with its own narrative that anchors, reporters, editors, and producers across the country completely ignored all the words around the phrase, which were entirely about strengthening communities in every part of the country:

> Americans want great schools for their children, safe neighborhoods for their families, and good jobs for themselves. These are the just and reasonable demands of a righteous public.
>
> But for too many of our citizens, a different reality exists: mothers and children trapped in poverty in our inner cities; rusted-out factories scattered like tombstones across the landscape of our nation; an education system, flush with cash, but which leaves our young and beautiful students deprived of knowledge; and the crime and gangs and drugs that have stolen too many lives and robbed our country of so much unrealized potential. This American carnage stops right here and stops right now.
>
> We are one nation—and their pain is our pain. Their dreams are our dreams; and their success will be our success. We share one heart, one home, and one glorious destiny.

Trump has felt the pulse of the country since before he announced his candidacy, and he clearly understands the pain and heartache of Americans. Despite the media's portrayal, President Trump actually delivered a tremendously uplifting speech. When historians study it in the future, they will describe it as an incredibly positive and visionary speech that helped set our nation on a bold new course. And their assessments will be supported by this quote:

> The time for empty talk is over. Now arrives the hour of action. Do not let anyone tell you it cannot be done. No challenge can match the heart and fight and spirit of

America. We will not fail. Our country will thrive and prosper again.

We stand at the birth of a new millennium, ready to unlock the mysteries of space, to free the earth from the miseries of disease, and to harness the energies, industries, and technologies of tomorrow. A new national pride will stir our souls, lift our sights, and heal our divisions.

This is something President John F. Kennedy might have said to rally America during the Cold War. It is optimistic, positive, and challenges Americans to make the next great discoveries in science and technology to help make a dramatically better future for the United States. This quote particularly excites me, because it shows the president's desire to bring Americans together to develop a totally new approach to accelerate science in curing disease, getting into space, creating jobs, and strengthening national security.

So, this was not a divisive speech. This was a speech that talks about bringing us together, strengthening our position in the world, and creating a better future. Throughout the address, the president focused on the nation as a whole—not Republicans or Democrats.

In fact, I was struck with President Trump's deliberate use of "we"—since we just had a president who found it hard to get through a sentence without the word "I." Sean Hannity told me once he counted seventy-nine uses of "I" in one of President Obama's speeches. But Trump, whom the media often caricatures as focused on himself, opened his first speech as president by saying, "We, the citizens of America, are now joined in a great national effort to rebuild our country and restore its promise for all of our people."

Notice how he continues with this language: "Together, we will determine the course of America and the world for years to come."

Here he showed his understanding that as president of the United States, he ultimately, inevitably, is a leader for the planet. We're too big an economy, we're too strong militarily, we have too great a dominance in culture to think just of ourselves. While President Trump wants to put America first, he wants to put America first within a world system in which he's deeply aware. Here he recognizes we are tied to the entire planet.

What he said next spoke directly to his unshakable resolve: "We will face challenges. We will confront hardships. But we will get the job done."

This line reminds me of a conversation I had with President Trump during one of the low points of the campaign. It was October, and most polls were showing Clinton with a several-point lead. Then-candidate Trump told me, "Remember, I will win." Even at one of his very lowest moments, he was determined. He didn't yet know how he would win. The campaign had not yet finalized its strategy to fight for Pennsylvania, Michigan, and Wisconsin, but Trump knew his success was a question of "how," not "if."

This is a deep part of Trump's personality, one that he wants to imbue on the entire country. Trump doesn't want Americans to talk about disabilities, he wants to talk about capabilities. For instance, Trump sees the success of the Wounded Warrior Project and compares that with our Social Security disabilities program. He wants to change the culture of this population. It's not about what America's disabled people can't do, it's about what they can do. Trump thinks about how we can train people to provide for themselves and their families despite their hardships.

In the same way, when he looks at the welfare and food stamps systems, he doesn't ask how to put more money into those programs to support more people, he asks how we can help these people find good-paying jobs. He asks how the president or Congress can make it easier and more affordable for small businesses to hire people.

Along those lines, I had a conversation with Colorado senator Cory Gardner, who pointed out that there are about 200,000 businesses in Colorado. If each business was able to hire just one more person, you could add 200,000 people to the workforce in Colorado. That would be 200,000 more people paying taxes—200,000 people taking care of their families, homes, and neighborhoods. This thinking is perfectly in line with the Trump mind-set: look at problems and turn them into opportunities.

In closing, Trump said, "Together, we will make America strong again. We will make America wealthy again. We will make America proud again. We will make America safe again. And yes, together we will make America great again."

With his inaugural address, Trump built on his "Make America Great Again" slogan, to reinforce that he wants America to be great for all Americans. It was a very conscious statement by Trump at the very beginning of his presidency, that his commitment is to all Americans.

This inclusive, inspirational message was the theme that allowed President Trump to succeed. And if President Trump keeps his focus on his effort to unify and strengthen America, he could easily build an eight-year administration around it—and America would become a much better place. It will be fascinating to watch how he directs and trains the people around him, because he has a vision of how to get this done.

Trump's inaugural described a fundamentally different direction for America by somebody who has earned the right to tell us what he honestly thinks. I don't know of anyone else who could have come out of nowhere and beaten sixteen Republican candidates. I don't know anyone else who could have taken on the entire elite media and beaten them. I don't know of any other candidate who could have taken on a billion-dollar Hillary Clinton campaign and won. Occasionally people tell me some other Republican would have won by a bigger margin. Baloney.

I've been through a lot of campaigns in my career. The 2016 victory took force of will. It took a willingness to confront his opponents. It took a willingness to be tough. I don't know of any other candidate who could have done it the way he did it. He will need to bring that same optimism, resolve, and confidence to the presidency to succeed in enacting his revolutionary agenda.

A HISTORICAL PERSPECTIVE

After President Trump's inaugural ceremony, I saw a parallel between Trump's inaugural speech and President Lincoln's 1861 inaugural speech. Both were clear statements of nonnegotiable principles to bitter opposition, both had survived some of the most divisive campaigns in American history, and both appealed to patriotism.

I wrote Dr. Allen Guelzo for his perspective. Guelzo is the Henry R. Luce Professor of the Civil War Era and the director of the Civil War Era Studies Program at Gettysburg College. He is one of the great students of Lincoln and one of the great historians in the country. Frankly, I expected Allen to respond, "Have you just lost your mind!?"

But he didn't.

Guelzo responded:

Your points are entirely on the mark. I have done a quick comparative outline of both inaugural addresses, and while the existential situation of the two are different, on

March 4th, 1861, Lincoln was already facing the secession of seven states, the official creation of a Confederate
States of America, and demands for the surrender of
federal property, there is this common thread, the sovereignty of the people. Lincoln used that principle to deny
that one part of the nation, the seven seceding states,
could break up the union without the consent of the
American people, as well as denying that one branch of
the government, the Supreme Court, could overrule the
American people's will.

This was enough to make me feel better. But Guelzo
continued.

Trump invokes that principle. To deny that a federal bureaucracy can enrich and empower itself at the
expense of the people, as well as denying that identity enclaves can overrule the fundamental unity of the
American people.

Guelzo went on to point out that Lincoln's inaugural was a
denial of radical intent, saying that the application of fugitive
slave law must incorporate due process. He said it highlighted
that secession was an impossibility, and that the Union was permanent. Guelzo said Lincoln pointed out that his administration threatened no one's rights, and that the people—not the
Supreme Court—are the ultimate arbiters in America.

Finally, he said Lincoln held that the nation belongs to the
people who inhabit it—rightly pointing out that this remark pre-
saged the Gettysburg Address, in which Lincoln spoke about
government "of the people, by the people, and for the people."

Trump's inaugural held many of the same themes, according to Guelzo.

He outlined Trump's speech as one that described people reclaiming government from the establishment, and repudiating the establishment for failing the citizens and enriching others. He said Trump reaffirmed that decisions would be based on the priority of American interests, and that the government would lead by example but not impose ideals on the people. And Trump stressed that American unity is based on patriotism, according to Guelzo.

Dr. Guelzo went on to say:

> There is one other point of relationship too, and that is the mix of confrontation and conciliation in Lincoln, without any hint of compromise. Lincoln appealed to the better angels of all Americans to promote unity, but along with that, he refused to endorse any compromise, short of a popularly endorsed Constitutional amendment. He, also, and this is more subtle, insisted that the application of the fugitive slave law be done with full respect for due process. This was a carefully calculated rebuke to Chief Justice Taney, sitting right behind him, who had insisted in *Dred Scott versus Sanford* that Blacks could not be citizens, and, therefore, could not claim due process rights.

Guelzo's assessment confirmed my own—that the Left and the media were completely off base, and that we can always learn from history no matter how unique the present seems to be. Guelzo had more to say, but I have included his additional thoughts in the next chapter.

Throughout the campaign, and in the early days of his presidency, I wondered why President Trump never backed off from a fight, or let even the most minor criticism slide. Anytime a pundit or a political opponent would cast him in a negative light, Trump would immediately respond—even if that brought more attention to the negative comment. Then, the answer became clear at one of his first presidential press conferences in February. As he stood for more than an hour speaking off the cuff—and voicing his criticism—to the press, he said "I love this, I'm having a good time doing it." I realized he likes the competition. That's good, because his opponents are going to fight him at every turn.

CHAPTER NINE

THE PERMANENT OPPOSITION

With Republican majorities in the House of Representatives and the Senate, President Trump is in a great position to enact policies that will dramatically improve our country. But he will face constant resistance from those in the permanent opposition. All the groups that opposed him during the campaign have and will continue to do so. The president must remember that this is just the start.

Every day of President Trump's administration, Washington inertia, the bureaucracy, the media—every fragment of the old order—is going to try to stop this badly needed political revolution. There's no doubt, Trump is going to find himself in a permanent fight.

President Trump is not the first president to lead a divided nation. The 1796 and 1800 elections between Thomas Jefferson and John Adams were incredibly close, divisive elections. In 1876, President Rutherford B. Hayes defeated Samuel Tilden by one electoral vote.[1] And a modern example is the 2000 election of George W. Bush, in which he defeated former vice president Al Gore 271 to 266.

However, the ideological divide now is more intense than it has been in over a century. Dennis Prager suggested in an op-ed he wrote for *National Review* in January 2017 that the political and ideological differences now amount to a second American Civil War.

Prager argues that today's divide is unique. First, he draws a distinction between liberalism and the Left. While liberals and conservatives historically have found common ground as Americans, the modern Left rejects American ideals and has abandoned the core principles of liberalism.

> Liberalism—which was anti-Left, pro-American, and deeply committed to the Judeo-Christian foundations of America, regarded the melting pot as the American ideal, fought for free speech for its opponents, regarded Western civilization as the greatest moral and artistic human achievement, and viewed the celebration of racial identity as racism—is now affirmed almost exclusively on the right and among a handful of people who don't call themselves conservative.
>
> The Left, however, is opposed to every one of those core principles of liberalism.
>
> Like the Left in every other country, the Left in America sees America as essentially a racist, xenophobic, colonialist, imperialist, war-mongering, money-worshipping, moronically religious nation.

To the modern Left, Prager says that the traditional melting pot on which American identity was founded, "is regarded as nothing more than an anti-black, anti-Muslim, anti-Hispanic meme." Where liberalism protects free speech for all, today's Left freely labels dissenting opinions that promote traditional American principles as "hate speech."

And Prager says the Left so far is winning the war by injecting its views into students. Children in school, he says, learn that "virtually every war America fought [was] imperialist and immoral," that the free market is actually a system of oppression, that all the troubles that affect African Americans are the fault of racist white people, and that the "nuclear-family ideal is inherently misogynistic and homophobic."

"That is how it has been able to take over schools—from elementary schools to high schools to the universities—and indoctrinate America's young people; how it has taken over nearly all the news media; and how it has taken over the entertainment media," Prager wrote.

Conservatives, he said are losing because they aren't fighting back with equal measure.

"Name a Republican politician who has run against the Left, as opposed to running solely against his or her Democratic opponent. And nearly all American conservatives, people who are proud of America and affirm its basic tenets, readily send their children to schools that indoctrinate their children against everything the parents hold precious. A mere handful protest when their child's teacher ceases calling their son a boy or their daughter a girl, or makes 'slave owner' the defining characteristic of the Founding Fathers," Prager wrote.

Now, for perspective, 620,000 soldiers died during the American Civil War, and approximately 400,000 were missing or captured. Countless other noncombatants also lost their lives. It was the bloodiest, gravest conflict in our history. Casualties from all our other wars combined did not meet the Civil War's death toll until the Vietnam War.[2] I don't think our current political fray will devolve to that.

But Prager does have a point that the last time our country was this ideologically divided was in 1861. The Left was dealt a strong blow by the 2016 election. It was stunned for a moment but has recovered, ready to continue its ideological war. The following chapter looks at where the Left's legions are—and how President Trump should address them.

TWO AMERICAS

There is no doubt, the political gap has widened in American politics. Polls by Pew Research Center show the ideological American middle has largely evaporated, as Democrats have shifted heavily to the Left, and Republicans have become slightly more conservative over the last twenty-one years.[3]

In 1994, the research center reported that most politically engaged people in America had centrist views. According to Pew, 48 percent of politically active Democrats had "mixed" views on a five-category liberal-conservative spectrum. At the same time, 35 percent of politically engaged Republicans were in the middle. Most of the general population—those who did not identify as "politically engaged"—were also in the middle. Fifty-three percent of Democrats and 44 percent of Republicans were in the political center.

By 2011, the percentage of people who said they had mixed political views had dropped to 35 percent for politically active Democrats and 28 percent for their Republican counterparts. In fact, an equal percentage of Democrats at the time described their views as "mixed" and "mostly liberal," and most Republicans, 39 percent, had shifted to "mostly conservative." Meanwhile, the general population remained centrist at 42 percent and 40 percent for Democrats and Republicans respectively.

Since then, Pew reports that polarization among politically active Americans has widened greatly. As of 2015, the research center reports that only 25 percent of politically savvy Democrats and Republicans have mostly centrist views.

The polls track Democrats on a hard-left trajectory since 1994. Most politically active Democrats polled—42 percent—are now "consistently liberal"—which is as far left as the spectrum goes. This is significant, because in 1994 only 8 percent of politically active Democrats claimed to be on the far left wing. That is a 34-percentage-point shift that speaks to how drastically the activist base of the Democratic Party has changed in two decades. It also shows how out of touch left-wing politics are even among Democrats. Among all current Democrats polled—not just those who are highly engaged—Pew found that 34 percent are centrists compared with 27 percent who identify as being far left.

Republicans have shifted right, but it's less extreme than the Democrats' movement. A plurality of politically engaged Republicans—37 percent—say they are "mostly conservative," which is one step away from center on Pew's scale. This much more closely matches the ideological makeup of the Republican Party at large, among whom 32 percent identify themselves as "mostly conservative," than the corresponding ideological groups in the Democratic Party.

The number of "consistently conservative" politically active Republicans remains high, at 34 percent—12 points higher than the percentage of very conservative Republicans in the general population. In 1994, those figures were 23 percent and 13 percent respectively.

It should be expected that politically active participants deviate from the general populace. But while most political Republicans have drifted one step more conservative than GOP members in the public, the political left has left its constituency—and most Americans—in the dust.

The two Americas were most apparent the weekend of President Trump's inauguration.

On Friday, the day the president was sworn into office, one America that came to Washington was the country that had been forgotten by most politicians—on both sides of the aisle—and regularly overlooked by the major media outlets.

These were the people who have watched for years as the federal government has taken and squandered their tax dollars, and made it harder for them to get trained for careers, run their businesses, and earn decent livings.

Donning their red "make America great again" caps, they walked out of their hotels and headed to the Capitol to celebrate the inauguration.

Then the other America showed up—the one that blocked people from entering checkpoints to the Capitol grounds, harassed Trump supporters, set cars on fire, smashed storefronts, and hurled rocks at police.

CNN reported the following day that six police officers were injured and 217 protesters arrested after "ugly street clashes in downtown Washington."4

On Saturday, the less violent side of that America came. It was made up mostly of people enraged that the Trump-supporting side of America was being paid any attention.

Much of the news media covered the weekend with nothing short of petty vindictiveness. Instead of pointing out how gracefully the supporters at the Capitol handled being confronted with virulent hate and vulgarity from the Left's protesters (no Trump supporters were arrested) the media decided to focus on how big the crowd was compared with past inaugurations.

And this is something that's important to keep in perspective: Saturday's coverage was dominated by the crowd-size nonsense, but the day of the inauguration, police arrested left-wing protestors across the country in Washington, DC; New York; Dallas; Chicago; Portland; Seattle; and elsewhere. In Oregon, the protesters were armed with clubs, setting fire to American flags, and throwing rocks, bottles, and flares at police, according to local news reports.[5] Protesters at the University of Washington campus threw bricks at officers.

But according to the Left, it's the Trump supporters who are hateful, closed-minded, and dangerous.

THE CULTURAL LEFT

While some moderate Democrats will be able to work with President Trump—particularly those in politically divided states—the cultural left will obstruct and attack him at every turn.

I'm not talking about regular partisans. It's the job of Chuck Schumer, the Senate minority leader, to oppose the Republican president. Nor do I mean the millions of Americans who voted for Hillary Clinton, who are not in any way committed to left-wing principles. Those are people we need to work with. I mean the Elizabeth Warren–Bernie Sanders–Keith Ellison wing of the Democratic Party—those in Pew's out-of-touch 42 percent "consistently liberal" politically engaged Democrats I mentioned earlier.

The hyper-Left wants to create an America that's unacceptable to the vast majority of Americans. As was mentioned in previous chapters, they focus on insidiously divisive identity politics, branding all Republicans as racist, and keeping Americans dependent on the government. They want a socialist state wherein government rules and citizens obediently pay for all higher education, health care, and social services. Yet, the hard Left can't solve anything. The Left has no solutions for Chicago's violence, West Virginia's poverty, or disastrous schools in Baltimore. All they can do is yell "racism!" and "sexism!" and hope that holds their coalition together.

Just look at the overall messages from the Women's March the day after President Trump's inauguration. The organizers—of whom about fifty organizations were paid by George Soros, according to the *New York Times*[6]—advocated for things like additional abortion protections, allowing transgender people to use their restrooms of choice, providing federal labor protections to illegal aliens, and establishing rights for sex workers. These are not mainstream issues. There's no middle ground here. Either Trump surrenders or Trump wins, but there's not going to be any zone of compromise.

The truth is, if the Republican Party could shrug off the Left's brand and engage Latinos, African Americans, Asian Americans, and others, we would build a huge coalition of Americans who favor traditional values. These are Americans who want to work hard, provide for their families, and pursue their own happiness without government intrusion. Frankly, that needs to be one of President Trump's main goals. If he's successful, it would be the most important accomplishment he could achieve for the Republican Party as president.

THATCHER, TRUMP, AND THE LOONY LEFT

A week after the inauguration, I wrote a column in the *Washington Post* comparing President Trump with the former British prime minister Margaret Thatcher.

In that piece, I drew a parallel between the vicious hostility Trump has faced—the young liberal fascists wreaking havoc across the country on Inauguration Day—with the intensely bitter, unhinged actions of the British Labor Party under Thatcher. In Britain, as the Left drifted further away from normal Western society, its members earned the moniker "the Loony Left."

I got the idea after reading a brilliant book by Claire Berlinski called *There Is No Alternative: Why Margaret Thatcher Matters*. Berlinski was a graduate student at Oxford when Thatcher was prime minister. Interestingly, she was opposed to Thatcher, but later in life realized that Thatcher's leadership had been absolutely vital.

Berlinski's core argument is Thatcher faced two crises in England. The first was the crisis of socialism as an immoral, dictatorial, and dangerous movement.

Thatcher's response to socialism—which describes what President Trump's response to the hard Left should be—was to wage moral warfare. Thatcher attacked socialism as immoral, not just wrong or expensive. It's immoral to steal from one person to give to another. It's immoral to spend other people's money. It's immoral to engage in a philosophy that teaches dependence is better than work ethic.

In my op-ed, I wrote that Trump's focus on tearing down the Left's moral legitimacy and removing power from the lobbyist and Washington bureaucratic establishments is in line with Thatcher's model. Already, he has moved forward on controlling immigration, and accelerating important energy infrastructure— which America's Loony Left has bitterly opposed.

Negotiating with rational Democrats is one thing, but President Trump cannot allow the extreme views of the American Left to force Republicans to compromise on critical issues. When Prime Minister Thatcher passed away in 2013, Arthur C. Brooks, the president of the American Enterprise Institute, wrote about a time when Thatcher interrupted one of her Tory colleagues who was arguing that the party should move to the middle on several issues in the face of pressure from the English hard Left.[7] As Brooks wrote:

> She pulled a copy of Hayek's *The Constitution of Liberty* from her briefcase and slammed it on the table, exclaiming, "This is what we believe!"

Thatcher was aggressive about rejecting the socialist agenda, and Trump should be also.

This is vital because dependency is remarkably antithetical

to American culture. Our society is based on the work ethic and the notion that you can have big dreams, but then you have to go work to make them happen.

The second crisis that Thatcher faced, according to Berlinski, was an effort by the coal miners' union to essentially take over the country.

The coal miners' union believed—much like the US Professional Air Traffic Controllers Organization's strikers did in 1981—that they could force their will on the government by striking. Specifically, the coal miners thought they could strike and seal off the mines, causing Britain to run out of coal. Thatcher, with the aid of the military and police forces, convinced them they were wrong. She saw the strike as an open assault on representative government. Thatcher made sure the coal miners understood that they couldn't overrule the Parliament, which represents the will of the people.

Reagan sent the same message to the PATCO strikers. They were certain Reagan would fold to their demands, because it would otherwise end the air traffic control system. I was in Congress and represented both the Hampton Air Traffic Control Center and the Atlanta airport. I told the strikers their strategy might have worked with Jimmy Carter, but it wasn't going to work for Reagan. They were incredulous. They had their strike, and Reagan replaced them.

President Trump faces an analogous fight with hyper-Left employees throughout the federal government, particularly at the Environmental Protection Agency. Leftist EPA workers who refuse to implement President Trump's energy agenda should be fired. The next section discusses that further.

Thatcher was so clearly anti-Left, its members hated her from the day she was sworn in. Every element of the British news media, the British intellectual community, and the labor movement attacked her. She was constantly under siege, just like Trump.

THE OLD GUARD

President Trump is a change agent. So naturally, he will be resisted by those who do not want change. Washington's two biggest proponents of the status quo are old-guard lawmakers—those on both sides of the aisle who have become too comfortable to do anything to significantly change the culture of Congress—and the established bureaucracy.

When dealing with the old guard, President Trump should look out for two phrases when he meets with lawmakers. The first is "You really need to be reasonable, so we can work this out." President Trump's greatest asset as our top executive is his ability to negotiate. But he will recognize quickly that people on Capitol Hill don't negotiate like normal businesspeople—because lawmakers aren't using their own money. Ninety-nine times out of 100, when a politician says you should be reasonable, they mean you should sell out and come over to their side. The president will need to approach every negotiation with serious, exercisable leverage to keep pressure on Congress to do the right thing, the right way.

The second phrase President Trump should look out for is "We should really do this later." In Congress, later means never. Lawmakers who use this line are not interested in the bold changes President Trump wants and needs to make. So this will immediately signal to him that they are not serious, and need not be bothered with.

THE FOURTH BRANCH

Breaking through the intransigence of the federal bureaucracy—the unofficial fourth branch of government—is the greatest challenge President Trump will face. Make no doubt about it, large sections of the government Trump is trying to lead are committed to destroying his presidency.

Remember that 95 percent of all donations from the so-called fourth branch went to Clinton. The bias is incredibly clear at the Department of State, where 99 percent of campaign support went to Clinton, and at the Department of Justice, where 97 percent of bureaucrat donations supported her. We cannot expect these people to ever stop fighting President Trump.[8]

Republican Oklahoma senator James Lankford has warned, "Trump's EPA Secretary will have 16,000 employees working against him."[9]

The State Department has a long record of rejecting and undermining presidential foreign policy. When Truman wanted to recognize the state of Israel, the entire leadership of the State Department opposed him, and the State Department's employees at the United Nations actively supported a resolution to avoid recognizing Israel. Only President Truman's disciplined focus on recognition overrode the State Department.

When President Reagan wanted to visit Berlin and say "Mr. Gorbachev, tear down this wall," the State Department's censors took it out of his speech twice. Even after Reagan put it back for the third time, the morning of his speech in Berlin, every senior adviser argued for taking it out.

President Trump's dramatic changes in American foreign policy will almost certainly be undermined, resisted, slow-walked, and sabotaged by the career Foreign Service employees. The novels of C. P. Snow and the two BBC television series *Yes Minister* and *Yes Prime Minister* are filled with tales of clever bureaucratic resistance to elected officials' policies. The problem of career bureaucrats having an illegitimate sense of empowerment to ignore the will of the American people is not new. This group feels so entitled, they developed an acronym describing their relations with presidential administrations: WEBEHWYG ("Wee-beh-wig"). It stands for "We'll be here when you're gone."

Shortly after Trump took office, those who oppose him at the Federal Bureau of Investigation began leaking classified information about ongoing investigations to the press in an effort to discredit the president and halt progress on his agenda.

These leaks resulted in the resignation of Gen. Mike Flynn as national security adviser. That was no accident. Remember that 97 percent of political donations from the Department of Justice's employees went to Hillary Clinton.

Since then, the FBI has leaked like a sieve, anonymously providing the media with classified investigative materials about Russia's alleged influence on the election.

Federal employees who oppose Trump across the government—from the Environmental Protection Agency, the Department of Labor, the State Department, and the US National Park Services—began to organize via encrypted communication apps.

As *Politico* reported in February 2017:

> Federal employees worried that President Donald Trump will gut their agencies are creating new email addresses, signing up for encrypted messaging apps and looking for other, protected ways to push back against the new administration's agenda.
>
> Whether inside the Environmental Protection Agency, within the Foreign Service, on the edges of the Labor Department or beyond, employees are using new technology as well as more old-fashioned approaches— such as private face-to-face meetings—to organize letters, talk strategy, or contact media outlets and other groups to express their dissent.

The news service reported that such employees were mainly using the encryption apps "to discuss what they would do if Trump's political appointees flout the law or delete valuable scientific data."

Here's the sick irony: communication by federal employees discussed via encryption applications can't be reviewed under the Freedom of Information Act—the hallmark legislation of government transparency.

So in order to discuss what might happen if they potentially witnessed theoretical lawbreaking, these federal employees broke the law.

President Trump shouldn't expect—or force—federal employees to support him politically, or agree with all of his policies. But he should expect and force them to do their jobs. If they refuse, they should be fired, just as Acting Attorney General Sally Yates was when she instructed Department of Justice employees not to defend President Trump's temporary travel ban in January 2017.

To be clear, Yates wasn't fired for disagreeing with the president. The attorney general should advise the president anytime he or she finds legal fault in one of the president's actions. Yates didn't do that. She was fired for telling her staff to ignore his orders.

President Trump has initiated targeted cuts to reduce the number of nonessential federal employees whose work does not affect national security or the safety of the country, and I suspect there will be more firings to come. He has, after all, pledged to shrink the federal workforce.

Of course, the bureaucracy is alarmed. All these people have been untouchable for decades. No doubt, federal employees will continue to leak one-sided, inaccurate, or purely fake stories to the press to make the Trump administration appear disorganized, or make it appear that no president has ever been so aggressive with the civil service.

Ignore them.

For historical perspective, Lincoln fired 1,400 of 1,500 political appointees when he took office.

Without bold, dramatic civil service reform, the Trump agenda will prove impossible to formulate and implement.

THE DANGER OF AN ESTABLISHMENT COUP D'ETAT

By the time this book is published, the news of the day almost certainly will be substantially different. But I suspect that the media, the intelligence community, congressional investigators, and the judicial system will still be focused on an alleged connection between the Trump campaign and Russia.

For your context, I am writing this book in early April 2017. At this point, there is more and more evidence building that suggests a wide array of establishment players are trying to use this investigation to cripple or destroy the Trump administration.

For example, it has just been discovered that President Obama's National Security Adviser, Susan Rice, may have been using her position to tap the intelligence community for a remarkable amount of information about the Trump transition team. It may also be possible that she was leaking names from the surveillance of foreigners who interacted with the Trump team. The former would be inappropriate and an abuse of power. The latter would be a felony.

Rice has prevaricated about this on television. That would be typical since she took the lead in deceiving the public about the Benghazi attack.

However, the danger in this situation is that the entrenched establishment system has already defined the problem it wants to investigate—and it has predetermined that problem is centered on the Trump team.

By the system's definition, any Russian efforts to penetrate and shape American politics must be centered on Trump—

forget about the fact that the Russians tried and failed to hack Republican computer systems during the election.

This is the establishment presumption under which General Flynn and Jared Kushner have been asked to testify.

But no Trump team member should agree to testify without being granted immunity. Their careers and their very liberty may be at stake.

Fishing expeditions driven by the Justice Department, congressional staffs, and the news media take on a life of their own and can easily trap innocent people through procedural mistakes. There is a grave danger that Trump team members will testify as though they were participating in a benign or honest process. That can lead to disaster.

Every word someone says can be measured against all other testimony and all available evidence. Any discrepancy, no matter how innocent, can lead to a charge of perjury or obstruction of justice.

Ironically, there is vastly more evidence of Russian involvement with Hillary Clinton and the Democrats than with Trump and the Republicans.

But as a very senior former prosecutor said to me recently, "This has now become a blood sport. The goal is not justice or truth, the goal is destruction of conservatives."

We are not watching an unbiased, truth-seeking process.

Obvious system-wide bias aside, there is another profound flaw with the current parameters of the discussion.

There is indeed a grave threat to American freedom from foreign manipulation and foreign corruption—but it is vastly bigger than Russia, and has vastly broader focus than this election.

We need a deep, thorough exploration of foreign efforts to shape American politics and policies.

For instance, it is vital to look at the tools Russia is developing for hybrid warfare and how they are being applied in the United States, in Europe, and elsewhere.

Hybrid warfare is a system of using intelligence, information, cyberwar, economic pressure, corruption, diplomatic pressure, and subsidized low-level violence to gain ground. It has been used in Ukraine, Estonia, and several other places to advance Russian interests. Russia has relied on this method to avoid dangerous conventional conflict. The Kremlin wants to maximize its impact while minimizing the risk of a major war.

This wide exploration should also include China, the foreign advocates of radical Islam, and countries that seek specific influence on American policy as it relates to them.

This is the drama that is unfolding. We have no idea how it will evolve.

THE MEDIA

The media opposition will be the most constant—and the most ridiculous.

Early in the administration, the media willfully mischaracterized so-called mass resignations of senior staff at the Department of State in an effort to promote a narrative of chaos in the Trump administration. It was actually four political appointees who had been handpicked by President Obama—and they had been fired. There was no symbolic walkout. This will continue.

Just watch: the same pundits, reporters, and commentators who were wrong about Trump winning the Republican nomination, wrong about him winning the general election, and wrong about him getting his cabinet picks confirmed, will continue to be wrong about his ongoing agenda.

They will be wrong because they still have no real connection to normal Americans. During the campaign, those in the elite media wrote off Trump's candidacy because he was talking about issues that were in their minds inappropriate. They watched him talk at rallies about renegotiating our trade deals, restoring control and security to our immigration system, fighting Islamic supremacism, and giving people school choice. These topics are anathema to the elite. So, to the mainstream media, the thousands of people who were showing up to Trump rallies across the country couldn't possibly affect the election. This is the level of contempt they had for normal Americans.

There's no reason to think this will change. So far, not one major media outlet has stopped to consider that after having been completely wrong about the last two years of American politics, it might be time to reassess how connected it is with the American people.

Instead, following the election, reporters and commentators immediately blamed pollsters for the media's botched analysis and lazy, pretentious reporting.

Pollsters, as a group, erred by adopting a fixed idea about America's voting pattern. Many incorrectly assumed that the same number of African American voters would turn out in 2016 as they did when President Obama was elected in 2012. And they assumed that turnout for white voters would resemble Romney's support the same year. For some reason, they decided those two data points were constant.

Even in the early evening on election day, analysts were tweaking the numbers to support their 2012 model that said Hillary Clinton would win by a healthy margin and Republicans would lose the Senate. They repeated this with conviction—until the moment Trump secured 270 electoral votes and the Senate Republicans earned a fifty-two-seat majority. Pollsters were fixated on the past and rejecting everything the present was showing them.

This is a symptom of a big problem with modern polling— which is essentially part of the media. Pollsters used to make predictions based on what people told them in landline phone surveys. Historically, they were fairly accurate. But now, given the huge number of communication platforms out there— mobile phones, text messaging, email, social media, video chat services—everyone communicates differently. Many polling outfits haven't adapted to the new world of communication. So analysts now stare at computer models that run on old information and hope the country hasn't changed.

Only the Pew Research Center and Gallup had the foresight—and the integrity—to stay out of the day-to-day election numbers, because they realized any poll they created would add to the confusion. Instead, Gallup and Pew have focused on what Americans think about particular issues over time.

Rutgers University public policy professor Cliff Zukin pointed this out in a story *Time* published on October 15, 2015.

[Gallup and Pew] have contributed to the political process, they're not just in it for the short time," said Zukin. "They do not want to mislead the public and they don't want to take a chance of not being able to do it well—it takes a lot more resources to do it well now.[10]

I'm interested to see whom the news media will blame when they are wrong about President Trump's tax reform plan, or his infrastructure agenda, or his plan to eventually repeal Obamacare.

In the meantime, the entertainment media continue to viciously attack the president and his supporters.

On March 24, liberal host Bill Maher opened his show by insulting voters who voted for Trump—in other words, half of America.

"I know you real Americans hate being called stupid," said Maher. "But you gotta meet me halfway and stop being stupid."

Much of this opposition is to be expected.

Trump, to his credit, is threatening the Left, the media, and the old guard simultaneously. He's combating an established elite class, and a set of left-wing values that have been building in this country for decades. We have not seen anything like it in our lifetime. Studying Abraham Lincoln might provide a comparable sense of hostility.

Dr. Guelzo, the Gettysburg College professor and Civil War Era expert I mentioned in chapter 8, sent me a few newspaper clippings from just after Lincoln's election. It is remarkable how similarly they track with the Left's coverage of Trump after the election.

From the *Memphis Daily Appeal* on November 13, 1860:

> Within 90 days from the time Lincoln is inaugurated, the Republican Party will be utterly ruined and destroyed. His path is environed with so many difficulties, that even if he had the ability of Jefferson and the energy of Jackson, he would fail, but he is a weak and inexperienced man, and his administration will be doomed from the commencement. If he takes that radical section of the Republican Party, the conservative wing of it will cut loose and repudiate him. If, on the other hand, he courts the conservatives and pursues a moderate conciliatory policy, the radicals will make open war upon his administration.

Remember: This is about Lincoln.

Here is another from the South Carolina *Lancaster Ledger*, also in November 1860:

> There is intense excitement here. Large crowds have gathered in the streets. The pervading spirit among the masses is resistance to Lincoln's administration, and everywhere that determination is manifest.

This next one is most interesting to me. It was written by the *New York Herald*'s Charleston correspondent.

Thursday night the streets were filled with excited crowds. Till nearly midnight, the streets presented the most animated appearance. The crowd illuminated their passage by rockets and other fireworks, and made the air resound with their deafening cries. No one talks of anything but the necessity for prompt action. It is believed that separate and immediate action on the part of this state will be followed by action on the part of several other southern states forthwith. It is hardly prudent for any man to express his opinion adverse to immediate secession. So heated are the public passions, so intolerant of restraint is the popular will.

Think about university campuses. Think about the number of conservative young students who are ridiculed. Think about what happened the day of Trump's inauguration, when the violent young fascists took to the streets with clubs and bricks.

The scene in Charleston this correspondent is describing is so much like today's Left, which vehemently rebukes dissenting opinion.

It is hardly prudent for any man to express his opinion adverse to immediate secession. So heated are the public passions, so intolerant of restraint is the popular will.

Today's Left resembles Charlestonians about to secede in defense of slavery. I hope they will think about that comparison. Until Trump successfully realizes his bold new vision for America, the confrontation will continue. The following chapters are dedicated to exploring how President Trump can succeed.

PART THREE

THE FOUR-BOX MODEL FOR THE TRUMP AGENDA

President Trump will succeed at making America great again for all Americans if he can keep his policy focus and organize his efforts. The following chapters describe a model I've suggested to him that could help him strategize his policy goals. The model includes four boxes: safety, American competitiveness, health care, and making government work. President Trump needs to think about how every single policy he implements fits in each of those boxes.

When President Trump was selecting his cabinet, he was especially glad to get Generals Mattis and Kelly. He was in awe of Mattis as a real fighter who insisted on winning. He loved Mattis's phrase that the marines could be your best friends or your worst enemies—and you get to choose. President Trump felt he had really accomplished something when General Mattis said yes.

Similarly, the then-president-elect revered the sacrifice General Kelly had made in losing his son in Afghanistan in 2010. He felt that Kelly would bring a competence, a dignity, and a sense of honor that Trump really valued. It is from this sense of respect for those who risk their lives to defend America that Trump approaches rebuilding and strengthening our military.

CHAPTER TEN

THE SAFETY BOX

P resident Trump's first, and most important job, is to be the commander in chief of our military. And the primary role of the federal government is to keep Americans safe from all threats foreign and domestic. The founders framed our nation this way, because there is no effective freedom without safety. There is no ability to pursue happiness without safety. The poor are especially vulnerable and likely to be exploited when there is no safety.

So it is only logical that safety is the first box in the four-box policy model President Trump should adopt.

After years of President Trump's predecessor refusing to enforce immigration law; failing to properly support law enforcement in the face of open, visible lawlessness; allowing longtime alliances abroad to wither; and allowing investment in our military to degrade; Trump has his work cut out for him.

SAFETY AT HOME

Restoring the rule of law within our borders is critical to making Americans safe at home. Most Americans understand this, and that's why President Trump's pledge to be a law-and-order candidate resonated. Meanwhile, the elite were completely befuddled by Trump's pledge.

The reason for the disparity in perception is simple. After reaching a peak in 1991, crime rates had fallen in the United States through 2014. This trend of falling crime rates was considered such a well-established fact by the elites that nothing could shake them off it. They were blind to two realities that were obvious to normal Americans who were watching the news and in tune with their communities.

First, violent crime was beginning to tick back up again. FBI statistics released in September 2016 show that violent crime increased 3.9 percent in 2015 compared with the previous year.[1] Preliminary FBI data from the first half of 2016 show that violent crime again increased in all categories compared with the first half of 2015.[2] (Notably, it increased the least in the Northeast, which may have added to the elites' lack of awareness.)

The elites were so stuck in the conventional wisdom that they couldn't process this new reality. Remember in chapter 2 when we talked about the four-sided table of Trump, and that one of those sides was anti–political correctness? We reviewed how political correctness can also mean adhering to the conventional wisdom. Trump's ability to recognize that violent crime was on the rise before anyone else is a great example of that.

Second, Trump understood the power of television and knew how disturbing the violent protests related to police shootings across the country were to normal Americans. He watched in horror as five police officers were gunned down by a sniper in Dallas, and he was aghast at news reports of radical Islamic terror attacks in San Bernardino and Orlando. He also understood that the huge spikes in shootings in Chicago, St. Louis, and Baltimore were earning major media attention and making Americans nervous.

These two dynamics are why Americans' concern for crime and violence has risen to a fifteen-year high, according to results of a Gallup poll published in April 2016.[3] The pollster reported that 53 percent of adults asked say they worry "a great deal" about violence and crime in the United States, while 26 percent of adults say they worry "a fair amount"—making a total of 79 percent of concerned adults.

The elites were stuck on outdated conventional wisdom while Trump saw Americans being killed, families being devastated, and our country falling apart. President Trump quickly repudiated the "nothing to see here" elites and sided with the large group of Americans who rightly believed their country was becoming less safe and more insecure.

It's no surprise that more people are anxious about becoming the victims of violence after you consider the recent rise of open, visible, violent rebellions against law enforcement in this country. The public has always questioned police officers who use lethal force in the line of duty—and this should not change. But the culture surrounding how police are held accountable has taken a violent turn toward mob rule.

In 2014, protests erupted in Ferguson, Missouri, after an officer shot and killed Michael Brown. These demonstrations lasted for weeks, eventually turning into full-scale riots. People set fire to cars and buildings, looted stores, and attacked police. The violence continued even after the state's governor called in the Missouri National Guard.

Nearly a year later, after a grand jury decided not to indict the officer involved in the shooting, deciding that Brown had never surrendered to police and had tried to take the officer's weapon, the rioting erupted again. More buildings were burned and more stores looted.

In April 2015, after days of peaceful demonstrations in Baltimore, Maryland, over the death of Freddie Gray while he was in police custody, some protestors turned to rioting. After Gray's funeral, the BBC reported, "That afternoon and evening rioters tore through parts of Baltimore leaving a path of debris, burnt or smashed cars, and looted storefronts."[4] The riots lasted for days and left Baltimore looking like a war zone.

And similar riots erupted in New York, Chicago, St. Paul, Baton Rouge, and Milwaukee over the deaths of Alton Sterling and Philando Castile, both of whom were killed by police officers.

I am not arguing that the police acted appropriately in all these events. But rioting was absolutely the wrong response. Each of these shootings and subsequent riots were highly televised and shared across social media. The American people were seeing a wave of mayhem moving across the country. Trump saw it too. He tapped into the concerns of the American people and had the courage to pledge to put an end to the lawlessness.

Trump had lived in New York City when it seemed almost ungovernable with crime. In 1986, the *New York Times* reported, "The number of reported murders soared by 50 percent or more in 21 of New York City's 75 police precincts [since 1985], reflecting the pervasive impact of drug-related crime on neighborhoods." There was a serious sense of insecurity that was reducing tourism and frightening New Yorkers.

And he lived through a revolution in law enforcement that had almost miraculous results. He knows that we know what works.

In 1995, Mayor Rudy Giuliani and New York police commissioner William Bratton implemented a system called CompStat. As a result, the NYPD reports the number of murders in the city dropped by 85 percent from 1990 to 2014.[5]

If you have a violent community in your state, it should establish a CompStat commission to explore what works and apply it relentlessly until neighborhoods become safe.

Conservative states have used the right kind of criminal justice reform to reduce crime, reduce the number of prisoners, increase safety, and reduce costs for the taxpayer. When governors and former governors like Rick Perry of Texas, Nathan Deal of Georgia, and Nikki Haley of South Carolina can all point to less crime, more former prisoners transitioning to jobs and citizenship—and lower costs with fewer prisons—something profound is happening.

President Trump knows there are proven steps to build safer communities, and he knows it is a moral imperative to use those proven steps to save the lives of the poorest among us.

SECURING THE BORDER

President Trump has already taken the first steps toward fixing our immigration system by strengthening security at our borders. During his first week in office, President Trump signed executive orders to hire up to ten thousand more US Immigration and Customs Enforcement officers and up to five thousand more US Border Patrol agents.

This was a perfectly reasonable action to take—and long overdue. Heroin and opioid abuse are devastating communities across the nation. The Drug Enforcement Administration told Reuters in July 2013 that large-scale opium poppy farms, the plant from which heroin is made, are "very rare" in the United States, so most of the heroin is coming from outside our borders.[6]

It turns out, the same agency said two years later in its National Drug Threat Assessment of 2015 that most drugs, including heroin, in the United States are indeed sourced from Mexico. This includes traditional drugs that have been abused for years, such as cocaine, heroin, and marijuana. But the DEA reported Mexico is also the primary source of new drugs that have been wreaking havoc on a new generation of Americans, including fentanyl, a synthetic opioid that's one hundred times stronger than heroin, and methamphetamine, which has ravaged entire communities in Appalachia and elsewhere.

Democrats would like people to believe that Republican efforts to secure the border are some xenophobic attempt to halt all immigration. But that's just not the case. We are trying to stop dangerous people from bringing dangerous substances that destroy our families and communities into our country. Violent drug cartels that operate throughout South America and Mexico are principally responsible for the supply side of the US drug trade.

According to the DEA's report:

> The most significant drug trafficking organizations operating in the United States today are the dangerous and highly sophisticated Mexican transnational criminal organizations (TCOs) that continue to be the principal suppliers of cocaine, heroin, methamphetamine, and marijuana. These organizations are responsible for the extreme violence seen in Mexico, as these groups battle for turf and attack public officials and innocent civilians. Domestically, affiliated and violent gangs are increasingly a threat to the safety and security of our communities. They profit primarily by putting drugs on the street and have become crucial to the Mexican cartels.

President Trump signed a trio of executive orders on February 9 instructing his administration to find ways to help local and state police stop "the illegal smuggling and trafficking of humans, drugs or other substances, wildlife, and weapons"; "comprehensively address illegal immigration, drug trafficking, and violent crime"; and to look for ways to better protect police and increase penalties for crimes committed against officers.

Drug-dealing thugs are not our only problem. Radical Islamic terrorists know how permeable our borders are. At a Senate Intelligence Committee hearing in 2005, the former CIA chief Porter Goss said "it may be only a matter of time" before terrorist cells attempt to use weapons of mass destruction within the United States. Any chemical, biological, or nuclear weapon brought into the United States by a terrorist cell would not likely be flown in on a commercial airliner. The United States has spent billions securing airports across the country. Any weapon would come in on a ship at one of our ports, or in the back of a truck that is waived through at a border checkpoint. All the money we have spent to make our airports safe is wasted if we don't enforce our borders on land and sea. Goss's testimony alone should be enough reason to fully secure our border and get serious about closely controlling immigration.

President Trump's next step toward securing the border came in his budget proposal released in March. The president called for $1.5 billion in supplemental funding in this fiscal year to start construction on the border wall with Mexico. He's asking for an additional $2.6 billion for the wall's funding in the 2018 budget. He is also proposing roughly $400 million for border security technology and almost $300 million for Customs and Border Protection operations. Add to that the approximately $1.2 billion he requested to help Immigrations and Customs Enforcement successfully detain and deport illegal immigrants who commit other crimes.

The Left downplayed President Trump's budget proposal as little more than messaging, since Congress ultimately controls the government's purse strings. But the message itself—that the United States was going to take border security seriously— already seems to be helping reduce illegal immigration. The *Los Angeles Times* reported on March 9 that the number of immigrants attempting to illegally cross the border has been reduced by 40 percent since President Trump took office.[7]

Citing US Customs and Border Patrol figures, the newspaper reported illegal entry attempts at the border and in ports dropped from about 1,370 per day in January to about 840 people a day in February. This was remarkable, because "Border Patrol agents typically see a 10 percent to 20 percent surge of people making the journey in February," the paper reported.

President Trump should continue to send his strong-border message and continue efforts to tightly control the border. Until we have total control over who enters our country, we will never have an immigration system that benefits the United States.

Meanwhile, the Left will fight tooth and nail to reduce spending on border security, but I urge you to pay close attention to what President Trump achieves with the funds he is allotted. Previous estimates by the federal government have claimed the border wall could cost up to $22 billion. With Trump's experience building large structures effectively and efficiently, I predict the cost will be dramatically less than that amount.

STOPPING OUTLAW CITIES

Strengthened border enforcement will help stop drug cartels, terrorists, and other illegal immigrants from entering the country. But if so-called sanctuary cities—which should be called outlaw cities—continue to refuse to turn illegal and undocumented immigrants in their jails over to federal authorities, our immigration system will never properly function and our communities will not be truly safe.

According to the 2015 DEA report, we could greatly weaken these drug cartels by deporting those who are in their US networks.

"The foundation of Mexican TCO [transnational criminal organization] operations in the United States is comprised of extended family and friends. Families affiliated with various Mexican TCOs in Mexico vouch for US-based relatives or friends that are deemed trustworthy enough to help run various aspects of the drug trafficking operations in the United States. Actual members of Mexican TCOs are usually sent to important US hub cities to manage stash houses containing drug shipments and bulk cash drug proceeds," the DEA reported.

President Trump has already moved the country in the right direction on this front as well. Just days after his inauguration, President Trump wrote an executive order declaring local governments that "willfully violate federal law in an attempt to shield aliens from removal from the United States" will "not receive federal funds, except as mandated by law."

That included cities such as Chicago and Los Angeles, where instead of immediately turning immigrants in police custody over to federal agents, the noncitizen criminals are released back out on the streets.

The Left immediately went bonkers, sowing fear of mass deportations throughout immigrant communities, and claiming crime would spike because immigrants in the country illegally who were victims of crime would be afraid to call police. But Trump's order was very clear about who he was going after. According to the order, that group included "illegal immigrants who:

"have been convicted of any criminal offense;

"have been charged with any criminal offense, where such charge has not been resolved;

"have committed acts that constitute a chargeable criminal offense;

"have engaged in fraud or willful misrepresentation in connection with any official matter or application before a governmental agency;

"have abused any program related to receipt of public benefits;

"are subject to a final order of removal, but who have not complied with their legal obligation to depart the United States; or

"in the judgment of an immigration officer, otherwise pose a risk to public safety or national security."

How could any reasonable person argue against swiftly deporting any noncitizen who comes to the United States and commits a crime, misrepresents him- or herself to our government, or poses a risk to national security?

One important group President Trump did not include in his enforcement agenda is the group of immigrants who have registered through the Deferred Action for Childhood Arrivals program. The president has repeatedly said he wants to deal with those who were brought to the country as children, and their parents, with compassion.

Some municipalities that had not been enforcing immigration laws corrected their policies once President Trump came into office. Miami-Dade mayor Carlos Gimenez told local jails to cooperate with federal immigration authorities the day after President Trump signed his executive order to deny federal funding to outlaw cities.

But others, such as San Francisco, Boston, New York, and Chicago have opted to ignore the order and continue ignoring federal immigration law.

San Francisco has challenged the president's order in court, over protest from its residents.

The website Immigrationreform.com reported:

> San Francisco, which has defiantly maintained its sanctuary policies despite public outcry after the fatal shooting of Kate Steinle by an illegal alien, stands to lose millions of dollars in funding. San Francisco receives as much as $1.2 billion in federal funds currently. Kate Steinle's murder has motivated lawmakers around the country to introduce legislation to eliminate sanctuary policies. This year, at least 25 state legislatures are considering measures to prohibit sanctuary policies in their states and require law enforcement to cooperate with federal immigration officials.

Ultimately, the leaders of cities that continue to defy federal law and grant asylum to criminal immigrants must answer to their voters and will have to explain why the imagined rights of criminal noncitizens are more important than federal funding to build infrastructure, hospitals, or schools. Mayor Rahm Emanuel will have a tough time telling the families of the four thousand people shot last year in Chicago why the community needs more criminals.

Liberals have also fought two attempts by the president to temporarily ban travelers from several Middle Eastern countries that Obama administration officials said lacked adequate security screening capabilities. Liberal judges in Seattle and Hawaii have acquiesced and halted two executive orders that President Trump signed to temporarily bar travel to allow security to be improved.

No doubt, the Left will continue to oppose efforts to create a legal, safe, controlled immigration system, just as it has fought efforts to combat voter fraud. I'm convinced these two issues are related for the Left. President Trump is working to ensure that only living, legal citizens can vote in this country—reasonable criteria to most Americans which pose real problems for the Left.

SAFETY ABROAD

President Trump will find it much easier to make America safe at home if he also focuses on safety abroad. The president must restore America's reputation around the world by rekindling relations with our traditional allies—and by reasserting our strength to potential enemies. He also must revive the strength of the military by restoring defense funding and immediately changing the Obama-era rules of engagement so that our servicemen and -women can fully defend themselves and complete their missions while in harm's way. Once he begins these first tasks, seeking out and eradicating radical Islamic terrorism will be made much easier.

RESTORING AMERICA'S REPUTATION

President Trump has already begun the process of strengthening our ties with the United Kingdom and Israel—two of our strongest allies.

British prime minister Theresa May was the first foreign leader to meet with President Trump after his inauguration. While the two are very different people, they had an excellent visit. May said in February she looked forward to hosting President Trump in Britain later this year.

The United States–United Kingdom partnership is uniquely important now, since both countries stand to benefit from a future bilateral trade deal once Britain officially exits the European Union.

President Trump also had a positive early meeting with Canadian prime minister Justin Trudeau, who perhaps could play a role in making America's deal with Britain a trilateral deal with our northern neighbor. As I mentioned earlier, the Canada–United States part of the North American Free Trade Agreement has been an effective, mutually beneficial arrangement.

One critical relationship President Trump immediately started nurturing is our alliance with Israel. After meeting with Prime Minister Benjamin Netanyahu in February 2017, Trump pledged to put his deal-making skills to use and help negotiate meaningful peace between Israel and Palestine. This is important, because the president plans to reach out to other Arab neighbors of Israel to help in the negotiations. This is an incredibly adroit move from a president the elite love to label as a foreign relations novice.

And while liberals and the media wince at President Trump's forceful stance on foreign issues, American allies in other parts of the world value the strength he is projecting and his willingness to listen. Benny Johnson with the *Independent Journal Review* wrote in March 2017 about a dinner he shared with the Afghan ambassador to the United States.[8]

The ambassador, Dr. Hamdullah Mohib, hosted a dinner for Gold Star Wives—the spouses of American soldiers who had died in combat fighting in Afghanistan. During the dinner, he took questions from the dozen Gold Star Wives and other military members he invited. According to Johnson, Dr. Mohib "stunned those listening" when he answered a question about how the Afghan people viewed President Trump.

This is the ambassador's response, according to Johnson:

I've personally met with President Trump at Mar-a-Lago and the president has had two phone conversations with President [Ashraf] Ghani [of Afghanistan]. One call was after he won the election and one after [Trump] became president. Before the calls, we were advised to keep conversations short because, we were told, Trump will not be interested in the details of the call and does not have a long attention span, so it would be pointless to have a long call.

However, we were pleasantly surprised at how much time President Trump spent asking very informed questions. The first time the presidents spoke, the questions Trump asked impressed us. "How can you win in this fight [against terrorism]?" he asked. "What do you need to become financially independent?" and "How can American business invest in Afghanistan? How can we develop businesses and mining in your country?"

Trump would listen intently after each question, often asking follow-ups. Trump's second call with our president was even longer than the first. Asking these types of questions for our country is something the Obama administration never did. The Obama administration was the most academic administration we have ever had to deal with but the Trump administration has been the most thoughtful and intelligent.

Trump continually asked "How can you win? What does Afghanistan need to win?" in reference to our fight with terrorism. Trump wants to win. Sincerely. All the Obama administration wanted to do was not lose.

The Obama administration was hesitant with us. The enemy could sense that. When the Obama administration announced its plans to pull troops out of the region, they announced the exact date they would do it. All our enemies had to do was wait [Obama] out. They knew the date they had to hang on until—which gave them the will to fight. They used that time to recruit and build up resources.

To bring real reform, we must be able to defeat enemies outside our country and inside. We must overthrow the Afghan warlords who are profiteering off the war. Every time we tried to remove one of them from power, [Secretary John] Kerry would say "no" because it would potentially make it unstable and require more troops be brought in. The entire Obama administration was too cautious, but Kerry was the most cautious. Perhaps the Obama administration was fatigued by the time we assumed power. [President Ghani assumed power in September 2014.] But Trump is very different from Obama in this way.

This is good, for the future of Afghanistan.

I included Ambassador Mohib's full response, because it perfectly speaks to President Trump's approach to learning that we described in chapter 2—but it also highlights the completely out-of-touch way our intellectual yet idiot international affairs experts have treated our allies for the last decade. If President Trump continues to approach foreign conflicts with a real resolve to win, our foreign allies will recognize and appreciate it, and our enemies will be deterred from bad behavior.

When all our allies respect the United States again, it will be easier to deal with countries like North Korea, which is the most dangerous place in the world. With a concerted, unified effort, Iran could be made to stop funding terrorism. Relations with

Russia will be much less complex when Vladimir Putin understands there are real consequences for acting like an aggressive imperialist.

REVIVING THE MILITARY

During his first week in office, President Trump ordered Secretary of Defense James Mattis to review the readiness of the US Armed Forces and our ballistic missile defense system, then report back with recommendations for how to rebuild our military. Trump's first presidential budget proposal included a $54 billion increase for the military to buy ships, planes, and necessary combat supplies.

There is no question President Trump will fully follow through on his promise to rebuild the US military into the world's standard. Our armed forces will be the strongest, smartest, and most effective they have ever been.

But we also need to overhaul the Pentagon by dramatically reducing red tape, and acquisition time and cost. Military contracts are notoriously overbudget and behind schedule. The F-35 program is only an extreme example of a widespread problem. President Trump is the perfect man to rein in out-of-control military spending. Because he knows how to negotiate, President Trump will not be caught in the typical political pitfall of being accused of being weak on the military matters for reining in defense contracts. Every dollar he saves by cutting regulations or negotiating military contracts will be another dollar that can be spent directly on our troops—either on equipment, training, or pay. Coupled with his willingness to increase spending in the right way, our military will soon be stronger than it has ever been.

The Pentagon also needs to modernize—technologically and in its thinking. Cyberattacks pose a serious risk to our economy and safety. Social media has helped terrorists take motivating propaganda to new levels. Russia has been pioneering a hybrid system of warfare that combines psychology, military power, and Internet-fueled propaganda that has helped it dominate in eastern Ukraine. A large, well-placed electromagnetic pulse could devastate our East Coast and cripple our civilization.

We need models to combat these new methods.

President Trump also needs to put an end to the rise of lawfare. The last thing we need when fighting a war is to have lawyers trapping us in red tape. Imagine how the Civil War would have gone had Lincoln's army been hamstrung by Obama-era rules of engagement.

Finally, we also need to reverse the trend of replacing uniformed military personnel at the Pentagon with civilian employees who can unionize. Under President Obama, who favored extreme civilian control of the armed forces, the number of professional military members at the Pentagon decreased, while civilian staff increased. Civilian leadership of the military is important, but it makes no sense to increasingly rely on civilians to plan and fight our wars. We must correct this imbalance. If President Trump's cabinet is any indication, we will soon see a lot more men and women in uniform in the halls of the Pentagon.

ELIMINATING RADICAL ISLAM

Once we strengthen our alliances and our military, permanently defeating ISIS and making radical Islamic terrorism unacceptable everywhere in the world will require supporting our Arab allies sufficiently to destroy the terrorists where they live.

But we need a successful, codified strategy for what happens next, so that power vacuums don't simply pave the way for the next brand of evil. Our current counterinsurgency model is totally inadequate, because it doesn't provide for a sufficiently vigorous replacement of the enemy system. When you try to secure places like Iraq or Afghanistan, the replacement system must be vigorous and able to solidify quickly. Terrorist cells like the Taliban and ISIS have been successful in taking control of war-torn regions, because they are able to regenerate more quickly than the budding governing regimes.

Developing a system wherein stable governments can outpace warlords and terrorist cells will mean our enemies will have fewer places to hide, and long-term direct US involvement will not be needed.

THE PERFECT TEAM

I am confident President Trump can achieve all these goals, and it is not just because I believe in his capabilities. It is also because he assembled the perfect team to do it.

Attorney General Jeff Sessions is an exemplary lawyer, with extensive law enforcement experience as a prosecutor for the United States government. He understands the unique challenge of balancing law and order with civil rights. Despite asinine attacks by the Left on his record, General Sessions cares deeply for all Americans and wants to see police and all our communities exist respectfully and peacefully.

General James Mattis is as good a senior officer as has served in the American military in the last generation. He's an astounding intellectual, he's a warrior, and he is totally patriotic. In selecting Mattis, President Trump asked for the first waiver since 1950 to allow a recent military member to serve as secretary of defense. Normally, military members must be out of uniform for at least seven years before they can lead the Pentagon. The only other general who was ever granted this waiver was General George Marshall during the Korean War.

Mattis's professionalism and reputation is so beyond repute that Democrats put up almost no opposition to his nomination or confirmation. The Senate confirmed his nomination by a vote of 98–1. Only Senator Kirsten Gillibrand, a Democrat from New York, voted no. And a spokesman for Gillibrand later said she opposed Mattis's confirmation only because she believed civilians should lead the military.

As an aside, keep in mind that President Trump's early opponents criticized his national security knowledge and experience. Then, one of his first actions as president was to nominate someone to lead our armed forces who was almost unanimously approved by the Senate.

Marine General John Kelly was the perfect pick to lead the Department of Homeland Security. I have known General Kelly since he was a colonel. When I was Speaker of the House, then-Colonel Kelly was the liaison for the Marine Corps. He has given his entire adult life to serving the country and remained steadfast even after he lost a son in combat. Before President Trump appointed him, General Kelly had just finished leading the Southern Command, which oversees US military operations in all of Latin America. There is no one more skilled, knowledgeable, or qualified than General Kelly to secure and protect our southern border, to implement and operate a safe immigration system; or to keep terrorists and drug dealers out of our country.

Some have questioned whether President Trump has leaned too heavily on former military members to lead his cabinet, but the American people don't think so. Pew Research Center released a report in October 2016 that found that almost 80 percent of American adults trust the military to act in their best interest.[9] According to the report, "one-third of the public (33 percent) has a great deal of confidence in the military and an additional 46 percent say they have a fair amount of confidence. The high ranking of the military is consistent with a 2013 Pew Research Center survey, which found 78 percent of the public said the military contributes 'a lot' to society."

Meanwhile, the October report found that only about 27 percent of Americans trust elected officials, and only 38 percent expressed trust in the news media.

Vice President Mike Pence could also be instrumental in developing meaningful immigration reform. When he was a congressman, Vice President Pence worked with Senator Kay Bailey Hutchison and Helen Kriebel of the Kriebel Foundation to develop an accurate picture of how normal Americans felt about immigration. Had President Bush worked with Pence and Hutchison, we might have solved many of our immigration problems in 2006.

Then you get to Rex Tillerson, who has had a tremendous career going around the world and successfully negotiating agreements with foreign countries on behalf of Exxon Mobil— an American company. This will be a significant change from the legacies of Hillary Clinton and John Kerry, who spent years unsuccessfully negotiating with foreign powers.

The most immediate change our allies and adversaries around the world are going to see is that Tillerson actually represents America and America's interests.

There is a great story former secretary of state George Schultz used to tell. When Schultz met new ambassadors before they were sent overseas, he would take them over to his globe and ask them to point to the country they were going to represent. Four out of five times, Schultz would say the new ambassadors would point to the country where they were going—not the United States, which is the country they would be representing.

The logical conclusion you can draw from that is for a long time there has been a systematic cultural problem in the State Department that has caused 80 percent of our ambassadors to be confused about what country they are supposed to be representing abroad.

We now clearly have a team that will ensure that the United States is safe again.

When we would talk during the campaign, Trump would emphasize that his experience as a businessman led him to understand the impact of both taxes and regulations. He was confident that he understood how business leaders think—and that an aggressive pro-American trade policy, combined with less regulation and lower taxes, would lead to a dramatic increase in economic growth.

CHAPTER ELEVEN

THE AMERICAN COMPETITIVENESS BOX

I n chapter 7, we established that for the last half century, the United States has adopted trade agreements that benefit our trading partners more than America.

With a few exceptions, the US trade balance—the amount of money we spend or gain in trade—remained positive from 1950 until the mid-1970s. During that time, the US trade balance ranged from $500 million to $1 billion, according to the website tradingeconomics.com.[1] The balance became erratic, running slightly negative, from 1977 through the early 1980s—dropping to an at-the-time historic low of −$15 billion. That was the start of a dramatic trend wherein the United States bought more than it sold and hemorrhaged jobs and money into the rest of the world, due to overgenerous trade agreements.

At the same time, we've also created the most antibusiness tax system in the developed world. Because of this, for the last decade we've experienced just 1.9 percent growth, dramatically less than the historic average. American competitiveness has withered, and it must be restored. Americans are gambling on President Trump to break the country out of this pattern. If he doesn't break us out, we will fail as a country.

TAX CUTS, MORE THAN TAX REFORM

Trump understands that job creation must be at the center of his presidency. As a candidate, President Trump said his economic agenda could be summed up in three words: "jobs, jobs, jobs."

If eight years from now, President Trump, like Reagan in the 1980s, can point to nineteen million new jobs, the American people will regard his presidency as a success.

It was the dramatic income tax cut in 1981 that led to the explosive economic growth under President Ronald Reagan. It was the capital gains tax cut in 1997 that led to the economic boom of the late nineties.

So, to boost job creation, President Trump will take a cue from history and work with Congress to cut taxes.

Tax cuts should be emphasized more than tax reform. Reforming the tax code will not create jobs on its own. Emphasizing tax "reform" will lead to Washington bean counters insisting on revenue neutrality—basically raising taxes in one area to cut taxes elsewhere. This is futile for job creation. In the short run, the tax increases always hurt more than the tax cuts help.

Instead of revenue neutrality, Trump and the Republican Congress should seek "deficit neutrality"—based on Obama's deficit baseline. This will create space for tax cuts by finding room elsewhere in the budget.

Unused federal assets should also be monetized to create nontax revenue that could offset tax revenue for tax cuts. This includes leasing non–environmentally sensitive federal lands for energy and mineral development and renting or selling federal housing stock and office space.

Trump and Congress should also insist on measures to crack down on waste and fraud, especially in our public health programs. There is an estimated $110 billion per year in fraud occurring in Medicare and Medicaid alone. Just cutting this in half would create room for over $50 billion more per year to be returned to the American economy via tax cuts.

By insisting on these steps and more, Trump and the Republican Congress could create room for a revolutionary job creating tax cuts without adding a penny to the deficit. Here is what that agenda could look like:

BUSINESS TAX CUT

The United States has the highest corporate tax rate among developed countries in the world at 38.92 percent, according to the Tax Foundation. It is the third-highest corporate tax overall. Only the United Arab Emirates and Puerto Rico tax businesses at higher rates. The world's average business tax across 188 countries and tax jurisdictions is 22.5 percent, and that is down from 30 percent in 2003, Tax Foundation figures show. Our rate is nearly 17 percentage points above average, and the average is dropping, so we are immediately at a disadvantage for attracting businesses. Meanwhile, Europe, as a region, has the lowest corporate tax rate at 18.88 percent.

If you were going to build a factory to make and sell widgets, where would you choose to set up shop: somewhere you would pay lower-than-average taxes, or the United States, where you would pay the third-highest rate in the world?

We must cut corporate taxes so businesses will want to invest in the United States and hire American workers. During the campaign, President Trump suggested lowering the rate to 15 percent, while Republican lawmakers are crafting a plan that would bring the rate to 20 percent. Either rate would be an enormous improvement that would immediately put the

United States in a better position to attract business and spur growth.

HOW A BORDER ADJUSTMENT TAX FITS IN

The United States is one of the few developed countries that does not tax imports and reward exports. Meanwhile, companies that remain in the United States and provide jobs to American workers are forced to pay taxes on their exports to other countries.

This means our current tax system is set up so that companies are better off manufacturing products in other countries, where they face lower taxes and fewer regulations, can pay lower wages to workers, and can sell into the huge US market penalty-free.

If we are serious about reversing the trend of jobs and money fleeing the country, we need to rectify this imbalance. Speaker Paul Ryan has a plan that involves implementing a border-adjustment tax, which is exactly the kind of system we need.

To be clear, the point of a border-adjustment tax is not to generate tax revenue to offset other cuts—we've discussed why this is harmful. It is to create jobs in America by putting us on an equal footing with other countries.

A border-adjustment tax is applied to all imported goods. Exports are not taxed. Naturally, this tax scheme incentivizes businesses that want to sell in the United States as well as in other countries to move here, because it allows them to avoid the import tax. Additionally, it gives large manufacturers good reason to expand their existing US facilities instead of outsourcing jobs to facilities in other countries.

More than 160 other countries have a value-added tax on imports, or a border-adjustment tax. Some have both. Countries aside from the United States that don't have such taxes include North Korea and South Sudan.

Critics of the border-adjustment tax say imported goods will be more expensive, because the border tax will be passed on to consumers. The standard counterargument is that the dollar will strengthen and balance out the price increases. But here's a simpler response for those concerned with expensive imports: we'd rather people buy American-made goods anyway. That aside, more companies coming to the United States means more American jobs. More Americans with jobs means more Americans with money in their wallets. If someone wants to pay more for an imported car, he or she would have that choice.

Some manufacturers who have built facilities in other countries would bear much of the burden early on, until they move more operations to the United States. But despite this, in February 2017, I met with thirty major American investors in Colorado. Nearly all of them voiced full support for a border-adjustment tax in America.

If President Trump and Congress are able to quickly cut taxes on businesses, and reform our tax system in a way that will attract business to America, our job market will see an immediate and lasting revival. According to the Tax Foundation, Speaker Ryan's tax plan could create about 1.7 million American jobs, and boost US production by more than 9 percent.

ELIMINATING THE CAPITAL GAINS TAX

Cutting the corporate tax rate and instituting a border-adjustment tax will incentivize American business investment and increase the number of jobs in the country, but we also must incentivize Americans to support business and their own retirements. The best way to do that is to eliminate the capital gains tax.

Scrapping the capital gains tax, lowering the corporate tax rate and initiating a border-adjustment tax would supercharge the American economy.

When I was Speaker of the House of Representatives, cutting capital gains was instrumental for balancing the budget. I will talk more about balancing the federal budget in chapter 13, but the impact of getting rid of capital gains taxes is relevant here.

The modern Left has convinced its voters that the capital gains tax isn't of interest to most Americans, because it is paid only by the wealthy. And it's true that households making more than $250,000 a year pay the clear majority of capital gains taxes. But the Left has also convinced liberal voters that increasing the tax would cause the wealthy to pay more in taxes—which is simply untrue.

The actual impact of increasing the capital gains tax is that wealthy investors, who hire smart accountants, invest less. They put their money elsewhere, and the US economy—and federal tax revenues—suffer. Higher taxes yield less investment, and lower taxes yield more investment.

Just look at what happened after we lowered the capital gains tax in 1997. According to the Tax Foundation, the effective capital gains tax rate in 1996 was 25.5 percent.[2] We were able to gradually lower it by 5 percentage points by 1999. *The Wall Street Journal* reported in October 2007 that the Joint Committee on Taxation said at the time the federal government would collect $195 billion in revenue from the capital gains tax from 1997 to 1999. In truth, lowering the rate spurred businesses to invest and we collected $279 billion in those three years.

More important than increased revenue, for three years, we saw over 4 percent GDP growth, with 6.7 million new jobs created[3] and median household incomes rising from $54,506 in 1997 to $57,909 in 1999.[4] The impact of the capital gains tax cut in the 1990s was an economic boost felt by the entire country, not just wealthy investors.

Cutting the capital gains by just 5 percent did all that. The economic growth that would result from eliminating the tax completely would drive the United States into a new era of prosperity.

As President John F. Kennedy said, the capital gains tax "directly affects investment decisions, the mobility and flow of risk capital" and limits potential economic growth. It is ironic that Kennedy understood what today's Democrats do not.

Congress and President Trump should act quickly to eliminate the capital gains tax, so investments and growth in America can begin as soon as possible.

REPATRIATION OF US MONEY HIDING IN FOREIGN COUNTRIES

President Trump also wants to offer companies a low-cost option to repatriate (or bring back to the United States) money they have earned overseas.

Repatriation of foreign earnings is really a no-brainer. According to the *Wall Street Journal*, over $2.5 trillion is being held overseas by companies that do not want to pay our high 35 percent corporate tax rate.

It's worth noting that the United States is one of only a few countries that tax active foreign earnings. This is part of the reason that the US system is so broken. First, we have trade agreements that encourage businesses to build outside our country, then we have a tax on foreign earnings, which gives them a reason to continue to invest outside the US rather than bring earnings home. Bringing that money back to the United States would spark an investment boom that would create jobs, raise the value of the dollar, and boost 401(k)s and pensions.

It is important, however, that corporate taxes are lowered and capital gains and foreign earnings taxes are abolished first before any one-time repatriation deal.

When Congress passed the Homeland Reinvestment Act, a tax holiday to repatriate earnings from overseas, companies brought roughly $300 billion back to the United States in 2005, according to a report by National Bureau of Economic Research.

The repatriated money went back to shareholders, who invested overseas again in anticipation of the next tax holiday, because American tax policy encouraged them to do so. For real, sustained investment, we need to create a strong business environment first.

CUTTING THE INCOME TAX

There cannot be a meaningful tax cut unless it grants relief to the middle class. President Trump has presented a plan to dramatically simplify the tax code and reduce the tax rates on income. The president's proposal would reduce the number of tax brackets from seven to three. The highest tax rate would be reduced from almost 40 percent to 33 percent. The middle-income tax bracket would be 25 percent, and the low-income bracket would be 12 percent.

Trump has also proposed eliminating the estate tax (also known as the death tax), the head-of-household filing status (which has had the perverse effect of incentivizing lower-income families not to marry), and, of course, all taxes associated with Obamacare. At the same time, he wants to more than double the standard deduction from $6,300 to $15,000 for single payers and from $12,600 to $30,000 for married couples.

Greatly reducing the tax burden on Americans will immediately spur savings, household buying power, and help reduce family debt.

In fact, President Trump's plan looks a lot like President Reagan's tax policy.

When Reagan took office, he was facing an economic disaster left by Jimmy Carter's administration. In 1980, inflation had reached 13.5 percent, and the prime interest rate was at 21.5 percent—which drove home mortgage interest to 14.7 percent. By the end of Carter's time in office, unemployment was nearing 10 percent, and 15.2 percent of Americans lived in poverty.

To spur economic growth, President Reagan immediately worked with Congress to cut the top tax rate from 70 percent to 50 percent. He then implemented a 25 percent across-the-board tax cut. With the passage of the 1986 tax reforms, there were only two tax rates: one at 28 percent and one at 15 percent.

President Reagan also aggressively cut spending, and greatly reduced red tape in Washington—all things President Trump has pledged to do. The result of Reagan's recovery was a seven-year boom that lasted from 1982 to 1990—until a tax increase that year ended the run. In that time, the US economy grew by one-third, the country added twenty million jobs, inflation dropped to 3.2 percent by 1983, and the prime interest rate dropped to 8.2 percent by 1987—eventually getting down to 6.25 percent by 1992.

At the same time—disproving the Left's dour predictions— federal revenue doubled from 1980 to 1990, reaching more than $1 trillion.

THE TRUMP RALLY

Business leaders and investors responded to the election of Donald Trump by betting on America again.

Just look at how the stock market has reacted to Trump's victory. On February 16, 2017, after Trump's first month in office, *CNN Money* reported that the S&P 500 increased by 3.8 percent. The S&P 500 index marks the performance of 500 commonly held stocks.

"That's the biggest increase for a new Republican president since the blue chip index that eventually became the S&P 500 debuted in 1923, according to S&P DJ Indices," wrote CNN's Paul R. La Monica.

That represented the largest postelection market rally on the S&P 500 since Lyndon Johnson took office after the assassination of John F. Kennedy in 1963.

The Dow Jones Industrial Average, the nation's oldest stock market index, closed at a record high of 21,115.55 on March 1, 2017, according to the website Thebalance.com. In fact, the Dow had thirty-two record-high closings from the 2016 election to March 1, the website reported.[5] The Dow tracks the average daily price changes of thirty large American businesses. This trend started just five days after Trump was elected, when the Dow closed above 20,000 points for the first time in its history. The Nasdaq 100, which is a measure of equity securities from 100 large nonbank businesses, also closed at a record high on March 13.

The US Bureau of Labor Statistics reported 235,000 new jobs in February 2017—well over the 195,000 expected by Wall Street bean counters. And the nation's economy added 227,000 jobs the month President Trump was inaugurated—which shattered the 175,000-job projection touted by economists.

The immediate growth to the economy following Trump's election has prompted the Federal Reserve Bank to increase interest rates for the third time since the Great Recession—and the second time in the previous three months.

The market quickly and enthusiastically reacted to Trump's election—along with the Republican majorities in the House and Senate—because business leaders know that they will soon see an end to anti-business, anti-growth, anti-investment policies in Washington.

This bull market and strong job numbers are a direct reaction to Trump's election, because businesses and investors across the world are more confident about the future of the United States than they have been in decades. Business leaders know that President Trump will make good on his promises to dramatically lower taxes and give US companies an option to repatriate money they've guarded overseas from liberal wealth redistributors.

REGULATIONS

President Trump has initiated a search-and-destroy mission to find and eliminate federal regulations that make it needlessly difficult to do business in the United States. As Trump promised during the campaign, "Any regulation that is outdated, unnecessary, bad for workers, or contrary to the national interest will be scrapped."

This is a serious challenge. According to the Competitive Enterprise Institute, in 2013, the Code of Federal Regulations—which catalogs every current federal rule—was more than 175,000 pages long. The group also estimated that the total cost of compliance to regulations is $1.8 trillion per year. In more personal terms, a family making $49,705 per year sees $14,768— 30 percent of their household budget—lost to the cost of regulations embedded in their normal expenditures. Meanwhile, small businesses face costs of over $10,000 per employee for regulatory compliance.

The compounding effect of this regulatory burden is astonishing. A study in the *Journal of Economic Growth* found that the growth in the regulatory burden in the United States since 1949 cost the country an average of 2 percent economic growth per year. Over nearly seventy years, that meant the US economy is only "28 percent of what it would have been had regulation remained at its 1949 level."

Reason magazine translated what that would mean for American families. According to its analysis, the median household income would be $330,000 a year had the regulatory burden not increased. Even if that analysis is off by 50 percent, and the median family income was $115,000 per year, how much better off would we be? That is the cost of the current insane regulatory regime.

If our country is going to continue to lead the world, the federal government needs to get out of the way of innovators, entrepreneurs, and others who are seeking to grow wealth in the United States and compete in science and invention worldwide.

Trump is off to a great start by working with Congress to use the Congressional Review Act to overrule Obama-era regulations issued by government agencies. The law, passed in 1996 when I was Speaker as part of the Contract with America agenda, had been used just one time before Trump assumed office. As of the date of this writing, Trump and the Republican Congress have used it six times. The regulations they have repealed include burdensome requirements on energy development, rules that removed authority from communities over zoning, and layers of bureaucracy imposed on state and local school systems.

Members of Congress could also help the president by aggregating bad regulations they hear about from constituents. Each congressperson should set up a website to crowdsource bad regulations from businesses and residents in his or her district. With enough forethought and organization, these websites could automatically find and sort the regulations that make it more difficult to grow and keep jobs in our congressional districts. From there, members of congress can compare notes and start tackling the top job-killing regulations.

To really end the job-killing nature of the regulatory state, however, it won't be enough to eliminate regulations one by one. The underlying philosophy behind how regulations are crafted will need to be changed.

The legal and political scholar Philip Howard wrote an op-ed in the *Washington Post* in December 2016 describing the over-regulation problem called "Six Presidents Have Failed to cut Red Tape. Here's How Trump Could Succeed."[6] In his op-ed, Howard said that for the last fifty years, leaders on both sides of the aisle have failed to cut unnecessary regulations, because they all approached the problem with a "flawed philosophy":

> What reformers have missed is that regulatory failure is not merely a matter of too much regulation but is caused by a flawed philosophy on how to regulate. Both sides assume that human responsibility should be replaced by what is called "clear law." By striving to prescribe every possible good choice, and proscribe every possible evil, U.S. regulation became an obsessive exercise in micro-management. That's why rulebooks are often 1,000 pages, while the Constitution is 15. The evil to be exorcised by all these legal dictates is human authority. Only by lashing each other tightly with detailed law can liberal and conservative politicians be sure that the other side won't do something bad.

Howard perfectly identified this pervasive philosophy of government control as the reason businesses in virtually every industry have to spend huge amounts of money on compliance, and why virtually every government-run initiative fails.

President Trump can change this system, Howard says, by getting rid of instruction-manual-style regulations and replacing them with simple regulations that allow human beings to focus on outputs—or results:

> The solution—the only solution—is to retool regulation to focus on results, not inputs. Find any good school, any good agency, and you will find people who take responsibility for getting the job done. Experts at the Federal

Aviation Administration certify planes as "airworthy" based on their expert judgment, not compliance with detailed specs on, say, how many rivets per square foot. Teachers at good schools typically say that the principal encourages them to do what they think is best and not worry about complying with many forms and metrics.

If President Trump can work with Congress to develop a doctrine and methodology of results, rather than input-focused regulations, he will have permanently changed the big-government, bureaucrats-know-best regulatory regime, and would put America on a path of sustained prosperity for decades to come.

JOBS, JOBS, JOBS

In some ways, Trump's focus on job creation has led him to behave more like a governor than a president. Governors spend much of their time searching for companies that are looking to relocate or build new facilities, then convincing those companies that his or her state is the best choice for them. Trump has been doing this since he was campaigning—only Trump has mostly been persuading companies that had announced plans to move operations outside the United States to stay.

In December, before President Trump took office, he and Vice President Pence worked out a deal with Carrier, which makes air conditioners and other heating- and refrigeration-related products, to save about eight hundred jobs that were slated to be moved from Indiana to Mexico. As part of the deal, the company would receive $7 million of tax incentives over ten years, in exchange for investing $16 million in an Indiana facility that manufactures furnaces.

In early January, Ford Motor Company's CEO, Mark Fields, said the automaker would cancel plans to build a plant in Mexico and instead invest $700 million in a Michigan plant. *CNN Money* reported the decision was made as a "vote of confidence" that President Trump would create a probusiness environment in the United States.

Critics on the Left have downplayed the retained jobs, saying that these instances won't greatly affect the overall job market. But these jobs make a huge difference to the people who live in Michigan and Indiana who were facing unemployment.

President Trump's plan to build $1 trillion worth of infrastructure will immediately create good-paying construction jobs all over the country. And this is a part of the president's agenda that will attract strong bipartisan support. There isn't a member of Congress or senator anywhere who doesn't need infrastructure improvements in his or her district or state. Implementing President Trump's infrastructure plan is going to be key to building and maintaining legislative momentum—and developing an environment in Congress in which Democrats and Republicans can start working together again.

JOB TRAINING AND EDUCATION

But it will do no good to create jobs if no one can do them. An often-overlooked problem with American employment is a serious lack of skilled laborers. According to Bureau of Labor Statistics data, there were 148,000 unfilled construction jobs and 325,000 unfilled manufacturing jobs in the United States in December 2016.[7]

One of the reasons these good-paying jobs are going unfilled is a growing lack of respect for vocational programs. We have missed out on nearly a generation of skilled workers who were convinced to attend a traditional four-year university. Curbed. com, a website that focuses on real estate and construction issues, said in an article on February 1, 2017, that this gap may come to the forefront of President Trump's agenda:[8]

The labor shortage in the construction industry is indica-
tive of a wider, decades-in-the-making gap in vocational
training that has had an impact on many sectors of the
U.S. economy. At a time when the incoming administration is talking about massive infrastructure investments
and helping the rural economy, action on this issue could
have a massive impact on the effectiveness of such programs. It may even impact his signature campaign promise and construction challenge, building the Mexican
border wall; many industry analysts and observers say
labor shortages and the need to vet legal workers for such
a massive public works project will be a huge challenge.

Aside from instructing Education Secretary Betsy DeVos to
look into ways to help states restore vocational training in K–12
education, President Trump could immediately start to solve the
shortage of skilled workers by reversing the Obama administration's debilitating policies over private career training programs.

The Obama administration shut down ITT Technical
Institute, which had helped train American workers in skilled
labor for more than fifty years. This pulled the rug out from under
about forty thousand students and eight thousand employees,
according to a September 20, 2016, *Washington Post* editorial.

And just before the end of his term, President Obama's education department pulled authority from one of the country's
oldest national academic accreditors, the Accrediting Council
for Independent Colleges and Schools (ACICS). The ACICS
accredits 725 schools, which serve more than 600,000 students.

These actions were part of what the *Washington Post* called
Obama's "ideological crusade" against private, for-profit
career-training institutions. If President Trump can quickly
remove federal hurdles to career-training institutions, we could
start to relieve the shortage of skilled labor in the United States.

Career training is also one of the best ways for those facing urban and rural poverty to improve their lives.

USA Today reported in 2014 that 2.5 million new special skilled jobs were expected to be available in 2017. These are good-paying jobs in construction, manufacturing, and other industries that require two-year degrees, certificates, or other noncollege training.[9]

The newspaper reported that all of those jobs would pay more than $13 an hour; many would pay much more and most require much less training than a four-year degree. After looking at 125 of the country's largest metropolitan areas, the newspaper found Houston would add 100,000 skilled labor jobs—40,000 of which would pay more than $20 an hour. Atlanta would be looking for about 77,000 workers for its budding film industry. The average pay for those jobs would be $84,000 a year. And "in most metro areas, some of the best-paying middle-skill jobs include radiation therapists, elevator installers and repairers, and dental hygienists, all with a median wage of more than $70,000."

Making sure Americans are trained and ready for these types of jobs is the best way to rebuild our middle class.

IMMIGRATION

At the same time, President Trump can help close the labor gap by focusing on improving legal immigration.

President Trump's proposal during his 2017 address to a joint session of Congress could help the United States achieve this. In his speech, the president suggested focusing on a merit-based system, similar to the one used by our northern neighbor, Canada. He said:

It's a basic principle that those seeking to enter a country ought to be able to support themselves financially.

Yet, in America, we do not enforce this rule, straining the very public resources that our poorest citizens rely upon. According to the National Academy of Sciences, our current immigration system costs American taxpayers many billions of dollars a year.

Switching away from this current system of lower-skilled immigration, and instead adopting a merit-based system, we will have so many more benefits. It will save countless dollars, raise workers' wages, and help struggling families—including immigrant families— enter the middle class. And they will do it quickly, and they will be very, very happy, indeed.

I believe that real and positive immigration reform is possible, as long as we focus on the following goals: to improve jobs and wages for Americans; to strengthen our nation's security; and to restore respect for our laws. If we are guided by the well-being of American citizens, then I believe Republicans and Democrats can work together to achieve an outcome that has eluded our country for decades.

A better guest worker program should include thorough criminal background checks for immigrant workers, identification cards encoded with workers' biometric information, and a more efficient process. Most immigrants don't want to turn to dangerous cartels to come to the United States, so they will be more likely to follow the rules to get a work visa if that process is expanded and made more efficient, and tailored to their skill set. And the immigrant workers who join the workforce would be paying taxes, operating in the full light of day, and helping reduce the demand for human smuggling, forged immigration documents, and other illegal activities that fuel business for criminal cartels. Once President Trump and Congress reduce taxes for businesses and individuals, repatriate US dollars being held offshore, eliminate burdensome regulations, make it easier for Americans to learn the skills they need to find jobs, and fix our broken immigration system, US productivity and trade will increase and America will be competitive again.

COMPETING FOR THE FUTURE

The United States can't focus solely within its borders if it wants to lead in the twenty-first century.

During President Trump's inaugural address, he invoked a part of the American spirit that has been silent for too long—its bold determination to reach for the stars.

"We stand at the birth of a new millennium, ready to unlock the mysteries of space, to free the earth from the miseries of disease, and to harness the energies, industries, and technologies of tomorrow," President Trump said.

The possibility of competing in space is one of the things about a Trump-Pence administration that excites me most. And to be sure, both President Trump and Vice President Pence are vital to space policy.

Vice President Pence has long believed in the space program. Even before he was elected to Congress he traveled from Indiana to Florida to watch rockets being launched. As a freshman in Congress, his number one goal was to get on the space subcommittee of the House Science Committee. The vice president is delighted that he is now the chairman of the Space Council, which brings together all the elements of the federal government's involvement in space.

I have been passionate about space since the Russians launched Sputnik in 1957. As an eighth-grader, I read *Missiles and Rockets* magazine—a periodical that covered the rapid evolution of our space capabilities. Like most Americans my age, I was fascinated by the Apollo program. I can still remember watching the first landing on the moon. At that time, everything seemed possible.

Then, NASA became bureaucratic. Funding was cut, and everything became slower, more expensive, and more risk averse.

Instead of the shuttle leading us into a bold new era, it became an enormously expensive system that absorbed money. NASA continued to fund science—and a lot of it has been extraordinary. However, the great adventure, the exploration of the unknown by humans, the spirit that got Americans to the moon in eight years, drowned in a sea of red tape.

In 1984, I hosted a series of dinners with Congressman Bob Walker, who later became chairman of the House Committee on Science and Technology and then led the Walker Commission on the Future of the United States Aerospace Industry under President George W. Bush.

At the dinners, we invited young NASA scientists. Most of them were under thirty-five years old.

The dinners were exciting and full of visionary ideas. I tried to capture them in a chapter of a book I wrote that year called *Window of Opportunity*. Unfortunately, the combination of bureaucratic inefficiency, lack of entrepreneurial daring, and timidity about risk taking on the part of the federal government guaranteed that thirty-three years later, most of the opportunities in space we discussed at the dinners are still unfulfilled.

In my 2012 presidential race, I went to the Space Coast of Florida and gave a boldly visionary speech about what was possible. I proposed:

> By the end of my second term we will have the first permanent base on the Moon, and it will be American.
>
> We will have commercial near-Earth activities that include science, tourism, and manufacturing, and are designed to create a robust industry precisely on the

model that was developed by the airlines in the 1930s, because it is in our interest to acquire so much experience in space that we clearly have a capacity that the Chinese and the Russians will never come anywhere close to matching.

And by the end of 2020 we will have the first continuous propulsion system in space capable of getting to Mars in a remarkably short time, because I am sick of being told we have to be timid, and I'm sick of being told we have to be limited to technologies that are fifty years old.

A few of my primary opponents attacked the idea of investing in space. In fact, their hostility was so great that Greta Van Susteren did an interview contrasting John F. Kennedy's bold, idealistic vision of going to the moon in 1961 with their penny-pinching, green-eyeshades reactionary attitudes.

Given that background, you can imagine how happy I was to see Trump's positive, visionary attitude toward space.

TRUMP AND THE BILLIONAIRES: A NEW ERA IN SPACE EXPLORATION

Two developments are reaching an intersection that will make it much easier and cheaper to achieve the dynamic future in space that Trump favors.

First, new technologies are creating capabilities that didn't exist before. Advances in computing enable engine and flight controls that were impossible a decade ago. New materials technology—including lightweight, moldable, woven carbon fibers—are creating dramatic new possibility for spacecraft design.

Composite technologies have reduced in cost and increased in practicality since the development of the space shuttle (look at the Boeing 787 Dreamliner as an example). Progress on the creation of carbon nanotubes will soon give us a material vastly stronger and lighter than steel.

The potential in robotics, autonomous systems, and 3-D printing could soon make manufacturing on the moon and in space entirely possible.

Second, these advances in technology are being matched by a new entrepreneurial enthusiasm for space—specifically among a key group of very successful people. Consider three examples:

Elon Musk developed the first consistent private space company. SpaceX was founded in 2002 with the specific goal of dramatically lowering the cost of access to space by developing reusable rockets. It has now had eight successful recoveries of rockets, and it launched and landed its first reusable rocket in March 2017. SpaceX expects to be able to use and retrieve the same rocket with a one-day turnaround by 2018. SpaceX has government contracts and has been launching satellites for a private Luxembourg company. It currently plans to take two private citizens around the moon in 2018.

Musk's stated goal is to build large enough spaceships to enable humans to colonize Mars. He is planning to develop what he calls the SpaceX Interplanetary Transport System that would take one hundred people at a time to Mars, with new engines that could get there in three months.

Space X still has a long way to go before it can get to Mars in three months. But for fifteen years, Musk has been steadily working toward that capability.

Jeff Bezos founded Blue Origin in 2000, two years earlier than Musk created SpaceX. However, Bezos has taken a very methodical capabilities-focused approach. His goal is to dramatically lower the cost of getting into space by having relatively inexpensive reusable rockets with short turnaround times.

Since Bezos is today one of the richest men in the world (his current estimated worth is $65 billion), he can pour a billion dollars a year into developing better, more powerful reusable rockets.

His first reusable vehicle, the *New Shepard*—named for Alan Shepard, the first American to go to suborbital space—first flew in 2015. It has achieved reusability with a two-month turnaround of the same rocket. Bezos hopes to start carrying space tourists into near space on suborbital flights in 2018.

Blue Origin is now developing a heavy-lift vehicle, the *New Glenn*—named for John Glenn, the first American to orbit the globe. This new, much bigger rocket will be competitive with the Titan IV as a lift vehicle for heavy satellites. Because it is reusable, it will be dramatically less expensive over time.

According to Bezos, it takes about $400,000 in fuel to launch a large satellite. However, since the current rockets can be used only once, the total cost is about $400 million. Therefore, Bezos reasons, if you could have a reusable rocket, the cost would drop by an order of magnitude to $40 million or less. Reducing the cost of getting into space by a factor of ten will open up massive potential for manufacturing, research, and space tourism.

While Musk focuses on Mars, Bezos looks to the moon. With 3-D printing and robotics, it will be possible to establish factories on the moon, which can use existing water and other resources to provide fuel for space activities. Since the moon only has one-sixth of earth's gravity and no atmospheric drag, it will be much easier to launch from the moon. This creates potential for building really large spaceships and even mining asteroids—one of which is estimated to have $9 trillion worth of rare minerals.

Remarkably different than Musk and Bezos is the approach being taken by Microsoft cofounder Paul Allen. Allen has already funded Bert Rutan's record-setting SpaceShipOne, which set the record in 2004 for flying to the edge of space twice. It is the first private vehicle to do so.

Now Allen is building Stratolaunch, the largest aircraft ever built. It will take rockets up to 35,000 feet and then launch them. As an airplane, it will be rapidly reusable and therefore much less expensive as a first stage, replacing the normal rocket first stage.

Allen's strategy coincides with the development of tiny microsatellites. As electronics have gotten smaller, the potential for effective satellites of small size has grown. There are now satellites the size of a loaf of bread that perform key services.

We are on the verge of launching hundreds of small satellites that can do the work of one huge, expensive satellite. Paul Allen's Stratolaunch may be a key enabler of this revolution.

In total, a team advising Trump has been able to identify sixteen billionaires with real interest in space. They are collectively worth $280 billion.

Vice President Pence may become the first vice president to lead a national space council of government agencies and a private entrepreneurial space council of major investors willing to go on their own, where no one has gone before (to paraphrase *Star Trek*).

Given President Trump's belief in space and his experience as an entrepreneur, he may lead an even more dynamic program in space than President Kennedy did.

If the entrepreneurs can be encouraged to move as fast as technology can be developed, Americans reoccupying the moon could occur late in Trump's first term. And this time, they would be there to stay. With a few breaks and some entrepreneurial daring, Americans could land on Mars either in Trump's last year of his second term or in the first term of his successor.

NASA will be revolutionized by the need to strip away bureaucracy and focus on achievements rather than paper studies. The speed and energy of the entrepreneurs will force NASA to eliminate bureaucracy or become irrelevant.

President Trump's entire career has involved dreaming big and undertaking bold projects.

As he carries this pattern into space, some of my childhood dreams and the dreams of millions of Americans will be coming true.

In every conversation I have had about health care with Trump, both when he was a candidate and as president, he has emphasized the importance of getting great health care for every American. He simply doesn't accept that we can spend this much money and do such a bad job of helping people. He is a naturally generous person, and there are an amazing number of people who can tell you how he has helped them when they had a medical crisis. He will try to bring this personal care approach to getting the American health system to work for everyone.

CHAPTER TWELVE

THE HEALTH BOX

Obamacare, in the words of President Trump, is a "disaster."

It is a disaster for two reasons.

First, the law creates a set of rules that make it impossible for insurance companies to offer low-cost plans to people who buy health insurance directly, instead of through their employer. These high-cost plans cannot attract enough healthy people to offset the health care costs incurred by the sick people enrolling who desperately need the coverage. The result has been a "death spiral" of rapidly rising premiums that prevent healthy people from signing up, and the problems worsen. That's why premiums increased by an average of 22 percent in the individual marketplace from 2016 to 2017.

Second, Obamacare was primarily health insurance reform, not health care reform. This distinction is important. Obamacare focused on the rules governing health insurance and largely ignored the underlying problems in the health care system that increase health care costs. Those rising costs are responsible for the huge rise in premiums over the past several decades—the dynamics of the insurance marketplace play only a minor role.

The American Health Care Act, which President Trump and Speaker Ryan attempted to pass in March 2017, would have been a good first step to address the first problem. The law, combined with administrative actions at the Department of Health and Human Services, would have led to price stabilization and more insurance choices in the individual marketplace.

However, the law still suffered from the second problem with Obamacare—it dealt primarily with financing health insurance; it wasn't actual health care reform. So, the failure to pass the American Health Care Act should not be treated as the end of health reform. In fact, it may have been the best thing that could have happened to get something much better.

WHY THE AMERICAN HEALTH CARE ACT FAILED

Before exploring what real health reform would look like, it is important to examine the effort to pass the American Health Care Act to avoid repeating the mistakes that were made that led to its failure.

The Republican congressional leadership's mistake was trying to repeal and replace Obamacare under the business-as-usual rules of Washington.

First, they allowed the Congressional Budget Office to score the bill. Even though the Republicans rejected the CBO's fake estimate, simply allowing it to exist in the first place gave the Democrats and the media the gift of being able to quote "the nonpartisan CBO" to attack the bill.

Second, they accepted the limitations of the Senate reconciliation rules even though that guaranteed the bill would be insufficient to satisfy conservative members.

Third, they rushed the bill by setting a deadline. This contradicts everything we know about what it takes to pass big reforms. President Reagan took eight months to pass his tax cut, which was very popular. When I was Speaker of the House of

Representatives, we took eighteen months to pass welfare reform, which was at 92 percent approval. In contrast, Republican congressional leaders tried to pass a very complicated repeal and replace bill in less than three months.

Fourth, they focused on a complex Washington insider argument and process involving a "three-step plan" and arcane Senate rules while their opponents in the media and in left-wing groups hammered away at the alleged human cost of their bill. The old rule in Washington applies: "If you are explaining, you are losing."

Finally, and most important, after an election in which a total outsider, Donald J. Trump, was elected president because Americans don't trust politicians, congressional leadership drafted a bill in secret, skipped hearings, minimized open debate, and made vague promises about future actions to try to whip up support, which amounted to, "Trust us, we're in Washington." No surprise, no one did.

The result was that President Trump and congressional Republicans lost the argument so badly that the bill was at 17 percent approval (less than one out of five Americans) the day it was pulled.

REFORM IS POSSIBLE, BUT WILL REQUIRE A DIFFERENT APPROACH

Successful health care reform can be achieved, but it will require a very different approach from the one taken with the failed American Health Care Act.

COMPREHENSIVE DOESN'T WORK IN WASHINGTON

First, Trump and congressional Republicans should abandon Washington's obsession with comprehensive reform. Health is the largest sector of the American economy—18 percent of GDP—and the most complex. Comprehensive legislation that affects one-fifth of our economy would be so complicated no one would understand it, and gaining majority support—much less bipartisan support—would be impossible.

Instead, health reform needs a slower-paced, transparent, simultaneous, issue-by-issue legislative approach. A series of hearings must be held to gather information and develop specific reforms that will improve health and health care. These hearings should have geographic as well as topical focuses so different citizens in different regions of the country will understand how the bill will affect them personally.

Some doubt that any health care legislation can pass Congress or garner the sixty votes needed in the Senate to avoid a filibuster. But there are recent examples of major health care bills that passed with significant bipartisan support.

The 21st Century Cures Act passed the House on November 30, 2016, by a vote of 392 to 26 and the Senate on December 7 by a vote of 94 to 5. The bill dedicated funds for biomedical research and updated Food and Drug Administration processes for approving cutting-edge therapies and treatments.

The Helping Families in Mental Health Crisis Act of 2016 passed the House on July 6, 2016, by a vote of 422 to 2 and the Senate by 94 to 5 (as a part of the 21st Century Cures Act). This nearly $4 billion reform in mental health programs was the most important in a decade.

Every Republican House and Senate member, and the Trump administration, should point to these reforms to remind Americans (and especially the news media) that Republicans are committed to work on a bipartisan basis to achieve a better health future for all Americans.

Right now, there are 25 Senate Democrats (including two independents who caucus with them) up for reelection in 2018. An effective, sustained grassroots program can force a number of them either to vote with our better Republican ideas or face defeat back home. This is a key component for Republican legislative success in 2017 and 2018.

LEARNING TO COMMUNICATE EFFECTIVELY

Second, successful health reform will require a much more morally compelling, persuasive style of communication than Republicans are used to. Eight years of opposing Obama and the temptation to remain negative will be hard to unlearn, but it is essential to governing.

The most effective conservative reformers of the past forty years all understood the importance of effective communication.

Margaret Thatcher had a rule for winning campaigns: "First you win the argument, then you win the vote."

Ronald Reagan, in his farewell address, explained how he succeeded in pushing conservative reforms through Congress: "I've had my share of victories in the Congress, but what few people noticed is that I never won anything you didn't win for me. They never saw my troops, they never saw Reagan's regiments, the American people. You won every battle with every call you made and letter you wrote demanding action."

When we passed welfare reform in 1996, we had explained our case so thoroughly that 92 percent of Americans favored reform, including 88 percent of those on welfare.

Thatcher, Reagan, and the Contract with America Republicans successfully communicated with the people by focusing on moral, human-focused arguments to achieve legislative success. Donald Trump and congressional Republicans must follow the same model. Winning the support of the American people for health reform will require a positive, morally centered, and human-focused vision of what such reform would mean for every single American.

Trump's instincts, I believe, are correct on this. During his winning campaign, Trump usually focused on the emotionally powerful theme of making sure people got the health care they needed. Insurance came second.

In September 2015, for instance, Trump was being interviewed by Scott Pelley of CBS and was asked about his health care plan.

"I am going to take care of everybody. I don't care if it costs me votes or not," he said.

Pelley asked a follow-up question, trying to turn the discussion to insurance, but Trump refocused on making sure people get treatment.

"They're going to be taken care of. I would make a deal with existing hospitals to take care of people," Trump responded.

In his postelection interviews as well, president-elect Trump repeatedly emphasized his plan would offer "better health care, for less money."

Notice that Trump put better health care first, money second. People get lost in the details when politicians focus on the technical details of insurance, because it doesn't relate directly to their lives. Painting a positive vision of how every American's health and health care will be better is how to communicate successful reform, not getting lost in abstraction about financing models.

President Trump and the Republicans in Congress lost this moral, personal focus once they started pushing the American Health Care Act. They became drowned in the details of refundable tax credits, continuous coverage, and changing the actuarial value of plans. The predictable result was that they could not garner support for the bill. The next health care reform effort must turn the focus back to health and health care rather than insurance financing.

Another principle to winning the support of the American people is for President Trump and the Republican Congress to discuss health care as an opportunity, not as a problem that needs to be solved. In addition to improving people's health, an American health system that is once again the most innovative and effective in the world would be a huge source of high-paying jobs and foreign exchange.

A VISION FOR AMERICAN HEALTH CARE IN THE AGE OF TRUMP

Health is a moral issue. It is about life and death first. Money comes second.

Trump and the Republicans' vision for health care reform must be about more than repealing Obamacare. It must be about more than insurance. It must create a clear, positive path for twenty-first-century health and health care.

Fortunately, we are entering an age of medical miracles that should give Americans reason to be excited.

Advances in science and technology have brought us to the brink of a miraculous future.

With the discovery of CRISPR, we may have opportunities to edit DNA to change, activate, and shut off genes that cause disease.

With immunotherapies, we are stimulating patients' immune systems to attack and kill cancer with biology instead of using radiation and chemotherapy that damage healthy cells.

Already, we have built bionic eyes—cameras that transmit vision directly to the retinas of the blind. And that is nothing compared with the gene therapies for blindness that are working in clinical trials today.

In labs across the country, doctors are growing new, replacement organs for patients whose bodies are failing. Even now, there are patients walking around with bladders that were grown in incubators more than a decade ago.

Breakthroughs in neuroscience could soon slow or even halt the onset of Alzheimer's and other dementias.

Miniature sensors can already monitor our vital signs around the clock, transmitting them wirelessly to our phones to alert us—and our doctors—of any sign of trouble. Soon, nano-sensors in the bloodstream will offer continuous access to every conceivable metric of health.

These are the scientific miracles before us. This is the future that every American could have. It would be a tragedy to abandon it. And yet we are in real danger of doing just that.

TWENTY-FIRST-CENTURY HEALTH AND HEALTH CARE RIGHTS AND RESPONSIBILITIES

The imaginations of our nation's entrepreneurs, coupled with the constant discoveries of our scientists, can lead us to this future. But our twentieth-century policies, regulations, and market approaches cannot solve our twenty-first-century challenges. We are also hindered by our big, bureaucratic government and special interests that protect the past at the expense of progress. We must urgently rethink these failing systems and outdated regulations if we are to clear the way for a revolution in health science and technology.

President Trump and congressional Republicans, therefore, must think much bigger and broader than changes in insurance financing to enact real reform that will save lives and save money. Instead, their number one priority should be to replace our current health bureaucracy with a flatter, more transparent, and more accountable health system that embraces innovation.

Every American should be able to expect certain standards, freedoms, benefits, and opportunities from a twenty-first-century health system. If they are willing to participate and be responsible, they will gain:

- improved health;
- longer lives with a much better quality of life;

- a more convenient, understandable, and personalized experience—all at lower cost;
- access to the best course of treatment for their particular illness and their unique characteristics;
- a system that fosters and encourages innovation, competition, and better outcomes for patients;
- a system that truly values the impact that medical innovation has on patients and their caregivers, as well as on society as a whole;
- a government that facilitates and accelerates extraordinary opportunities to improve health and health care;
- continuous but unobtrusive 24/7 monitoring of their general health, chronic conditions, and acute health problems;
- access to the most modern medical knowledge and breakthroughs, including the most advanced technologies, therapies, and drugs, unimpeded by government-imposed price controls or rationing;
- the chance to increase their personal knowledge by learning from a transparent system of information about their diagnosis, costs, and alternative solutions;
- a continuously improving, competitive, patient-focused medical world in which new therapies, new technologies, and new drugs are introduced as rapidly and safely as possible—and not a day later;
- greater price and market competition, innovation, and smarter health care spending;
- a system of financing that includes insurance, government, charities, and self-funding that ensures access to health and health care for every American at the lowest possible cost without allowing financing and short-term budgetary considerations to distort and weaken the delivery of care;

- genuine insurance to facilitate access to dramatically better care, rather than the current system, which is myopically focused on monthly or annual payments;
- a health system in which third parties and government bureaucrats do not impede the best course of treatment that doctors and their patients decide on; and
- a health system in which seniors, veterans, or others under government health programs receive the same quality of care as their children in private market systems.

Big reforms are required to transform today's expensive, obsolete health bureaucracy into a system that conforms to these principles.

REFORMS TO ACHIEVE THIS VISION

President Trump's new approach to reform will have to be much different from what has passed for health care reform in Washington for the past two decades.

Instead of arguing over how to afford our broken health care system, he must focus his administration and congressional Republicans on actually fixing it.

We discussed why focusing on insurance financing is counterproductive to the goal of effective political communication—people care about their health, not abstract funding models. However, it is also self-defeating from an effective policy perspective.

First, most dysfunctional systems are starved for money because they are dysfunctional—not vice versa. Our broken health care system is a perfect example. Some analyses have shown that nearly $1 trillion per year is lost to waste and fraud in the health care system. You read that right: $1 trillion *per year*.

It is impossible to adequately finance a health system that bleeds $1 trillion annually. Costs will always overwhelm our resources. And we can't fix our health care system solely by reducing the amount of money being spent by the government or insurance companies on health care. To use a medical analogy, trying to cure our health care system of what ails it by focusing on financing is treating the symptom, not the disease.

The disease in our health care system is a toxic mix of:

power centralized in large bureaucracies instead of the individual patients and doctors;
cultural and societal patterns that lead to poor health; and
a dysfunctional health delivery system that encourages waste, maximizes defensive medicine because of a broken litigation system, and tolerates fraud.

Only by focusing on solving these three challenges can we solve the problem of escalating costs. Figuring out how to pay for coverage and health care for the poor will be much easier if it is dramatically less expensive.

This leads us to the second reason why focusing narrowly on money is self-defeating: arbitrarily decreasing or increasing funding across an ineffective system does no good. But spending money in an effective health care system can have second-order economic benefits that end up paying for itself, or at least offsetting the costs. Effective health care spending directly saves lives, which go on to years and years of productivity instead of being cut short. Therefore, it is critical that lawmakers take a smart, strategic approach when it comes to making the health care system work, rather than waste time bickering over dollars and cents.

The following are a series of strategies and reforms I have shared with President Trump and his team. They are focused on fixing the root causes of the health care systems' dysfunction rather than trying to tweak public and private insurance rules and funding.

These reforms are not a one-size-fits-all, Washington-knows-best model. They would give every single American the power to affect the health care marketplace. This is the only way to have a system that responds to the needs of patients instead of bureaucracies, adapts quickly to new information and innovation, encourages competition, and drives down prices while delivering better results.

STRATEGY 1: MAXIMIZE INNOVATION

Maximizing innovation and the speed at which medical breakthroughs can reach patients must be the number one priority of a twenty-first-century health care system.

The explosion of new scientific and medical knowledge we are seeing worldwide will do little good for patients if it takes decades for those advances to reach them. Yet that is the situation we are in today. Numerous studies have estimated that it takes seventeen years for research evidence to reach clinical practice.

Rapidly accelerating this process will—most important—save lives, and it will save money.

The benefit of quickly getting new treatments to patients is clear.

As Thomas Peter Stossel of the American Enterprise Institute wrote in February 2016, there is significant evidence that "the introduction of new drugs and devices has been the dominant factor behind a ten-year increase in U.S. longevity, a marked reduction in mortality from cardiovascular disease and cancer, and improved quality of life due to reduced morbidity caused by afflictions such as arthritis."

And maximizing innovation would save money.

Innovation creates "cost collapses"—dramatic reductions in (or virtual elimination of) the costs of treatments for expensive diseases. Allowing market factors like innovation to cut costs is much more effective than "cost control," which usually consists of large bureaucracies arbitrarily reducing funding across the board to try to save money.

The creation of the polio vaccine offers a simple example of how cost collapses work. The US health care system spends almost zero today on iron lungs to help polio victims breathe. One study published in PubMed estimated that the $35 billion the United States has spent on polio vaccinations since their invention has prevented 1.1 million cases of paralysis, 160,000 deaths, and created a net economic benefit to the United States of $180 billion. That's a remarkable return on investment.

There are more recent examples of new treatments producing huge cost collapses.

A study in *Health Affairs* estimated that the use of statins (a cholesterol-lowering drug) in 2008 translated into a 27 percent reduction in health care costs per patient due to fewer strokes and heart attacks. This produced a net savings within the health care system itself of $5 billion.

The benefit is even more pronounced if you look at the broader benefit to society. The same study also estimated that the use of statins between 1987 and 2008 generated $1.25 trillion in economic value from years of life saved for those taking the medicine. During that time, approximately $200 billion was spent on statin drugs, meaning a net benefit to society of $947 billion. That is roughly a 4:1 benefit to cost ratio.

Another study in the *Journal of Managed Care* showed that the $14 billion that has been spent on treatments for chronic myeloid leukemia (CML) since 2001 has created $126 billion in economic value for patients. That doesn't even account for the full societal benefits, such as reductions in the burden on caregivers or reduction in other medical costs due to improved health.

President Trump and congressional Republicans need to take aggressive steps to maximize innovation in the health system so new treatments can be developed and reach patients faster.

Dramatically Increase Funding for Scientific Research

One of the biggest mistakes people in Washington make is to get trapped in short-term budgetary crises that prevent the type of investments in research and treatments that produce huge long-term savings. This is another reason why a myopic focus on money is counterproductive to fixing our health care system.

Alzheimer's and other forms of dementia, for example, are projected to cost the United States more than $20 trillion over the next four decades. A great deal of this cost will be absorbed by Medicare and Medicaid. Current spending levels in the two programs are already at $154 billion—almost 15 percent of their total combined budgets—and those costs are projected to increase 420 percent and 330 percent, respectively.

Considering this massive current and future financial tsunami, you would think that developing a cure for these brain diseases would be considered an urgent national priority. Even delaying the onset of Alzheimer's by just five years would cut costs by one-third.

Yet the National Institutes of Health (NIH) is spending only $1.3 billion per year on research into Alzheimer's and dementia— less than 1 percent of the federal government's expenditures on the diseases alone. The National Science Foundation is similarly underfunded when it comes to brain research.

The federal government has an irreplaceable role to play in funding this sort of "upstream" research, which private companies can then take and develop into cures and treatments. It cannot be done entirely by the private sector, because this sort of early-stage research rarely produces profits in an amount of time acceptable to investors. This partnership between the public and private sector has allowed the United States to be the epicenter of biopharmaceutical research and development for decades.

One of the great struggles in the Trump administration will be between those who want an innovative, creative science-and-technology strategy and those who are desperate to cut everything but defense. In his campaign speeches, President Trump was clearly in favor of a dynamic, research-oriented effort to cure diseases. In the initial budget, the green-eyeshade accountants won out with what I believe was a truly mindless and destructive set of cuts to the National Institutes of Health. Since the budget came out, there has been no defense of the cuts, and there is growing evidence that the innovative wing is winning.

In addition to federally funded research, we need creative new ways outside the normal budgeting process to fund research into areas that are urgent national priorities, such as brain science, heart disease, diabetes, and cancer.

Dr. Michael Burgess, a Republican congressman from Texas, introduced a bill in 2011 called the MIND Act that would create "Alzheimer's Bonds." The money raised by selling the bonds would go directly to brain research. Breakthroughs that reduce the projected costs associated with the disease would go to paying back the bondholders.

The NIH should also explore the use of cash prizes to incentivize the development of specific cures identified by its researchers. Throughout history, cash prizes have been an alternative means to focus creativity on solving complex challenges, although they are not a substitute for the private research ecosystem that fuels the discovery of most new biopharmaceuticals. A large cash prize would be paid out only once an achievement is realized, so it can be an effective means of a financing cure. The government pays only for the cure, and the projected savings from the cure can justify the payment for the prize. Any such system, however, must maintain incentives for private-sector involvement, or else such cures will never be developed into actual, marketed products.

These are all creative ways to break out of short-term thinking that saves a penny today at the cost of a dollar tomorrow.

New Methods for Paying for Certain Expensive Drugs

Short-term thinking can also prevent Americans from benefitting from breakthrough cures and treatments that are already available.

For example, the Gilead pharmaceutical company recently released two new drugs for the treatment of hepatitis C, a disease that affects three million Americans. The disease carried an estimated economic burden of $6.5 billion in 2011 alone.

The drugs—called Sovaldi and Harvoni—are a quantum leap beyond the previous standard of care. Rather than a 50 percent rate of effectiveness, the two new drugs cure 95 percent of patients. They also work faster and produce fewer side effects. However, the drugs are also expensive. Full-course treatments were listed at $86,000 and $95,000 respectively when they were first released. Even though the list price of a brand-name drug is almost never the price ultimately paid after rebates and discounts negotiated by various actors in the distribution chain, the high list price for these game-changing drugs caused quite a shock.

But criticism over the initial high list price did not acknowledge how much money would be saved by actually curing patients with hepatitis C. The older course of treatment for the disease was far costlier over the long term. It didn't help that most of those who would benefit from the new hepatitis C treatments were on state Medicaid programs that would be put in short-term financial distress by these new expensive cures. However, even as competition has driven down the price (Dr. Steve Miller, chief medical officer of Express Scripts, recently said the costs of hepatitis C drugs are now lower in the United States than in Europe[1]) some plans still refuse to cover the drugs until the disease causes late-stage liver deterioration.

President Trump should instruct Tom Price, the secretary of health and human services, to work with insurers to develop new actuarial, reinsurance, and other financial methods that can help finance the high upfront costs of specialty drugs, whose costs are higher than anticipated by today's insurance company risk models, and cannot be afforded by state and federal public health programs in the near term.

One concrete idea is for health insurance companies to study the reinsurance models of the property and casualty insurance industry. Property and casualty insurance companies know how to price their premiums to cover payouts for catastrophic hurricanes, terrorist attacks, and other low-frequency but potentially costly risks. Similarly, health insurance companies should be able to develop reinsurance models to cover the payments for the low-frequency but expensive cures that come along from time to time that can dramatically improve the health of certain subsets of their covered populations.

State and federal health programs could employ similar models, or even use the type of bond program described earlier in this chapter to finance research applied to maximizing the use of certain game-changing cures among the patient population. The eventual savings from curing diseases like hepatitis C would pay off the bondholders over time.

As a builder, entrepreneur, and businessman, Donald Trump understands that costs must often be borne upfront in order to achieve profits and savings later. He and his administration should recognize that breakthrough medicines offer the same opportunity.

Getting Breakthrough Drugs to Patients Faster

A recent study estimated that it currently costs an average of $2.6 billion to bring an FDA-approved medication to market.[2] Lowering the cost of bringing a new drug to market is one of the best ways to accelerate the development of new cures and lower overall health care costs.

The 21st Century Cures Act was a major step forward in allowing the FDA to use more modern tools to validate the effectiveness of treatments, which should speed the development of new cures and lower research and development costs. Congress should build on this success with further reforms.

For example, the FDA needs enhanced hiring flexibility to ensure that the agency's talent and expertise can keep up with the innovations occurring in the biomedical research and scientific communities and in our private biopharmaceutical industry.

Advances in genetics-based medicine and the use of adult stem cells to regrow body parts such as cartilage, bladders, retinas, optic nerves, and kidneys have the potential to revolutionize the way we treat disease and injury. However, these tailored therapies do not fit the standard FDA clinical trial models that are based on the idea of testing the effectiveness of the same pill or device being given to every patient. As a result, much of the cutting-edge development of these new procedures is occurring overseas. New rules must be written to speed these breakthrough therapies to patients.

In addition, adults with fatal diseases should be allowed to exercise informed consent to access experimental new drugs and off-label drugs whose effectiveness have not yet been evaluated by the FDA.

Accelerating the FDA's Approval Process for Generic Drugs

In testimony before Congress in February 2016, Dr. Janet Woodcock, the director of the FDA's Center for Drug Evaluation and Research, explained the stakes in the rapid approval of generic drugs.

She observed that 88 percent of all drugs dispensed in the United States are generic, up from 30 percent in 1990. From

2005 to 2014, the use of generic drugs has saved the US health system $1.68 trillion.

This two-decade-long growth in the generic drug industry brought its own challenges. As more and more generic drug manufacturers entered the market, the FDA could not keep up with its approval pipeline. Hundreds and hundreds of generic drug applications were backlogged.

Finally, Congress acted in 2012 to impose user fees on generic manufacturers, which allowed the FDA to restructure its approval process and hire hundreds of new examiners to speed up the pipeline of new generics.

The stakes are high for the FDA to follow through and achieve real breakthroughs in the approval of new generic drugs. This is especially true for the class of generics known as "first generics." These drugs are the first to come on to the market as a generic in competition with the brand-name drug whose patent has expired. The Manhattan Institute reported a finding that a one-year acceleration in bringing FDA-approved drugs to market could deliver to patients an estimated $4 trillion worth of value annually as measured by living longer lives with better health.[3] This is an extraordinary estimate of individual and social savings that should focus everyone's minds on the importance of reforming FDA practices.

Make Foreign Countries Pay Their Fair Share for US-Developed Drugs

As a candidate and as president, Trump has promised to negotiate better trade deals with other countries. He can start with pharmaceuticals. The "free ride" that foreign countries enjoy by benefiting from US pharmaceutical innovation while refusing to pay a fair price must come to an end.

As President Trump explained after a recent meeting with pharmaceutical companies, "We're going to be ending global freeloading. Foreign price controls reduce the resources of American drug companies to finance drug and [research and development] innovation. I think you people know well, it's unfair to this country. . . .

"Our trade policy will prioritize that foreign countries pay their fair share for U.S.-manufactured drug[s], so our drug companies have greater financial resources to accelerate development of new cures, and I think that's so important," Trump said. "Right now, it's unfair what other countries are doing to us."

American companies shouldn't be coerced into selling their products at unfair prices in foreign countries. Our trade policy should prioritize that foreign countries pay their fair share for US-manufactured drugs. In addition, it is shortsighted for foreign countries to free ride on US drug research and development, because these countries could help add to the societal benefits from faster development of new cures through their own research. The end of foreign price controls on US-manufactured drugs would serve as a significant accelerant of new drug development.

Protect Innovation from the Old Order

You may be wondering, Who could oppose innovative new therapies that save lives and save money? Who could oppose eliminating the $1 trillion in waste and fraud from the health care system?

The answer is obvious: all those who profit from the current system.

When innovation and costs collapses occur in any industry, there are real institutions and real interests on the other side of the equation that are decimated. I often joke that if the stagecoach industry had had a powerful lobby in Washington during the 1850s, we would never have had the intercontinental railroad, or later the automobile.

I recently got into a public fight with the optometrist lobby over an app called Opternative that uses the camera on your phone and laptop to deliver a refractive eye exam to get glasses or contact lens prescriptions. The service costs less than a traditional eye exam and is much more convenient.

This service does not replace an eye health exam, but those are recommended by the American Optometric Association only every two years. Meanwhile, contact lens prescriptions need to be refilled every year, and while the patient is there, optometrists usually conduct a full eye health exam anyway. So optometrists have been benefiting from this steady stream of medically unnecessary exams.

Faced with the potential loss of half their members' eye exam business, the optometry lobby mounted campaigns to convince lawmakers that the new technology was unsafe. Unfortunately, they succeeded in banning the use of the service in several states, including my home state of Georgia. The fight is ongoing in several other states.

This nakedly self-interested protection at the cost of patients' convenience, well-being, and resources is a small taste of what is to come.

Kidney dialysis, for instance, is an over $40 billion industry ($34 billion is spent per year by Medicare, which absorbs most dialysis costs due to the average age of the patients who receive treatment). Imagine replacing years of painful and expensive kidney dialysis with new kidneys grown from a patient's own cells. The kidney dialysis industry would evaporate.

Efforts to eliminate the upward of $1 trillion of waste and fraud in the health care system will also be met with bitter opposition. All those who profit from this waste—the blood analysis and imaging centers that profit from unnecessary tests, the claims processing centers that handle all the paperwork that could better be done with digital systems, and the hospitals that bill huge amounts for emergency room visits that could better be done at urgent care clinics—will seek to protect their incomes. The first place they will turn will be to lawmakers to help.

As an entrepreneur, President Trump understands how new competition and innovation can disrupt old systems, and the result is better services and better results for customers. He must resist attempts by the old order to rig the game against the forces of innovation to the detriment of patients.

STRATEGY 2: REWARD HEALTH AND WELLNESS

The United States spent more than $3.2 trillion on health care in 2015. This is a shocking amount of money—almost 18 percent of our economy. What is most shocking, however, is how much of that money is spent on the treatment of largely preventable diseases.

According to the US Centers for Disease Control and Prevention (CDC), nearly one out of every six of those health care dollars was spent treating just three chronic conditions—cardiovascular disease, diabetes, and cancer. That's around $500 billion.

The CDC also estimates that through changes in diet, exercise, and smoking habits, nearly 80 percent of heart disease and stroke cases, 80 percent of type 2 diabetes, and 40 percent of cancer cases could be prevented. This likely means that more than $300 billion per year could be saved in treating just these three diseases if Americans adopted healthier lifestyles. More important, tens of millions of Americans would be healthier, happier, and more productive.

These data illustrate why it is paramount to put the individual back at the center of the health system and start paying attention to the cultural and societal patterns that lead to poor health decisions.

Regulatory changes should be pursued to allow—and incentives established to encourage—health plans, employers, and

Medicare and Medicaid to make encouraging healthy behaviors a priority. Patients should be encouraged and expected to engage in self-monitoring and self-care. The minor additional costs associated with these incentives are dwarfed by the potential savings.

These programs and initiatives can be partially funded by the federal government but must be designed and implemented at the local level. Studies have shown that a person's zip code is as strong a predictor of health outcomes as any other factor. Community-based programs can do a better job targeting high-need individuals, who represent about 5 percent of patients but 50 percent of health expenditures. Working with these patients by making sure they are complying with their medicine and other therapy regimes will improve health outcomes and reduce expenditures. The federal government's role should be to incentivize the adoption of these programs and be a source of data collection and analysis to identify the best-performing programs for other communities to implement.

Increase Transparency

Patients can't be actively engaged with their health and be informed consumers if the real cost of their health care is hidden from them. Patients will be empowered purchasers when they can compare their actual costs in real time. Reforms designed to create more market competition must include greater cost transparency at the patient level as a fundamental value.

In addition, current regulations should be changed to allow far more robust communication among drug manufacturers and drug payers and providers about the performance of drugs, both prior to and after FDA approval. This also should cover truthful information about FDA-approved uses of drugs, as well as non-FDA-approved but medically accepted uses of drugs. Removing the threat of legal action from these conversations ultimately will allow patients to have greater access to the drugs most appropriate for their condition, allow payers and providers to plan better for handling the introduction and financing of new drugs, and lower overall health costs.

Reorient Our Public Nutrition Programs toward Nutrition

In addition, supplemental nutrition programs like SNAP and WIC should be overhauled to encourage healthy eating. The operative word in these programs' functions is "nutrition." The idea that food stamps can be used to purchase junk food with little nutritional benefit that leads to health problems down the road (which may also need to be paid for with public funds through Medicaid and Medicare) is both financially stupid and morally irresponsible.

To be clear, I support consumer choice and am not advocating the taxation or banning of sugary foods. However, we should draw the line at using taxpayer money that is supposed to be dedicated to nutrition to subsidize unhealthy eating habits.

Confront the Addiction Crisis

Over the past fifteen years, the number of drug-overdose deaths in America has doubled. With more than 52,000 deaths in 2015, overdose is now the leading cause of accidental death in America. The opioid epidemic is driving this problem, accounting for about two-thirds of the increase. Over 33,000 Americans died in 2015 from opioid overdose, and 2.4 million Americans are struggling with an opioid use disorder. Overall, more than 7 million Americans battled a drug use disorder—over 20 million if you include alcohol—in 2014.

President Trump made it clear during the presidential campaign and during his early presidency that he was going to confront the addiction crisis facing America. Half of the challenge is preventing the flow of drugs from the southern border, which

I addressed in chapter 10, and the steps he has taken there are promising. The other half is how to deal with those who are already addicted.

In March, President Trump tapped New Jersey governor Chris Christie to head a commission on opioid addiction. To be successful, the commission will need to do more than advocate for increased funding for treatment; it will need to look at how to change underlying attitudes about addiction and mental health. Too many of our medical rules and practices surrounding addiction grow out of outdated and inaccurate dogmas that are not based on science or medicine.

For instance, there is no scientific evidence that suggests the standard twenty-eight- or thirty-day drug and alcohol detoxification program model is the optimum length of time for ridding the body of toxins or to fight addiction. It came about because of armed forces personnel rules that did not require service members to be reassigned if they were away for less than thirty days. In fact, the evidence shows that the longer a person stays in rehabilitation, the less likely they are to relapse.

Ultimately, confronting the addiction crisis will require confronting the false dichotomy present in the health system between mental and physical health. Modern medicine is more than two hundred years old, but scientists have had imaging equipment sensitive enough to monitor what is happening in the brain only over the past three decades. This relative gap in understanding led the medical community to treat mental health and physical health as two different things. Now we know that a person's mental state is largely governed by physical phenomenon in the brain that can be positively affected with medicine.

Addiction is a disease of the brain that can be treated with medicine to curb cravings. We have known for decades that medication-assisted treatment has higher success rates at getting addicts to complete their treatment and avoid relapses, yet less than 15 percent of Americans seeking treatment for addiction receive medication assistance.

This is because addiction is still treated as a weakness or character flaw that must be confronted through willpower alone. In fact, addiction causes physical and chemical changes to the brain that make it difficult for addicts to stop taking the drug. Genetics also plays a huge role in who gets addicted, so everyone is not on equal footing.

President Trump should work with Congress to break down the barriers in public and private insurance that create unnecessary hurdles to accessing these types of therapies. It makes zero sense that patients can easily obtain prescriptions for the opioids that cause addiction but face huge hurdles in trying to access medicine that can help them overcome their addiction.

In addition, as part of his health deregulation agenda, President Trump should also instruct Health and Human Services Secretary Price to lift the outdated caps on the number of patients that doctors can treat with medication-assisted addiction treatments. Many of these caps were put in place to prevent diversion (the medicine being resold illegally on the black market) but there are now implantable versions of the medicine that last for several months and make the concern over diversion irrelevant.

President Trump should also work with Congress to enact prison reform to move nonviolent individuals with mental health and addiction issues into separate programs designed to treat their conditions. The Federal Bureau of Prisons reports that roughly 64 percent of the jail population nationwide suffer from mental health conditions. Treating those offenders as patients rather than prisoners could end up saving billions of dollars at expensive state and federal correctional facilities. Many conservative governors in Republican states have enacted similar reforms and have had great success. This is an issue that could attract a large bipartisan majority.

Rethink Disabilities

More than ten million people receive disability payments from the federal government every month—approximately one in twenty working-age adults in America. This ratio has doubled since 1990, when one in forty received disability benefits, despite rising health outcomes and safer jobs during that period.

Some of the increase can be explained by the aging of the baby boomers and the increased number of women in the workforce. However, an analysis by the Federal Reserve Bank of San Francisco shows that at least half of the increase is due to fraud. This is not only outrageous, it is tragic.

Once people go on disability, they are unlikely to come off it. An analysis by the *Washington Examiner* showed that only 13 percent of these Americans have worked for pay since they started receiving benefits. These benefits are small—only about $13,000 per year—but it also includes Medicare. That means a person on disability likely receives more value by not working than he or she would with a minimum-wage job earning $15,000 per year.

So, instead of helping people, our disability program is a poverty trap for millions of Americans. And it stands to get only worse—the number of children receiving disability payments has increased 700 percent in the past thirty years. They are being taught as children to live a life of dependence.

Tackling this challenge will not only require tougher enforcement. We also need a cultural change in the way we think about disabilities in America.

Disabilities have to be rethought into capabilities. Our wounded warriors teach us every day that focusing on what you can do leads to a dramatically fuller, better life than being supported in dependency, focusing on what you can't do. We need to create this same spirit and expectation in our families and communities that the "pursuit of happiness" in America is not just a right, it is an expectation.

In the 1990s we reformed welfare to include an expectation that you either worked or pursued a certificate or degree to enable you to get a job. We should expect the same of those on disability, except for those in the most extreme of circumstances.

Breakthroughs in health also offer the possibility of people with debilitating medical conditions being able to make faster and fuller recoveries, so they can more quickly return to being happy and productive citizens.

STRATEGY 3: GO DIGITAL—BUT INSIST ON INTEROPERABILITY

The most effective way to improve the patient experience and eliminate waste and fraud in the health care system is to make it a seamless digital experience for patients, providers, and payers.

The vision for a digital health system is for patients to be able to control all their own health data, and for them to enable any doctor or provider in the country access to that information at his or her discretion. This would eliminate duplicate care and time spent filling out and processing paperwork. It could be achieved through a smart card system similar to ATMs.

Fully digital systems for claims submission, insurance eligibility verification, and most other interactions between payers and providers would eliminate enormous costs and speed access to care. Hospitals could take most of the money they spend on administration and divert it to hiring doctors and nurses.

Digital systems would also allow for the use of big data to discover other inefficiencies, quickly identify pandemics, and create a process of perpetual learning so doctors and providers can constantly migrate toward best practices.

A provision in the 2009 stimulus set aside tens of billions of dollars to incentivize doctors and providers to adopt electronic health records and e-prescribing. Unfortunately, this potentially game-changing initiative was implemented in a way that frustrated doctors and didn't achieve the interoperability goals required to make that vision a reality. In fact, the degree to which hospitals contracted with IT companies to deliberately create systems that could not communicate to trap doctors and patients within their hospital networks is a scandal worthy of hearings in Congress.

Still, President Trump and Congress should resist the temptation to impose a one-size-fits-all digital solution on the health system. We want variety and competition to create better and better products. In addition, the disastrous launch of Healthcare. gov shows that the government is not particularly good at developing its own information technology.

The federal government should, however, set clear standards for interoperability that providers and their digital contractors must meet on all their digital initiatives. In other words, the electronic medical record system of two hospitals does not need to be the same, but they do need to be able to communicate with each other so that patients' data can be seamlessly transferred between them. Setting that clear standard is the type of regulation by results rather than by process discussed in an earlier chapter.

Stopping Health Care Fraud

The FBI estimates that between 3 and 10 percent of all health care spending in America is lost to fraud. That's between $100 billion and $300 billion per year.

This problem is particularly pronounced in public health programs. Jim Frogue, my former colleague at the Center for Health Transformation, wrote a book called *Stop Paying the Crooks*, identifying between $70 billion and $110 billion Medicare and Medicaid fraud annually. This represents $1 trillion in savings over ten years without touching a single honest person's benefits. Making progress in eliminating fraud in public health programs would free up significant resources, some of which could be used to help low-income Americans access and afford the best treatment.

The solution to stopping health care fraud is to look at what works in other industries. The fraud rate in the credit card industry is a miniscule one-tenth of one percent. That's because it is almost completely digital, and expert systems have been designed to detect anomalies in spending patterns. The American health care system, meanwhile, is still mostly paper-based, and detecting fraud is difficult.

President Trump should enlist Visa, MasterCard, and American Express to design a digital system for Medicare billing that allows the detection of fraud in real time, similar to the credit card industry. States should do the same for their Medicaid programs.

STRATEGY 4: ENCOURAGE THE ADOPTION OF BEST PRACTICES

Numerous studies have shown there is enormous variability in the quality of care that patients receive throughout the country. This variability is both dangerous for patients receiving lower-quality care and expensive for the health system at large.

The National Committee for Quality Assurance estimates that 57,000 lives are lost per year because physicians aren't using evidence-based care. Meanwhile, analysis of Medicare spending data shows that even after controlling for variables such as age, sex, and race, Medicare spending is almost two times greater in Miami than in Minnesota.[4] The Dartmouth Atlas of Health Care also estimates that adopting the same quality of care as Intermountain Healthcare in Utah or the Mayo Clinic in Minnesota across all of America's 5,500 hospitals, Medicare alone would save 32 percent—with better health outcomes.

Part of the reason for this huge level of variation is the explosion of new science and knowledge. Doctors and provider associations have not yet implemented the sort of continuing education practices necessary for physicians to stay informed enough to make sure they are practicing best-in-class medicine.

President Trump should work with Secretary Price to encourage the development of best-practice initiatives that would educate physicians about what the latest evidence shows is the best care. However, this initiative must be located in the private sector and not be used to ration care.

Value-Based Purchasing

While we must avoid rationing care, it is imperative that the health system move away from payment models that compensate doctors and providers based on the number of procedures they perform rather than the results of the care they deliver.

There has been some modest progress on this front in the private insurance industry. Blue Cross Blue Shield of Massachusetts implemented Alternative Quality Contracts, which have financial rewards for providers who reach certain quality benchmarks and save money. The program produced significant savings and improvements in the quality of care by its fourth year. Blue Cross Blue Shield of Michigan created a patient-centered Medical Home program that demonstrated improvements in quality and prevention and saved an estimated $155 million over its first three years.

Medicare has also begun to experiment with value-based purchasing through accountable care organizations that have achieved better patient outcomes with lower costs. These pilot projects are one of the few parts of Obamacare that should be kept. In fact, President Trump should expand them to the Federal Employee Health Benefits, the Department of Veterans Affairs, and Indian Health Service to test and source good ideas.

Doctors' offices are also embracing economic models that emphasize keeping people healthy rather than the quantity of visits and procedures. Some practices have stopped taking insurance and instead charge an annual membership fee for patients. In this model, doctors are incentivized to keep people healthy. Plus, they avoid the expensive overhead required to handle the endlessly complex billing and compliance issues associated with public and private insurance.

Legal and regulatory changes should be explored that allow drug manufacturers, payers, and providers to tailor arrangements among them to incentivize payments for drugs based on measurable improvements in health outcomes. This will improve health outcomes and lower overall health costs.

Medical Liability Reform

The adoption of best practices and value-based purchasing will be much more likely to succeed if other incentives for doctors and hospitals to waste money are removed from the health care system. One of the most significant reasons providers waste money on unnecessary tests and other procedures is to avoid the threat of lawsuits. This practice, called defensive medicine, is estimated to cost $46 billion per year.

The fear of malpractice lawsuits does not protect patients. Instead, it drives up costs and threatens patients' care by distorting doctors' decision making. Addressing the medical liability crisis will bring down the cost of care, and improve it as well, by returning doctors to making medical rather than legal-defense decisions.

President Trump and Congress have several good models from which to design potential medical liability reform legislation. Several states have implemented reforms that protect doctors if they follow clinical care standards, cap noneconomic damages, and reduce junk lawsuits through "loser pay" laws. They have seen doctors flood into their states for the lower cost of insurance, and the residents are benefiting from increased access to care. States should also look at implementing medical malpractice models similar to workman's compensation boards, which would resolve patients' complaints faster and with far less money going to expensive lawyers.

Making Coverage Affordable for Those in Need

If Donald Trump and the Republicans enact these and other reforms to solve the cost crisis in health care, it will free up hundreds of billions of dollars a year in federal and state resources, making the challenge of helping the poor afford care and coverage much easier.

Medicaid programs need to continue to protect those who currently rely on them while adopting long-term changes designed to give states flexibility to implement them and give much greater choice. Governors and local leaders understand the needs of their people better than bureaucrats in Washington do. A recent study of the Oregon Medicaid system showed that while the program did improve financial outcomes for those in the system, it did not actually improve health outcomes. All fifty states need to focus on quality-of-care reforms, like those outlined earlier in this chapter, to actually deliver better health for their poorest residents. Part of this effort should be rethinking how we use our eight thousand federally funded community health centers.

Medicare should provide seniors with new choices. They should have the option to choose whether to remain in the existing program, or to transition to a more personalized system in the private sector. If they select the personalized system, beneficiaries should be able to receive a voucher equal to the average cost per enrollee in Medicare to help cover their private sector premiums.

High-Risk Pools: An Alternative to "Guaranteed Issue"

To deal with the challenge of those with preexisting conditions driving up costs for everyone if insurers are required to sell them coverage, Maine implemented an invisible high-risk-pool model, which is showing great results. The model is called an "invisible" high-risk pool because customers don't know if they are part of the pool or not. To them, it is just regular insurance.

Five percent of patients consume 50 percent of all health care resources. The state works with insurers to separate out the costs of the sickest patients, so that the premiums of everyone else are dramatically lowered. The state then subsidizes the expenses of the sickest patients. Since the adoption of this program, premiums for those in their early twenties have dropped by almost $5,000 per year, while older customers in their sixties have seen savings of more than $7,000 per year.

THE WAY FORWARD

As of the day this book is going to print, the fate of the American Health Care Act is uncertain. There have been several attempts to revive the bill with changes and amendments to make it more palatable to the conservatives and moderates in the House Republican caucus who would not support the original bill. Of course, even if the House manages to pass an improved version of the bill, the Senate then needs to pass its version, and then a final bill needs to be produced by the conference committee and then voted on by the House and Senate.

Regardless of whether the bill has passed the time you are reading this, there is still much more to be done to truly reform our health system. A dramatically better health system with better outcomes and lower costs is possible. The evidence is all around us in real practices and real systems working every day to improve lives while lowering costs.

These four strategies outlined in this chapter and the measures contained within are not an exhaustive list, but they do provide the framework for a real health care reform agenda.

President Trump and the Republicans in Congress should spend the next three and a half years holding hearings and gaining support for these reforms, passing as many of them as possible as freestanding bills.

Trump is quickly learning Washington the way he learned the hotel and real estate businesses, and his ability to get things done will be amazing. One key to his success is that Trump hires really good people and demands a lot from them. He also delegates details to competent people. But he always gives credit to those who earn it. Callista and I were at the grand opening of Trump International Hotel, and Trump made a point of getting pictures with everyone who works there. He kept telling the members of the staff that they had done a great job and were the key to the hotel's success. His enthusiasm and his interaction with the workers says a lot about how he invests emotionally in his employees.

CHAPTER THIRTEEN

THE MAKING-GOVERNMENT-WORK BOX

P resident Trump has the opportunity to bring the same "ahead of schedule, under budget" doctrine he applied to his real estate projects and election campaign to the federal government. However, it will require an enormous fight with entrenched interests throughout the federal bureaucracy.

The experience of Governor Scott Walker in Wisconsin proves that reforms can be passed, but it takes enormous courage and determination.

Walker campaigned on a set of reforms from the day he announced to the day he was elected. I know because Callista and I did one of his first big fundraisers in Milwaukee, and I did one of his last campaign rallies in Waukesha. Walker was very consistent about what he would do if elected. When he was sworn in, he proposed the very reforms he had promised in the campaign. The Left was horrified. Its members had hoped to intimidate him into backing down.

Madison, Wisconsin, was filled with left-wing, union-led protests. Over 100,000 people took to the streets. The capitol was occupied by demonstrators for six months. Both the governor and his wife received death threats. His private home in Milwaukee was picketed, to the surprise of his parents who were living there at the time (he was in the governor's mansion in Madison).

Having failed to stop the governor and the legislature (including Democratic state senators leaving the state to try to deny a quorum), the Left then forced a recall election, which Governor Walker won. It turns out that despite all the bitterness and huge crowds showing up to protest Governor Walker, the views of the radical left and apologists for the bureaucracies were a minority.

President Trump should take this lesson to heart as he approaches the issue of making government work again. Take the difficulties Governor Walker had to overcome in Madison and multiply by at least twenty or thirty to get some notion of the intensity he will face to implement real reform of the federal bureaucracy. However, this is not a fight that President Trump can avoid.

No matter how big the difficulties, it will require profound reform for President Trump to manage the government, implement his policies, and efficiently and effectively serve the American people.

GOVERNMENT PERFORMANCE: A LONG-IGNORED ISSUE

The federal government's disastrous response to Hurricane Katrina in August 2005 was probably the moment when the federal government's incompetence became impossible to ignore. Americans saw in painful, vivid detail just how ineffective our federal government had become at performing its basic functions. Viewing this incompetence in combination with the failure to secure the peace in Iraq, Americans began to demand change.

Inexplicably, President Bush failed to propose the type of sweeping reform agenda on the government that would have shown Americans he understood their concerns. Americans reacted to this failure by punishing the incumbent president's party. Republicans lost the House and Senate in 2006, as well as most governorships and state legislatures in the United States.

Yet even after this stinging defeat, during which the issue of government performance was front and center, the Bush administration failed to get serious about proposing a plan for reform.

In 2008, dismayed by the president's inaction and worried about Republican prospects due to President Bush's continued unpopularity, I wrote a book called *Real Change: From the World that Fails to the World that Works*. In it, I argued that Americans were hungry for change and that dramatic measures to improve government performance were a critical part of what they wanted. I also argued that this change had to come from the Right because the Left was so captured by the government employee unions—which are a major inhibitor of reform—that they could never be anything more than enablers of the status quo.

Unfortunately, Republicans failed to make a dramatic change agenda the centerpiece of their fall campaign. As a result, Americans elected a president in 2008 whose slogan was "Change you can believe in." Then, being a left-wing ideologue from a left-wing party that is in the thrall of government employee unions, President Obama totally failed to deliver real change to make government work again—just as I predicted. Because of this, the high-profile failures continued to mount and the frustration of Americans deepened.

Two government failures, in particular, stick out due to the amount of attention they received.

The first was the disastrous launch of Healthcare.gov, which kept crashing and even months after it stabilized still could not accurately verify people's vital information. Obamacare was badly designed, but there was no reason within the law from a public policy perspective that the technical launch of the website was destined to be a mess. That was purely a function of the government's ridiculous contracting rules and lack of accountability.

The second was the wait time scandal at the Department of Veterans Affairs. In 2014, we learned that dozens of VA facilities had been falsifying their records to hide outrageously long wait times for veterans to receive appointments. The VA's inspector general reported in 2015 that 307,000 veterans may have died waiting for care. The Obama administration reacted by firing Eric Shinseki, the VA secretary, but this was a purely symbolic gesture. Nothing actually changed. Two years later, in March 2016, a fifty-one-year-old veteran actually set himself on fire in front of a VA facility in New Jersey in protest of the bureaucracy's coldhearted incompetence.

This escalating series of scandals, breakdowns, and calamities is why Americans overwhelmingly view the federal government as incompetent. The 2016 Forrester Research US Customer Experience Index found that the federal government was ranked last by survey respondents out of twenty-one major industries. In fact, of the 319 brands tested, five out of eight of the worst-performing brands are run by the federal government.[1] And according to Pew, just 20 percent of Americans believe that federal government programs are "well run."[2]

UNACCOUNTABLE BUREAUCRATS

Right after World War II, the US government was an amazingly effective system. However, as the bureaucracy grew, it became steadily slower and less competent.

The problem is bigger than just the sheer size and complexity of the bureaucracy. The federal workforce has become a powerful interest group more interested in self-protection than in serving the American people. It has negotiated ridiculous rules on terms of employment that make it nearly impossible to fire or discipline anyone.

For example, disciplinary actions, including termination, are subject to lengthy and expensive appeals processes, during which the employee is entitled to keep receiving his or her salary.

Over the past few years, the Department of Veterans Affairs has been the most visible and scandalous example of management paralysis due to a combination of civil service and union contract rules.

Last year, the *Washington Post* reported:

> More than 2,500 employees at the Department of Veterans Affairs were placed on paid leave for at least a month last year, and the agency acknowledges it did not track the details of why they were sent home, according to newly released information.
>
> The total tab in salary alone for these absences—ranging from 30 days to more than a year for 46 employees—came to $23 million, according to a report provided to several congressional Republicans.[3]

Amazingly, even some of the people involved in the VA wait times scandal continued to collect their six figure salaries on paid leave before being fired.

Sharron Helman, the Phoenix VA Hospital director during the wait times scandal was on paid leave for seven months.[4]

Lance Robinson, Associate Director at the Phoenix VA hospital and Brad Curry, Chief of Health

Administration Services at the Phoenix VA hospital were both put on paid leave for 19 months after the scandal broke, then got put back to work for two months before being fired in June 2016.[5]

Dr. Darren Deering, the Phoenix hospital's chief of staff, was put on paid leave in May of 2014 and not fired until June 2016.[6]

This pattern is not limited to the troubled Phoenix facility:

Ed Russell was the director of the regional benefits office of the VA in Reno, NV. After years of poor performance, Mr. Russell was put on paid leave for several months, and then as part of a court settlement was given a new, work-from-home advisory position which never existed before.[7]

Terry Wolf, the Pittsburgh VA hospital director during an outbreak of Legionnaire's disease, spent five months on paid leave.[8]

Frederick Harris, a nurse's aid at the Alexandria VA Hospital, continued to be employed for four years despite being criminally charged with manslaughter after beating a patient to death in 2013. He was finally suspended indefinitely on February 14 after being indicted on a new charge of negligent homicide. His trial is scheduled for May 1.[9]

Even negligent doctors at the VA are protected:

David Houlihan, a doctor at the Tomah, Wisconsin, VA, was on paid leave for over a year despite having his medical license suspended for drugging veterans with

massive amounts and dangerous combinations of opioid
painkillers.[10]

Daniel Kim, an ophthalmologist at the Jackson,
Mississippi, VA, was put on leave with his full salary
after blinding a patient during routine cosmetic surgery.
The incident mirrors another one from his career in
which he forged a patient's consent form, who then died
in routine cosmetic surgery.[11]

Jose Bejar, a neurologist at the Topeka, Kansas, VA,
received more than $330,000 while on paid leave for
two years after five women accused him of sexual
misconduct. He finally pleaded no contest to the
charges.[12]

President Trump has expressed nothing short of outrage
at the scandal-wracked VA, pledging to find and fire corrupt
employees at the organization, empower Veterans Secretary
David Shulkin to bring the sprawling bureaucracy under control and provide better care for veterans.

While the Department of Veterans Affairs is the most visible example of federal management collapse, similar examples
can be found in virtually every federal department and agency.

The Department of Defense was recently exposed burying
a report that outlined how to save $125 billion over five years
in administrative waste. The report was hidden out of concern
that Congress would use it as an excuse to cut the department's
funding.

Medicaid made $36 billion (6.25 percent of its budget) in
improper payments in 2016 alone.

I was recently told (on a confidential basis) of another agency
that has two federal employees who have failed to work for two
years. One simply stays home. The other turns up, puts his or her

head on the desk and goes to sleep. Despite daily photos of the sleeping employee, neither has been fired, since the human relations department has either slow-walked or bungled the paperwork over and over. Furthermore, it has proven impossible to fire or discipline the nonperforming personnel employees themselves either for incompetence or nonperformance.

So, the head of the agency can't fire the sleeping or absent employees and they can't fire the people who refuse to fire them.

No statistic better illustrates the disparity between the federal workforce and the private sector than the fact that the monthly layoff and discharge rate in the private sector is more than three times the annual firing rate in the federal government.[13]

Not only is it nearly impossible to fire or discipline a federal employee, it is enormously time consuming to even let an employee know that he or she is underperforming.

Federal managers are required to produce individualized performance-improvement plans for employees whom they rate as less than "fully successful" in their reviews. Furthermore, even those reviews are subject to an appeals process that can take months.

This helps explain why, per the Government Accountability Office, 99 percent of the members of the federal workforce are given scores of "fully successful" or above on their performance reviews. In fact, 74 percent are given above-average ratings.[14]

Another study, this one by the Office of Personnel Management, showed that even though 80 percent of all federal managers say they have managed a poorly performing employee, only 15 percent have given an employee a less than "fully successful" rating. Worse, less than 8 percent attempted to discipline the employee, and among those who attempted to do so, 78 percent said their efforts had no impact.

Imagine the effect of this management dysfunction and paralysis on the federal employees who want to do a good job.

The 2016 Federal Employees Viewpoints Survey showed that only 29 percent of employees believe that "in my work unit, steps are taken to deal with a poor performer who cannot or will not improve."[15]

As the system continues to decay, if you have a system that defends incompetence with bad people, then good people will leave. The system gets sicker and sicker.

HOW TRUMP CAN TELL FEDERAL BUREAUCRATS, "YOU'RE FIRED"

President Trump can follow two paths in his approach to civil service reform.

The first, articulated by the legal scholar Philip Howard, would be to change the civil service system by executive order. Howard argues in an op-ed for the *Wall Street Journal* that the decades' worth of laws and executive actions that have insulated bureaucrats from accountability are unconstitutional.

Howard says that such protections for federal employees violate the Constitution's mandate that "the executive power shall be vested in a President."

Invoking the ideas of James Madison, Howard writes:

Taking away the president's power over executive branch employees is synonymous with removing his executive power altogether. Yet this is exactly the case today. Because of civil-service laws passed by Congress many years ago, the president has direct authority over a mere 2% of the federal workforce.

The question is whether those laws are constitutional. Does Congress have the power to tell the president that he cannot terminate inept or insubordinate employees? The answer, I believe, is self-evident. A determined president could replace the civil-service system on his own,

by executive order. The move would doubtless be challenged in court, but it would likely be upheld, especially
if the new framework advances legitimate goals, honors
principles of neutral hiring and is designed to foster a
culture of excellence.

An executive order may be tempting for its simplicity; however, the experience that President Trump had over his immigration executive order suggests that it may not be the most
effective. The legal process would take a long time, and there is
no guarantee of success.

The better strategy, I believe is to rally the American people to insist on dramatic, deep reform of the federal civil service.
Citizen activists and interested groups can be aroused and coor-
dinated to build powerful grassroots pressure for "an honest,
effective, accountable civil service." The reforms can either be
passed in 2018 or it will become a major referendum issue in the
2018 elections and lead to the defeat of antireform, procorrup-
tion, prowaste House and Senate members.

Trump should be a champion of civil service reform in the
broadest sense, but he should not allow the effort to become
known as the "Trump plan." Instead, he should work with congressional leaders to hold a series of hearings, debates, and public events highlighting the issue so that it is the American people
insisting on reform, not the president. Rallying the American
people should not be too difficult for President Trump, especially in this case.

SUFFOCATED BY PROCESS

The lack of accountability within the federal bureaucracy is a
major component of the government's dysfunction, but so is
the stultifying set of rules and processes under which the government must operate. This problem is most apparent in fed-

eral, state, and local government's inability to build bridges, roads, and other infrastructure improvements on time and on budget.

President Obama summed up the endless amounts of red tape binding the government from completing projects when he said about the 2009 stimulus bill's failure to produce construction jobs, "Shovel ready was not as shovel ready as we expected."

When crafting his infrastructure agenda, President Trump should remember this lesson.

Trump has discussed plans for a $1 trillion infrastructure plan. Spending money under the current rules will be a recipe for failure, just as the stimulus was. If he hopes for it to succeed, Trump will need to insist that the metric for success of this plan be $1 trillion in results rather than in federal dollars spent. In other words, the goal should be for the bill to "cause" $1 trillion in infrastructure to happen. That means that the focus of the bill should be to overhaul the bad rules that slow down contracts, permitting, and building. If he does this correctly, the amount of federal money spent could be very small, since new rules would inspire the private sector and state and local governments to invest much more in projects they have avoided due to the huge amount of regulatory overhead.

When looking for solutions, the Trump administration and Congress should look to successful examples of state-level projects that cut through regulations to finish very fast.

In 1994, after Northridge, California, experienced a major earthquake, Governor Pete Wilson waived a number of rules and regulations that could slow down the rebuilding effort. It also established performance incentives that were not allowed under normal rules. The result was that massive sections of major highways that normally would have taken years to build were replaced within months.

Governor Arnold Schwarzenegger used similar emergency

measures to speed up the contracting process for repairs of a section of on-ramps onto a major highway after a gasoline truck blew up and caused them to collapse. They were repaired in a week instead of months.

Governor Mike Leavitt of Utah rebuilt the highway system for the Winter Olympics. He used incentives and metrics to get the job done ahead of schedule, under budget, with minimum impact on rush-hour traffic.

Governor Mitch Daniels of Indiana leased a failing toll road that had been managed by the state to a private company for $3.8 billion. As part of the lease agreement, the company also committed to making $4 billion of highway improvements. Daniels used that money to renovate one-third of the state's bridges and half of its roads. Because the projects could be built without the long, expensive, time-consuming federal red tape, they were completed in half the time, at two-thirds the typical cost.

In Ohio, Governor John Kasich leased the states' liquor stores and used some of the money for highway improvements. Because they were using nonfederal money, they could skip the time-consuming and cost-increasing federal red tape, and they were able to complete the construction for about 40 percent less and in dramatically less time.

Phillip Howard, a leading expert on regulatory reform, estimates that consolidating all federal requirements into a one-stop office could save 40 percent in construction costs. The lengthy, repetitive, and at times contradictory federal bureaucratic process takes a lot of time, and the time value of that money is enormous.

Any infrastructure bill should have a very strong, decisive opening section on regulatory reform. That will enable the federal government to create many more projects per billion dollars than it can under the current red-tape-ridden bureaucratic system.

Beyond infrastructure, President Trump and his team

should also encourage federal managers to expose as many rules and processes that slow down their work as possible. They should make sure they all know the story of Wollman Rink and feel empowered to make that same standard for faster, cheaper achievement than the standard bureaucratic model in their departments.

A TRUMPIAN LEGISLATURE

For Trump's agenda to last, he will need to cultivate a legislature that works. This will require a cultural change in Congress that is a long time coming.

Congress is far too insular and isolated to be effective in the twenty-first century. The world is too complicated, there are too many new things happening. Ninety-nine point nine percent of all knowledge is outside Washington, but Congress keeps relying on the same revolving door of lobbyists and staff to shape its thinking.

Congressional hearings are also overwhelmingly used to investigate and castigate failure rather than to learn from success. Oversight is important, but the committee hearing process is a huge opportunity to marshal the best experts and practitioners from all over the country. There is too much focus on failure and not enough on success.

The story of Wollman Rink is again applicable. Trump recognized that he didn't know anything about skating rinks, so he looked to Canadian experts to figure out how to fix Wollman Rink. Congress's approach, if it had been given the project, would have been to call up all the people that already failed to fix the rink and learn what they did.

Our success in reforming welfare was due to a deliberate strategy of bringing in stakeholders and experts from across the country to help draft the bill. At the time, we had on our team governors such as Tommy Thompson, John Engler, George

Allen, and Mike Leavitt, who had all experimented with welfare reform at the state level. They were prepared to loan us their state welfare directors, who then came up to Washington with us to help reform welfare the right way. We wanted state-level people, because they were the ones actually implementing welfare on the ground. They were the ones actually helping poor people in their states.

Many of the federal committee staff members resented the access and authority we gave the state people. They felt that they were the smart people who had spent their lives studying the national system, and they disliked having to share legislative drafting power with people whose only credentials were that they had actually run welfare systems. It was a good reminder of the insular jealousy and isolation of Washington staffs from the rest of the country.

As a result, we produced a welfare-reform bill that turned out to be the most successful social conservative reform of the last half century. Welfare offices across the country became employment offices. Instead of teaching people how to be efficiently dependent, our welfare system taught people how to find and get stable jobs.

President Trump, his senior staff, and congressional leadership also need to realize that you cannot run over people to get what you want. We have already discussed how the American Health Care Act failed because of secret negotiations and artificial deadlines that rushed the process of getting the best ideas and forming consensus.

Every member of the House and the Senate has a measure of power that he or she can exercise to either help you or keep you from your goals. If you run over someone, that person may stand aside just long enough to put a legislative knife in your back when you pass by.

When I was Speaker of the House, we developed a model: listen, learn, help, and lead.

We reached out to as many of our fellow members of Congress as possible, listened to their problems, learned from their situations, offered to help however we could, and used what we learned from the experience to lead in legislating.

We constantly focused on unlocking people rather than trying to bypass or run over them. It was tremendously helpful.

Over the multimonth process of working with people, we trained ourselves to always ask, "Under what circumstances could you do this?" This was an important tactic, because it got the members in the mind-set of saying "yes, if" rather than "no, because."

Most of the time, this helped both parties get a result they liked. Saying, "Yes, I can do that if . . ." immediately starts a productive negotiation. We had virtually every Republican in the House constantly engaging, looking for "yes, if" answers, because we knew really changing the federal government was going to be a huge task.

BALANCING THE BUDGET

As a candidate, Trump never emphasized balancing the budget. He talked constantly about the scale of the federal debt and Obama's deficits. However, he seldom discussed balancing the budget, possibly because it would have seemed unrealistic in the middle of a campaign. Just stopping the deficits seemed like a huge task.

Since his first appeal to the American people, he has focused on making America great again, controlling immigration, creating an America-first trade policy, and repealing and replacing Obamacare. Balancing the budget sounds boring. President Trump wants to create jobs, boldly reform the tax system, aggressively deregulate our business sector, and dramatically improve American competitiveness.

Here's the thing: doing all those things will naturally shrink the deficit and help balance the budget. Simply put, a balanced budget is a product of making government work.

This is the same principle San Francisco 49ers coach Bill Walsh wrote about in his book *The Score Takes Care of Itself: My Philosophy of Leadership.* Walsh wrote that he didn't focus on the score of the game. When he coached, he focused on making sure the team executed every play perfectly. If each play was perfectly executed, they would win.

In 1994, just before our Republican majority was elected, the federal deficit was $276 billion. That is a huge number, but we were able to bring the budget to a surplus by 1998. President Trump, however is facing a projected budget shortfall of $559 billion, according to the Congressional Budget Office. At the same time, the national debt has risen from $4.7 trillion in 1994 to more than $19.5 trillion in 2017.

President Trump has a much steeper challenge than we had, but our model is still useful for him to enact the policies that will lead to a balanced budget.

This is how we did it: first, we built a team of House Republicans—and that was very important. Trump should start by working to build strong teams within the House and Senate that work well with his administration.

If Trump doesn't build effective teams, he will fail. French infantry colonel Charles Jean Jacques Joseph Ardant du Picq said, "Four brave men who do not know each other will not dare attack a lion. Four less brave, but knowing each other well, sure of their reliability and consequently of mutual aid, will attack resolutely."

For our team in the 1990s, our lion was balancing the budget. We tried passing a Constitutional amendment requiring a balanced budget, which was approved in the House with more than 300 votes, but it failed in the Senate with only 65 votes when we needed 67. We were really only one vote away, but Senator Bob Dole voted with the Democrats to keep the procedural power to bring the matter up again in the Senate. At that point, we could have thrown our hands up and said, "Well, we did what we promised. We had a vote." But instead, we recognized that while we didn't have support from two-thirds of the Senate, we still had a large enough majority to overcome filibusters. We leveraged that support and balanced the budget anyway through regular spending legislation.

When we started, the combined budget deficit from 1992 to 1995 was $1.26 trillion. No one in Washington thought we could balance the budget—the same way no one had thought Americans would elect the first Republican majority in the House of Representatives in forty years the year before. But beginning in fiscal year 1998, we created four years of consecutive surplus totaling $659 billion.

Keep this in mind as President Trump is enacting his policies. Remember that before the election, virtually no one in Washington thought he would be elected.

THE IMPACT OF A WORKING GOVERNMENT

Once President Trump makes the bureaucracy accountable, reforms regulatory philosophy, and establishes an effective working structure with Congress, American enterprise will be unshackled and will drive innovation and economic growth.

This is supported by history.

The balanced budget and reforms we put in place strengthened the dollar and allowed for lower interest rates. The practical result was that people did dramatically better, but we followed Ronald Reagan's principle that a job is the best social policy.

Even liberals were stunned by the success of balancing the budget for four straight years and creating jobs. In 1999, Jack Lew, the former chief of staff for President Clinton and the treasury secretary under President Obama, and Bob Rubin, who was Clinton's secretary of the treasury, wrote an op-ed in the *Washington Post* praising the balanced budgets we created:

> The president's plan to retire such a large amount of debt is also the best pro-growth strategy for our economy. . . . When the government adds to private savings rather than drawing from it, more resources are available for private economic growth, higher standards of living and increased revenues—without any increase in tax rates.

They called high deficits, "a straight jacket on investment and economic growth," saying that "the deficit reduction achieved by Clinton and the Republican Congress led to economic growth."

It makes you wonder if Lew forgot these benefits when he was presiding over President Obama's deficits.

So, to those who will undoubtedly tell President Trump that it's impossible to make significant changes in Washington, remember that we balanced the budget at a time when it was considered impossible. We know how to effect real change because we've done it before.

As always, the prodebt, prospending model will ultimately collapse. Margaret Thatcher captured it best when she told Llew Gardner, a journalist with Thames TV, "Socialist governments traditionally do make a financial mess. They always run out of other people's money."

This is the interview from which the famous Thatcher-attributed aphorism "The problem with socialism is that eventually you run out of other people's money" was born.

The United States used to be a country in which people worked and saved to pay off the mortgage, then left the farm for their children. After decades of liberalism, we have become a country in which people sell off the farm today so they can mortgage their children's future. It's fundamentally wrong. We need to understand that in many ways, balancing the budget is a moral, not an economic, issue.

Outside of war and emergencies, it's simply wrong for us to spend our children's money.

It will no doubt be a difficult task, but President Trump has the unique opportunity to right America's fiscal ship. With the help of Congress and the American people, he can make the federal government effective, accountable, and adherent to the same economic principles that guide responsible American families and businesses every day.

Trump has always worked with state and local leaders on his various real estate projects. He has a very practical understanding of what you can and can't get done. At one point, he was trying to rezone a property, and he was being blocked by a small rural county commission—despite his best efforts. I asked what he was going to do about it, and he said, "You know, sometimes you have to accept reality and be very, very patient. You focus on the projects you can make progress on, not the ones you can't." He has a real feel for the depth of state and local leadership and the fact that we should get a lot of decisions out of Washington and bring them back home.

CHAPTER FOURTEEN

BRINGING TRUMP TO STATES AND COMMUNITIES

P resident Trump's election is an opportunity to reestablish America as the single most successful, wealthy, powerful, and free country on the planet. I spent much of the previous chapters talking about what Trump and the Republican Congress should do at the federal level to take advantage of our current situation.

But lasting changes in our country don't start in Congress, they start in our states and communities.

State legislatures, governors, and local elected leaders across the country have a unique opportunity to help establish an alternative model of society and government to replace the bureaucratic welfare state and left-wing value system that has been growing since President Franklin Delano Roosevelt won election in 1932.

For the last eighty-four years, the Left has had enough strength in Washington to keep state and local officials trapped within the rules and regulations of Washington bureaucrats and Washington politicians. They don't anymore.

Republicans control the legislatures and the governorships in twenty-five states. As Chris Cillizza of the *Washington Post* has reported, there are ten states in which the Republican majorities are so massive that the Democrats are virtually powerless to block reforms and new ideas.

As Cillizza outlined in his article, here are the ten states, along with their percentages of Republican officeholders:

STATE	STATE SENATE	STATE HOUSE	STATEWIDE	CONGRESS
Wyoming	90%	85%	100%	100%
South Dakota	83%	86%	100%	100%
Idaho	83%	84%	100%	100%
Utah	83%	83%	100%	100%
Oklahoma	88%	74%	100%	100%
North Dakota	81%	86%	93%	100%
Arkansas	74%	76%	100%	100%
Tennessee	85%	75%	100%	78%
Indiana	82%	70%	89%	78%
Missouri	74%	72%	75%	75%

With President Trump and Vice President Pence in the White House, and Republican majorities in the US House of Representatives and the US Senate, these "red states" and others have a genuine opportunity to redefine government's relationship with society and replace eight decades of bureaucracy and regulations with bold, modern approaches.

This chance mainly comes from finally having a federal government that won't get in the way of states that want to develop new solutions for the problems they are facing.

THE RED STATE OPPORTUNITY

This chapter outlines the general principles of this "Red State Opportunity." It also includes a series of key projects that could help state and local governments begin to replace bureaucratic, left-wing programs with those built on historic American values, entrepreneurial models of achievement, and modern science and technology.

The historic principles and values that made America more prosperous and free than any society in history—along with the liberating potential of new science and technology—will lead to more jobs, with higher take-home pay for workers; greater opportunities for retirement; better, more convenient and lower-cost health care; more effective learning; and greater safety.

President Trump can set the direction, rally his supporters, enact significant changes, and recruit a team of like-minded citizens. But to fully implement Trump's vision for America, an amazing amount of invention and creativity must occur at every level. There are more than 500,000 elected officials in the United States. Only one of them is president. He is the most visible and most powerful official, but he can't invent and implement a new governing system—that works in every state—by himself.

As the new Red State Opportunity system is developed, it should attract leaders from other states to participate and create a series of insights and lessons that could be applied to rethinking and transforming the federal government.

As the new system clearly produces better outcomes in people's lives, it will be the basis for campaigns in 2018, 2020, and beyond—which we must win to make this system last.

THE LEFT IS CORNERED

We must remember that the Left is cornered but still dangerous.

For eight decades, the Left has ruled. Bureaucracies have grown bigger, and so have their budgets. For years, they have been able to increasingly dedicate tax dollars to left-wing ideals. Conservatives occasionally slowed down or trimmed this process but have not yet reversed it.

At the same time, the ideals of the Democratic Party have become more extreme. They have evolved from providing limited government welfare during a crisis under Franklin D. Roosevelt, to creating systems of lifetime dependency on government under Lyndon B. Johnson, to rejecting the whole notion that people should have to work, under the Elizabeth Warren–Bernie Sanders model.

Contrast the American patriotism of Franklin D. Roosevelt, Harry Truman, and John F. Kennedy with the globalist, anti-American views of modern Democrats. The shift from traditional to radical values has been striking. Just look at public employee unions as an example. Franklin D. Roosevelt completely rejected them, and now those public employee unions dominate his party. And no Democratic president through Lyndon B. Johnson would understand or accept the social radicalism and hate speech of the modern Left.

The election of Trump is, in part, a deeply emotional rejection of this shift in the Left. Those who voted for Trump are tired of the Washington-centered, bureaucratically imposed, court-enforced, radical redesign of America by left-wing intellectuals, activists, and media organizations.

If executed properly, the Red State Opportunity and Trump will do much more than trim the excesses of the Left. These related movements aim to spur a profound, passionate return to the core American principles of the Founding Fathers, Andrew Jackson, and Abraham Lincoln—not simply a rehash of modern conservative ideology.

Those on the left understand that Trump represents a deep repudiation of their values, world, and power structure. The viciousness, bullying, intimidation, vulgarity, and explosions of rage we have seen since Trump's election all reflect the Left's clear understanding that the world Americans have chosen is incompatible with their left-wing values and institutions.

Under President Obama they thought they were on the verge of redefining America. If Hillary Clinton had won, they might have succeeded. Their very closeness to victory fills them with desperation as defeat sets in. The Left knows the governmental system they have worked to implement for the last half century is endangered. They will not go quietly.

THE GUIDING PRINCIPLES

The modern Left deliberately repudiates American history. It refuses to teach it, study it, or learn from it. At every turn, the Left diminishes the lessons of America by insisting they represent the work of slave owners and "old white men."

On campuses across the country, weird courses and bizarre definitions of history have replaced the study of the culture, history, and personalities that made America the freest, most prosperous, and safest society in history.

This initial look at principles will make clear why Trump is such a threat to the Left.

Some of these will invoke topics discussed in earlier chapters, but they are summarized here for convenience. This is also only an introductory set of examples. As people rethink modern government and society from a Trumpian perspective, they will inevitably add principles and expand the analysis and interpretation:

- American history is at the heart of what makes us Americans. The core principles American history teaches are timeless and apply today as much as in 1776—or 1861. That our unalienable rights come from our Creator makes us unique. We must reemphasize learning what makes us American.
- Work is good. Everyone should expect to work. People have responsibilities as well as rights. A key part of work

is learning. Everyone should expect to learn all their lives.
Trump does this. He is constantly learning and adapting
on a daily basis.

- Everyone has strengths. Gallup's Strengthfinders
works, because it focuses on enhancing strengths—not
wallowing in weakness. This leads to profound rethinking
of disabilities, welfare, impoverished communities, and
criminal justice reform.

- Pragmatism is the core American philosophy. Facts drive
and define theory. Determining the facts is the necessary
first step toward real analysis.

- Entrepreneurial behavior characterized Presidents
Washington, Jefferson, Franklin, and Lincoln, and
millions of successful Americans. These presidents
applied common sense, rapid learning, hard work, and
constant innovation. None of them favored bureaucratic
behavior. President Trump continues this legacy by
bringing his unique business background and skill to
the White House.

- Output is more important than input. Phillip Howard,
with his idea of output-focused regulations, is
suggesting a profound revolution in how we think about
bureaucracies and regulations. As a real estate developer,
Trump understands this. The important part of building
a building is that it stands up when you are finished.

- Winning is important. Failure is often a necessary step
toward winning. This is a clear repudiation of the anti-
competition, everyone-is-a-winner mind-set of modern
academics. The president thrives in competition and
knows how to overcome hurdles.

- Because failures often precede success, frugality is
important. We must save resources for repeated efforts.

The Wright brothers would have never flown if they operated on NASA's model.

- Finding the best expert and cutting through the red tape saves enormous amounts of time and money. Every government should adopt the Wollman Skating Rink model I discussed earlier. All state and local leaders should read the chapter on Wollman in *The Art of the Deal* and apply it to their projects.
- If something is stupid, say so.
- If something doesn't work, quit doing it.
- If something is working, do more of it.
- Define measurable metrics. Common sense beats academic theories that do not work in the real world.
- Look to the past to solve future problems. Imitation is cheaper than invention. The Founding Fathers studied history extensively. Lincoln studied the history of war extensively. A lot of smart people have solved a lot of hard problems. Learn from them.
- Dream big. Creating America in 1776 was a big dream. Doubling the size of America with the Louisiana Purchase in 1803 was a big dream. The transcontinental railroad was a big dream. Preserving the Union in 1861 was a big dream. Building the Panama Canal was a big dream. Going to the moon in eight years was a big dream. The creation of mass-produced cars, electric lights, movies, flight, and the Internet were big dreams. It is time for America to have big dreams again.
- Big dreams require bold, daring projects, a willingness to accept failure, and an eagerness to apply the lessons of failure to trying again until the dream becomes real.
- The Declaration of Independence applies to all Americans. There are no hyphenated Americans. We

are all endowed by our Creator with certain unalienable rights. Trump's agenda should be dedicated to turning this into a reality for every American.

- We believe in science, technology, engineering, and innovation. This is why the American Constitution includes a provision for a patent office. Innovation- and technology-based breakthroughs should be a continuous part of our thinking.

- America is much bigger than the federal government. Your state is much bigger than the state government. The local community is much bigger than the city or county government. We should limit the size of government across the board. The federal government in 1900 spent 2.7 percent of the gross domestic product. The 1930 federal number had only grown to 3.5 percent of GDP. In 2012, the government spent 24 percent of the GDP. Meanwhile state and local governments grew from 9.1 percent of GDP in 1930 (the earliest year numbers are available) to 14.8 percent in 2012. So, government as a share of society has grown by more than a factor of 300 percent. Inventing patterns, institutions, and habits to return power and resources from government to the private sector, individuals, and local communities will be one of the biggest challenges of Trump's and one of the most intensely contested.

- The will of the American people is more important than the advice of the elites. This core belief in the common sense and legitimate right of opinions and values by everyday citizens was at the heart of the farmers at Concord and Lexington. It was why bringing judges under control and guaranteeing jury trials ranked second only to no taxation without representation as a demand in the American Revolution. It was at the heart of the

Jacksonian rebellion against Eastern elites. It was the key to Lincoln's ability to hold the Union together through four years of war. We the people trumps you the elites.

- Because people matter as individuals, not "the people," policies should be tested against their micro effect as well as their macro effect. "How will this policy work in the real world with everyday folks?" should be a required test for any big macro proposal.

- The Founding Fathers had a passionate belief in the rule of law. They saw the law as the protector of the weak, the bulwark against corruption, the guarantor of a reliable process of commerce and life itself. We have to reassert the sanctity of the law against political corruption, bureaucratic tyranny, and judicial dictates.

- As part of the rule of law, your physical safety is the first obligation of government. A government that can't keep you safe has failed in its most important duty. This is made clear in the preamble to the United States Constitution.

POSSIBLE PROJECTS

The following are examples of the kind of bold projects and new thinking that the application of Trump's principles might lead to at the state and local level. They are listed in no particular order of priority, and some have been more fully detailed in earlier chapters.

REGULATORY PROJECTS

Project 1: Get the people to help kill regulations. President Trump has launched a bold initiative to require bureaucracies to kill two old regulations for every new one they issue. Every state and local government should adopt the same rule for its bureaucracies. Furthermore, state legislatures and city councils should develop online mechanisms to let citizens list the regulations they most want to see repealed. The bureaucrats we are trying to reform should not pick which regulations are cut. Really taming bureaucracies and the administrative state at all levels will be a huge job. It will require projects beyond reducing two old for each one new regulation.

Project 2: Move from input-focused regulations to outcome-focused regulations. In virtually everything the government regulates there is a bias toward prescribing inputs and prescribing step by step what has to be done. Phillip Howard's concept of outcome-based regulations is potentially powerful. Every state legislature and city council should develop a working group on replacing input-focused regulations with outcome-focused regulations. Every governor should appoint a state government-wide focus on the same transformation.

Project 3: Infrastructure projects should begin with a focus on dramatic regulatory reform. States and local governments should adopt Phillip Howard's proposal to consolidate all permitting into one shop, with one-time reviews. This could reduce time and costs dramatically. Second, the experiences of Governors Wilson, Schwarzenegger, Leavitt, Daniels, and Kasich should be codified into dramatic reforms. In all cases—but for different reasons—they avoided federal regulations, and had projects come in under budget and ahead of schedule. Some projects saved 40 percent over federal estimates. States should share new infrastructure approaches with the Trump administration and the new Republican Congress, to help them develop a new infrastructure program.

Project 4: Cut costs by cutting federal red tape. It is estimated that universities may spend as much as 15 percent of their overhead cost in meeting federal requirements. Doctors take home less money, because they have to hire more clerical staff to deal with paperwork from the federal government and insurance companies. Small businesses, small towns, and family farms all find federal red tape more and more burdensome. Every state should initiate a project to recommend dramatic streamlining to the Trump administration and Congress.

Project 5: Devolve power from the state capitol to local governments, private organizations and citizens. The same principle of decentralization we are applying to Washington bureaucrats should be applied to state government bureaucrats.

TECHNOLOGY PROJECTS

The technological revolution is immense, but its impact on public policy has been minor.

Project 6: Establish an advisory group of entrepreneurial innovators and ask them to rethink government in the age of mobile, digital, virtual, and personal (to borrow Carly Fiorina's phrase). This group should look at four profoundly different possibilities arising from this technological revolution:

- How will these systems empower individuals so we can achieve personal and societal goals in dramatically better, more effective ways?
- How can we automate yet personalize government activities and services?
- How can we achieve savings in personnel and bureaucratic costs comparable with those being achieved in business?
- What are the government-imposed limitations and inhibitions on achieving these goals?

Project 7: Establish working groups to explore the potential of smartphones in particular and mobile devices in general. The smartphone is the most powerful, liberating, and innovating device we have.

LEARNING PROJECTS

A major breakthrough will occur if we shift from talking about education to talking about learning.

President Abraham Lincoln estimated he had three years of formal schooling but he learned his entire life. Pioneers like Sebastian Thrun at Udacity are developing online learning systems much more powerful than traditional education systems. Obsolete government rules and institutions are major obstacles to shifting from a late-nineteenth-century education bureaucracy to a continuously evolving twenty-first-century learning system.

Project 8: Challenge every current accrediting system. They protect the past, block the future, and give enormous self-protecting power to professors to block competition. Each state should work with its employers to create a new achievement-based accrediting system. We don't care how many hours you sat in a classroom. We care what you learned and what you can do.

Project 9: Emphasize science, math, and engineering. Establish a letter jacket program for bright students parallel to that for athletic programs. Encourage schools to recognize high achievers in math, science, and engineering. This worked for Governor Mitch Daniels, who pioneered this area.

Project 10: Every state should review the tax paid curriculum and ask if taxpayers' money and students' time is being wasted on destructive detours from useful learning. As universities have grown bigger, the dominance of the weird and the fake has grown. The Ohio State University offers a course on "the problem of Whiteness" (this is a current fad, with the Universities of Southern California, Wisconsin, and others joining in). When black students demand a segregated space on a public campus to exclude whites, taxpayers have every right to demand an integrated America. We do not have an obligation to fund the destruction of our civilization. Taxpayers have no obligation to subsidize or support the intellectual narcissism of the

Left and the tyranny of radicals.

Project 11: Require all new higher-education construction to be fully funded and include a maintenance and upkeep trust. Some colleges have doubled their buildings without adding a single student.

Project 12: The College of the Ozarks is a remarkable work-study institution. Over 92 percent of the students graduate debt-free. Every state should establish one or more work-study colleges so anyone willing to work can get an education.

Project 13: Replace tenure for college professors with five-to seven-year revolving contracts comparable with contracts for sports coaches. Both teaching effectiveness and ideological honesty require a more disciplined approach to education staffing. Academic freedom has mutated into freedom to coerce by left-wing factions.

Project 14: Establish a student's right to complain. The amount of ideological bullying and one-sided fake lecturing present today is intolerable. Students should be entitled to complain about bad and bullying professors, and the professors should face sanctions.

CAPABILITY PROJECTS

Our Wounded Warrior programs offer vivid proof that people can overcome extraordinarily difficult challenges. Modern medicines and technologies can enable people to be productive when they have conditions that a generation ago would have taken them permanently out of the workforce.

Project 15: Each state and local government should get one-year and ten-year assessments of the direct and indirect costs of the dependency-disabilities culture. Indirect costs would include lost tax revenue from people not working. This sets the scale of both the human and financial opportunity for a successful capabilities-focused program.

Project 16: Retrain every human resources manager dealing with workers' compensation and disabilities to approach each person by asking how to maximize their independence, productivity, and achievement

Project 17: Create centers for capabilities where modern science, technology and experience working with people with special needs can be combined to develop the most powerful possible program to help people truly pursue happiness whatever their challenges.

WORK PROJECTS

For more than two generations, we have adopted antiwork, propassive dependency policies. We separated children from their fathers to get welfare. We made it harder and more expensive to open small businesses. Big cities are especially anti–small business, with arrogant bureaucracies, licensing fees, taxes, and red tape. Los Angeles mayor Richard Riordan once told me a friend tried to build a factory in the poorest part of LA and gave up after eighteen months because the bureaucracy was unresponsive.

Project 18: Review every licensing requirement and eliminate, shorten, or simplify virtually all of them. Licensing and permitting became a creative tool to minimize competition. There are more than 100,000 licenses in America today, and a large percentage have absurd requirements that restrict trade. Virtually all licenses make it harder and more expensive for minority members to enter trades.

Project 19: Review all laws that inhibit work. Recognize that modern technologies allow young people to be productive safely at a much earlier age. Laws growing out of child labor in coal mines and sweatshops may now hurt young people more than help them. Establish apprenticeship and internship rules to get willing young people into productive behavior.

Project 20: Ask small businesses which procedures, regulations, and taxes make it harder to start up and harder to hire more people. Establish websites where bad, arrogant, and rude bureaucrats can be reported.

Project 21: Anywhere you see a line of people interacting with government representatives, ask why. Technology enables us to have people online instead of standing in line. Every bureaucratic line in state and local government offices should be replaced with smart technology that allows people to instead easily interact with government online. Global Entry for returning to the United States is a good example of how technology can streamline a long government process. The goal should be to focus on making life easier for citizens rather than for bureaucrats.

Project 22: A job remains the best welfare policy. A goal should be set to make all government assistance tied to some level of effort. America Works is a remarkably successful company in New York City that specializes in getting the hard-core unemployed back to work and helping prisoners transition from jail to full employment. Its founder is adamant—after more than thirty years of experience—that everyone should be required to do work to receive aid (with the sole exception of the most severely challenged).

JOB-CREATION PROJECTS

It is virtually impossible to overstate the critical role that job creation plays in a healthy, stable, free society. New jobs improve take-home pay, wealth creation, and retirement funds, and increase revenue for government and charity, as well as fostering a sense of upward mobility and declining social tension as people believe their lives and their children's lives will improve.

Project 23: Every state and local government should authorize a special commission of job creators to measure every policy and regulation against its impact on job creation.

NEW BUSINESS PROJECTS

For long-term job and wealth creation, small businesses are far more important than big businesses. Yet governors and mayors spend more time wooing big businesses rather than thinking about how to launch the maximum number of young businesses, which can grow into medium-size and big businesses.

Project 24: Establish an annual survey of business start-ups. Interview founders and find out what helped and hurt them. Canvass for potential start-ups and find what is holding them back.

Project 25: Ask every small and medium-size business under what circumstance they would hire more people every year.

Project 26: Use an entrepreneurial survey to identify young people and link them with early entrepreneurship opportunities—starting their own companies in middle school or high school. Gallup's Builder Profile 10 is a survey that has a good track record of identifying entrepreneurial talent.

FAMILY PROJECTS

Families are the bedrock of our society. Strong families create strong, safe, prosperous communities.

Project 27: Review every law and regulation to determine whether they undermine and weaken families. Then recommend steps to make them profamily instead of antifamily rules.

ANTICORRUPTION PROJECTS

Historically one of the key differences between third-world societies and the United States has been the difference in corruption. The United States was founded in part in response to the corruption that held together the British government.

Five different forces have led to a dramatic increase in corruption as government has grown—crony capitalism, special interests, fast technology, slow bureaucratic adaptation, and dependency-based culture—all of which encourage theft and dishonesty.

At the federal level, it's estimated that theft and fraud add up to more than $200 billion a year, which is well over $2 trillion a decade. That doesn't count cost overruns.

Project 28: Bring in the most effective antifraud systems in your state and ask them how they would design your payment systems to minimize theft and corruption.

SAFETY PROJECTS

There is no effective freedom without safety. There is no ability to pursue happiness without safety. The poor are especially vulnerable and likely to be exploited when there is no safety.

Project 29: State and local governments that have a violent community should establish a CompStat commission to explore what works and apply it relentlessly until neighborhoods become safe. (CompStat was the system used by Mayor Giuliani to achieve a huge reduction in crime in New York City.)

Project 30: Review the actions of conservative states that have used the right kind of criminal justice reform to reduce crime, reduce the number of prisoners, increase safety, and reduce prison costs for the taxpayer. When governors like Rick Perry of Texas, Nathan Deal of Georgia, and Nikki Haley of South Carolina can all point to less crime, more former prisoners transitioning to jobs and citizenship, and lower costs with fewer prisons, something profound is happening.

Project 31: Establish a working group on the opioid epidemic and the emerging potential to use medication-assisted treatment to dramatically save lives, return people to work, and create healthier communities.

Project 32: Review prison populations to determine how many prisoners need mental health treatment. In some states over half the prisoners are mental patients who should not be imprisoned. It is more humane and much less expensive to develop an effective mental health strategy rather than to lock up noncriminals.

Project 33: Each state should review its Medicaid program to ensure that true mental health parity is being enforced, so we can help people cope with mental health and addiction strategies before they become prisoners.

Project 34: Develop multiyear budgeting at the micro level to measure the true costs of incarcerating rather than treating people.

STATE CAPABILITY PROJECTS

Liberals have a bias against state and local government—and a deep commitment to centralizing power in Washington. Consequently, they ignored state achievements and favored federal bureaucrats even when the results were weaker or more expensive. In fact, a number of state forest departments keep healthier, more effective forests at lower costs than the National Forest Service does.

Project 35: Assess every aspect of duplicative state and federal activities. In instances in which the state is doing a better job, the state should offer to contract with the federal government to take over the activity for a fee. The federal government can set standards and monitor outcomes while the state government handles the work. This is the Phillip Howard model.

* * *

If our leaders at the state level can take these principles to heart—and put these projects to the test—it will dramatically improve people's lives and solidify Trump's vision for the country. This is a watershed moment. This is our chance to make America great again.

CHAPTER FIFTEEN

THE ROAD AHEAD

I hope *Understanding Trump* has given you a better sense of the extraordinary figure who has become the forty-fifth president of the United States.

Keep this in mind: his presidency is a work in progress.

Every day, he learns more about the complexities of the government, the country, and the world he is trying to lead.

The hypernegative media will continue to attack every change, every evolution, every twist and turn.

The media's passion to find or interpret Trump negatively is amazing.

As I was writing the concluding chapters for *Understanding Trump*, one reporter attacked the president for praising President Andrew Jackson one week (while in Jackson's home state of Tennessee) and then praising Henry Clay the following week (while in Clay's home state of Kentucky). According to the reporter, this showed ignorance. Jackson and Clay were bitter enemies. How could President Trump praise both of them, the reporter asked in scornful language.

When I read this, I became very angry. The arrogance and shallowness of his column got to me.

First, it is normal for presidents to say nice things about great men whose home state they visit. Jackson and Clay may have been bitter opponents, but both were great Americans.

Second, you can praise political opponents for different characteristics and be totally coherent. Jackson was a great populist. Clay was a great advocate for putting America first in economic policy. President Trump can praise each for his policies in different areas.

Similarly, it is totally legitimate to admire Thomas Jefferson's political commitment to having every person participate in the republic and Alexander Hamilton's dedication to economic growth through market-oriented capitalism. The two men may have been bitter rivals, but Jefferson focused on making us free while Hamilton focused on making us economically strong enough to maintain our freedom.

In fact, you can argue that the genius of Lincoln was his ability to synthesize Jefferson's government of, by, and for the people with Hamilton's and Clay's style of economics and nationalism.

My advice to analysts is to quit overanalyzing and trying to diminish President Trump.

The key to our future is not changing Trump.

The key is changing Washington and America. We must get back to a healthier path to make America great again.

There are five key challenges for President Trump on the road to success:

1. Creating jobs
2. Maintaining global stability
3. Learning to lead Congress
4. Learning to profoundly change the entrenched bureaucracy
5. Establishing goals so large they build *huge* momentum for a better future

Let's explore each one.

First, if President Trump can get America back to the 5 percent or greater annual growth it achieved under Reagan, he will be reelected in a landslide in 2020. Americans want jobs for themselves and their children. They want higher take-home pay, and increasing wealth for their 401(k)s and pension funds.

If President Trump can deliver that kind of economy, people will overlook almost everything else and vote to keep him and the "Trump prosperity." On the other hand, if he can't create this kind of economic growth, almost nothing else will build an electoral majority.

Second, I am writing in early April during the Syrian and North Korean flashpoints. It is not clear what the outcome will be. What is clear is that the United States is the indispensable leader. When only North Korea, Iran, and Russia joined Syria in complaining about the US Tomahawk missile response to the use of poison gas, it was clear a new global community was emerging. Ironically, it was a Trump-led rather than an Obama-orated community.

It was clear that the Chinese visit to Mar-a-Lago paid dividends when China abstained rather than opposed the United States on Syria in the UN Security Council. Russia was left isolated.

As I write, the vice president is in South Korea, the secretary of defense is in Saudi Arabia, and the National Security Adviser is in Afghanistan.

It is increasingly clear that Trump's vision of America First involves leading the world rather than withdrawing from it. It is also clear he is rapidly building worldwide friendships that will help him in that leadership.

If he can strengthen the forces of freedom, law, and prosperity while weakening the forces of terrorism and tyranny—and do so without a major war—he will be seen as a remarkably successful president by 2020.

Third, the initial failure of the House Republican health bill was a sign President Trump had not yet mastered the art of leading the legislative branch. As I write, a number of very smart, serious people in the legislative and executive branches are working to redraft the health bill. They are working to make it stronger and to enable it to pass the House, the Senate, and a conference committee, which then must again pass both the House and the Senate.

Legislating major change is an extraordinarily difficult and challenging art form. Health care is one-fifth of the economy and a matter of life and death. It should not shock us that it is hard to reform—or that many powerful interests get involved because they think it is their money.

Also, repealing Obamacare is inherently and unavoidably partisan.

However, most legislating can be bipartisan if it is set up correctly. When we passed welfare reform in 1996 (the largest conservative policy reform in our lifetime) we split the Democrats exactly evenly with 101 for and 101 against. When we passed Reagan's tax cuts in 1981, one out of every three House Democrats voted for the Reagan bill.

President Trump has the potential to reach out and build Trump majorities in the House and Senate. He could potentially gain a 275-seat Trump majority in the House and a 65-vote bloc in the Senate. It would require a Reagan-like focus on arousing the grassroots and running public campaigns to build support for ideas and legislation. Of course, that is something candidate Trump did brilliantly.

Fourth, the depth of bureaucratic resistance is only beginning to be obvious. A successful Trump administration will have to develop very profound reforms to gain control of the civil service and ensure it is both modernized and responsive to the values of the American people. This zone may be the greatest test of whether President Trump is merely a successful commander in chief or a truly historic one.

Fifth, making America great again requires doing great things. Washington is a city that loves to bog leaders down in gossip, petty squabbles, and irrelevant noise. The greatest American leaders somehow cut through all that distraction and focus on big breakthroughs.

In his historic February 2017 address to a joint session of Congress, President Trump described the 250th anniversary of the Declaration of Independence in 2026. He noted that on the 100th anniversary there had been a great exhibition of progress in Philadelphia.

Now, at the beginning of the Trump administration, is a good time to set great goals for 2026.

Imagine the following very real possibilities for the 250th anniversary:

- A nonaddictive painkiller will have replaced opioids, saving thirty-three thousand lives a year.
- Alzheimer's will have been detected early and contained for five years or longer, cutting the costs of treatment by 50 percent and eliminating a huge amount of pain for caregivers and loved ones.
- Self-regenerating kidneys will have replaced kidney dialysis, saving billions of dollars and giving millions more complete, independent lives.
- Brain science will have revolutionized our understanding of autism, depression, Down syndrome, and dozens of other brain activities.
- Prescribers will be able to look at a patient with osteoarthritis, a disease affecting more than 30 million in the US, and offer medication that stops or reverses

damage, whereas today they can only provide relief of mild symptoms.

- We will have landed on Mars and established a permanent base.
- We will have manufactured the first large spaceships on the moon with robotics and 3-D printing.
- The first asteroid mining systems will have generated huge profits.
- Virtually every third-grader will have the ability to read and write.
- Chicago and other dangerous cities will have experienced a dramatic decline in violence.
- Jobs will have proliferated in rural, small towns and in poor urban neighborhoods.
- Every adult will have access to job training, and the middle class will have grown.
- The military will have streamlined red tape and procurement, so we get far more combat power per dollar.
- Those dollars will have been invested in new twenty-first-century capabilities, so we once again have an unchallengeable military advantage.
- Islamic supremacists will have been destroyed everywhere. The radical Islamist movement will have been reduced to scattered remnants living in hiding.
- Post-Putin Russia will have decided to become normal and join Western countries.
- China will have decided that a revitalized America can't be defeated and is operating collaboratively with the United States.

These are the kind of breakthroughs a successful Trump administration could develop.

This is the path that would make America great again.

Following are a collection of essays and speeches that I found useful in *Understanding Trump.*

THE INTELLECTUAL
YET IDIOT

From *Skin in the Game*
by Nassim Nicholas Taleb

What we have been seeing worldwide, from India to the UK to the US, is the rebellion against the inner circle of no-skin-in-the-game policymaking "clerks" and journalists-insiders, that class of paternalistic semi-intellectual experts with some Ivy League, Oxford-Cambridge, or similar label-driven education who are telling the rest of us 1) what to do, 2) what to eat, 3) how to speak, 4) how to think . . . and 5) who to vote for.

But the problem is the one-eyed following the blind: these self-described members of the "intelligentsia" can't find a coconut in Coconut Island, meaning they aren't intelligent enough to define intelligence hence fall into circularities—but their main skill is capacity to pass exams written by people like them. With psychology papers replicating less than 40%, dietary advice reversing after 30 years of fatphobia, macroeconomic analysis working worse than astrology, the appointment of Bernanke who was less than clueless of the risks, and pharmaceutical trials replicating at best only 1/3 of the time, people are perfectly entitled to rely on their own ancestral instinct and listen to their grandmothers (or Montaigne and such filtered classical knowledge) with a better track record than these policymaking goons.

Indeed one can see that these academico-bureaucrats who feel entitled to run our lives aren't even rigorous, whether in medical statistics or policymaking. They can't tell science from scientism—in fact in their image-oriented minds scientism looks more scientific than real science. (For instance it is trivial to show the following: much of what the Cass Sunstein–Richard Thaler types—those who want to "nudge" us into some behavior—much of what they would classify as "rational" or "irrational" (or some such categories indicating deviation from a desired or prescribed protocol) comes from their misunderstanding of probability theory and cosmetic use of first-order models. They are also prone to mistake the ensemble for the linear aggregation of its components as we saw in the chapter extending the minority rule.

The Intellectual Yet Idiot is a production of modernity hence has been accelerating since the mid-twentieth century, to reach its local supremum today, along with the broad category of people without skin-in-the-game who have been invading many walks of life. Why? Simply, in most countries, the government's role is between five and ten times what it was a century ago (expressed in percentage of GDP). The IYI seems ubiquitous in our lives but is still a small minority and is rarely seen outside specialized outlets, think tanks, the media, and universities—most people have proper jobs and there are not many openings for the IYI.

Beware the semi-erudite who thinks he is an erudite. He fails to naturally detect sophistry.

The IYI pathologizes others for doing things he doesn't understand without ever realizing it is *his* understanding that may be limited. He thinks people should act according to their best interests *and* he knows their interests, particularly if they are "red necks" or English non-crisp-vowel class who voted for Brexit. When plebeians do something that makes sense to them, but not to him, the IYI uses the term "uneducated." What we generally call participation in the political process, he calls by two distinct designations: "democracy" when it fits the IYI, and "populism" when the plebeians dare voting in a way that contradicts his preferences. While rich people believe in *one tax dollar one vote*, more humanistic ones in *one man one vote*, Monsanto in *one lobbyist one vote*, the IYI believes in *one Ivy League degree one vote*, with some equivalence for foreign elite schools and PhDs as these are needed in the club.

More socially, the IYI subscribes to *The New Yorker*. He never curses on twitter. He speaks of "equality of races" and "economic equality" but never went out drinking with a minority cab driver (again, no real skin in the game as the concept is foreign to the IYI). Those in the U.K. have been taken for a ride by Tony Blair. The modern IYI has attended more than one TEDx talks in person or watched more than two TED talks on YouTube. Not only did he vote for Hillary Monsanto-Malmaison because she seems electable and some such circular reasoning, but holds that anyone who doesn't do so is mentally ill.

The IYI has a copy of the first hardback edition of *The Black Swan* on his shelves, but mistakes absence of evidence for evidence of absence. He believes that GMOs are "science," that the "technology" is not different from conventional breeding as a result of his readiness to confuse science with scientism.

Typically, the IYI get the first-order logic right, but not second-order (or higher) effects, making him totally incompetent in complex domains. In the comfort of his suburban home with 2-car garage, he advocated the "removal" of Gadhafi because he was "a dictator," not realizing that removals have consequences (recall that he has no skin in the game and doesn't pay for results).

The IYI has been wrong, historically, on Stalinism, Maoism, GMOs, Iraq, Libya, Syria, lobotomies, urban planning, low carbohydrate diets, gym machines, behaviorism, transfats, freudianism, portfolio theory, linear regression, Gaussianism, Salafism, dynamic stochastic equilibrium modeling, housing projects, selfish gene, election forecasting models, Bernie Madoff (pre-blowup) and p-values. But he is convinced that his current position is right.

The IYI is member of a club to get traveling privileges; if social scientist he uses statistics without knowing how they are derived (like Steven Pinker and psycholophasters in general); when in the UK, he goes to literary festivals; he drinks red wine with steak (never white); he used to believe that fat was harmful and has now completely reversed; he takes statins because his doctor told him to do so; he fails to understand ergodicity and when explained to him, he forgets about it soon later; he doesn't use Yiddish words even when talking business; he studies grammar before speaking a language; he has a cousin who worked with someone who knows the Queen; he has never read Frederic Dard, Libanius Antiochus, Michael Oakeshott, John Gray, Ammianus Marcellinus, Ibn Battuta, Saadiah Gaon, or Joseph de Maistre; he has never gotten drunk with Russians; he never drank to the point when one starts breaking glasses (or, preferably, chairs); he doesn't even know the difference between Hecate and Hecuba (which in Brooklynese is "can't tell *sh**t* from shinola"); he doesn't know that there is no difference between "pseudointellectual" and "intellectual" in the absence of skin in the game; has mentioned quantum mechanics at least twice in the past five years in conversations that had nothing to do with physics.

He knows at any point in time what his words or actions are doing to his reputation.

But a much easier marker: he doesn't even deadlift.

Postscript—*From the reactions to this piece, I discovered that the IYI has difficulty, when reading, in differentiating between the satirical and the literal.*

Post-Postscript—*The IYI thinks this criticism of IYIs means "everybody is an idiot," not realizing that their group represents, as we said, a tiny minority—but they don't like their sense of entitlement to be challenged and although they treat the rest of humans as inferiors, they don't like it when the waterhose is turned to the opposite direction (what the French call* arroseur arrosé*). (For instance, Richard Thaler, partner of the dangerous GMO advocate Übernudger Cass Sunstein, interpreted this piece as saying that "there are not many non-idiots not called Taleb," not realizing that people like him are < 1% or even .1% of the population.)*

Post-Post Postscript—*(Written after the surprise election of 2016; the chapter above was written several months prior to the event.) The election of Trump was so absurd to them and didn't fit their worldview by such a large margin that they failed to find instructions in their textbook on how to react. It was exactly as on* Candid Camera; *imagine the characteristic look on someone's face after they pull a trick on him, and the person is at a loss about how to react.*

Or, more interestingly, imagine the looks and reaction of someone who thought he was happily married making an unscheduled return home and hears his wife squealing in bed with a (huge) doorman.

Pretty much everything forecasters, subforecasters, superforecasters, political "scientists," psychologists, intellectuals, campaigners, "consultants," big data scientists, everything they know was instantly shown to be a hoax. So my mischievous dream of putting a rat inside someone's shirt (as expressed in The Black Swan*) suddenly came true.*

NOTE: this piece can be reproduced, translated, and published by anyone under the condition that it is in its entirety and mentions that it is extracted from *Skin in the Game*.

Publications banned from republishing my work without explicit written permission: *Huffington Post* (all languages).

SELECTED SPEECHES
OF DONALD J. TRUMP

Inaugural Address of
President Donald J. Trump
January 20, 2017

Chief Justice Roberts, President Carter, President Clinton, President Bush, President Obama, fellow Americans, and people of the world: thank you.

We, the citizens of America, are now joined in a great national effort to rebuild our country and to restore its promise for all of our people.

Together, we will determine the course of America and the world for years to come.

We will face challenges. We will confront hardships. But we will get the job done.

Every four years, we gather on these steps to carry out the orderly and peaceful transfer of power, and we are grateful to President Obama and First Lady Michelle Obama for their gracious aid throughout this transition. They have been magnificent.

Today's ceremony, however, has very special meaning. Because today we are not merely transferring power from one administration to another, or from one party to another—but we are transferring power from Washington, DC, and giving it back to you, the American people.

For too long, a small group in our nation's capital has reaped the rewards of government while the people have borne the cost.

Washington flourished—but the people did not share in its wealth.

Politicians prospered—but the jobs left, and the factories closed.

The establishment protected itself, but not the citizens of our country.

Their victories have not been your victories; their triumphs have not been your triumphs; and while they celebrated in our nation's capital, there was little to celebrate for struggling families all across our land.

That all changes—starting right here, and right now, because this moment is your moment: it belongs to you.

It belongs to everyone gathered here today and everyone watching all across America.

This is your day. This is your celebration.

And this, the United States of America, is your country.

What truly matters is not which party controls our government, but whether our government is controlled by the people.

January 20, 2017, will be remembered as the day the people became the rulers of this nation again.

The forgotten men and women of our country will be forgotten no longer.

Everyone is listening to you now.

You came by the tens of millions to become part of a historic movement the likes of which the world has never seen before.

At the center of this movement is a crucial conviction: that a nation exists to serve its citizens.

Americans want great schools for their children, safe neighborhoods for their families, and good jobs for themselves.

These are the just and reasonable demands of a righteous public.

But for too many of our citizens, a different reality exists: mothers and children trapped in poverty in our inner cities; rusted-out factories scattered like tombstones across the landscape of our nation; an education system, flush with cash, but which leaves our young and beautiful students deprived of knowledge; and the crime and gangs and drugs that have stolen too many lives and robbed our country of so much unrealized potential.

This American carnage stops right here and stops right now.

We are one nation—and their pain is our pain. Their dreams are our dreams; and their success will be our success. We share one heart, one home, and one glorious destiny.

The oath of office I take today is an oath of allegiance to all Americans.

For many decades, we've enriched foreign industry at the expense of American industry;

Subsidized the armies of other countries while allowing for the very sad depletion of our military;

We've defended other nations' borders while refusing to defend our own;

And spent trillions of dollars overseas while America's infrastructure has fallen into disrepair and decay.

We've made other countries rich while the wealth, strength, and confidence of our country has disappeared over the horizon.

One by one, the factories shuttered and left our shores, with not even a thought about the millions upon millions of American workers left behind.

The wealth of our middle class has been ripped from their homes and then redistributed across the entire world.

But that is the past. And now we are looking only to the future.

We assembled here today are issuing a new decree to be heard in every city, in every foreign capital, and in every hall of power.

From this day forward, a new vision will govern our land.

From this moment on, it's going to be America first.

Every decision on trade, on taxes, on immigration, on foreign affairs, will be made to benefit American workers and American families.

We must protect our borders from the ravages of other countries making our products, stealing our companies, and destroying our jobs. Protection will lead to great prosperity and strength.

I will fight for you with every breath in my body—and I will never, ever let you down.

America will start winning again, winning like never before.

We will bring back our jobs. We will bring back our borders. We will bring back our wealth. And we will bring back our dreams.

We will build new roads, and highways, and bridges, and airports, and tunnels, and railways all across our wonderful nation.

We will get our people off of welfare and back to work— rebuilding our country with American hands and American labor.

We will follow two simple rules: buy American and hire American.

We will seek friendship and goodwill with the nations of the world—but we do so with the understanding that it is the right of all nations to put their own interests first.

We do not seek to impose our way of life on anyone, but rather to let it shine as an example for everyone to follow.

We will reinforce old alliances and form new ones—and unite the civilized world against radical Islamic terrorism, which we will eradicate completely from the face of the earth.

At the bedrock of our politics will be a total allegiance to the United States of America, and through our loyalty to our country, we will rediscover our loyalty to each other.

When you open your heart to patriotism, there is no room for prejudice.

The Bible tells us, "How good and pleasant it is when God's people live together in unity."

We must speak our minds openly, debate our disagreements honestly, but always pursue solidarity.

When America is united, America is totally unstoppable.

There should be no fear—we are protected, and we will always be protected.

We will be protected by the great men and women of our military and law enforcement and, most importantly, we are protected by God.

Finally, we must think big and dream even bigger.

In America, we understand that a nation is only living as long as it is striving.

We will no longer accept politicians who are all talk and no action—constantly complaining but never doing anything about it.

The time for empty talk is over.

Now arrives the hour of action.

Do not let anyone tell you it cannot be done. No challenge can match the heart and fight and spirit of America.

We will not fail. Our country will thrive and prosper again.

We stand at the birth of a new millennium, ready to unlock the mysteries of space, to free the earth from the miseries of disease, and to harness the energies, industries, and technologies of tomorrow.

A new national pride will stir our souls, lift our sights, and heal our divisions.

It is time to remember that old wisdom our soldiers will never forget: that whether we are black or brown or white, we all bleed the same red blood of patriots, we all enjoy the same glorious freedoms, and we all salute the same great American flag.

And whether a child is born in the urban sprawl of Detroit or the windswept plains of Nebraska, they look up at the same night sky, they fill their heart with the same dreams, and they are infused with the breath of life by the same almighty Creator.

So to all Americans, in every city near and far, small and large, from mountain to mountain, and from ocean to ocean, hear these words:

You will never be ignored again.

Your voice, your hopes, and your dreams, will define our American destiny. And your courage and goodness and love will forever guide us along the way.

Together, we will make America strong again.

We will make America wealthy again.

We will make America proud again.

We will make America safe again.

And, yes, together, we will make America great again. Thank you, God Bless you, and God bless America.

Remarks by President Trump in a Joint Session of Congress
February 28, 2017

Thank you very much. Mr. Speaker, Mr. Vice President, Members of Congress, the First Lady of the United States, and citizens of America:

Tonight, as we mark the conclusion of our celebration of Black History Month, we are reminded of our nation's path towards civil rights and the work that still remains to be done. Recent threats targeting Jewish community centers and vandalism of Jewish cemeteries, as well as last week's shooting in Kansas City, remind us that while we may be a nation divided on policies, we are a country that stands united in condemning hate and evil in all of its very ugly forms.

Each American generation passes the torch of truth, liberty, and justice in an unbroken chain all the way down to the present. That torch is now in our hands. And we will use it to light up the world. I am here tonight to deliver a message of unity and strength, and it is a message deeply delivered from my heart. A new chapter of American greatness is now beginning. A new national pride is sweeping across our nation. And a new surge of optimism is placing impossible dreams firmly within our grasp.

What we are witnessing today is the renewal of the American spirit. Our allies will find that America is once again ready to lead. All the nations of the world—friend or foe—will find that America is strong, America is proud, and America is free.

In nine years, the United States will celebrate the 250th anniversary of our founding—250 years since the day we declared our independence. It will be one of the great milestones in the history of the world. But what will America look like as we reach our 250th year? What kind of country will we leave for our children?

I will not allow the mistakes of recent decades past to define the course of our future. For too long, we've watched our middle class shrink as we've exported our jobs and wealth to foreign countries. We've financed and built one global project after another, but ignored the fates of our children in the inner cities of Chicago, Baltimore, Detroit, and so many other places throughout our land.

We've defended the borders of other nations while leaving our own borders wide open for anyone to cross and for drugs to pour in at a now unprecedented rate. And we've spent trillions and trillions of dollars overseas, while our infrastructure at home has so badly crumbled.

Then, in 2016, the earth shifted beneath our feet. The rebellion started as a quiet protest, spoken by families of all colors and creeds—families who just wanted a fair shot for their children and a fair hearing for their concerns.

But then the quiet voices became a loud chorus as thousands of citizens now spoke out together, from cities small and large, all across our country. Finally, the chorus became an earthquake, and the people turned out by the tens of millions, and they were all united by one very simple, but crucial demand: that America must put its own citizens first. Because only then can we truly make America great again.

Dying industries will come roaring back to life. Heroic veterans will get the care they so desperately need. Our military will be given the resources its brave warriors so richly deserve. Crumbling infrastructure will be replaced with new roads, bridges, tunnels, airports and railways gleaming across our very, very beautiful land. Our terrible drug epidemic will slow down and, ultimately, stop. And our neglected inner cities will see a rebirth of hope, safety, and opportunity. Above all else, we will keep our promises to the American people.

It's been a little over a month since my inauguration, and I want to take this moment to update the nation on the progress I've made in keeping those promises.

Since my election, Ford, Fiat-Chrysler, General Motors, Sprint, Softbank, Lockheed, Intel, Walmart, and many others have announced that they will invest billions and billions of dollars in the United States, and will create tens of thousands of new American jobs.

The stock market has gained almost $3 trillion in value since the election on November 8, a record. We've saved taxpayers hundreds of millions of dollars by bringing down the price of a fantastic—and it is a fantastic—new F-35 jet fighter, and we'll be saving billions more on contracts all across our government. We have placed a hiring freeze on nonmilitary and nonessential federal workers.

We have begun to drain the swamp of government corruption by imposing a five-year ban on lobbying by executive-branch officials and a lifetime ban—thank you—and a lifetime ban on becoming lobbyists for a foreign government.

We have undertaken a historic effort to massively reduce job-crushing regulations, creating a deregulation task force inside of every government agency. And we're imposing a new rule which mandates that for every one new regulation, two old regulations must be eliminated. We're going to stop the regulations that threaten the future and livelihood of our great coal miners.

We have cleared the way for the construction of the Keystone and Dakota Access Pipelines thereby creating tens of thousands of jobs. And I've issued a new directive that new American pipelines be made with American steel.

We have withdrawn the United States from the job-killing Trans-Pacific Partnership. And with the help of Prime Minister

Justin Trudeau, we have formed a council with our neighbors in Canada to help ensure that women entrepreneurs have access to the networks, markets, and capital they need to start a business and live out their financial dreams.

To protect our citizens, I have directed the Department of Justice to form a task force on reducing violent crime. I have further ordered the Departments of Homeland Security and Justice, along with the Department of State and the director of National Intelligence, to coordinate an aggressive strategy to dismantle the criminal cartels that have spread all across our nation. We will stop the drugs from pouring into our country and poisoning our youth, and we will expand treatment for those who have become so badly addicted.

At the same time, my administration has answered the pleas of the American people for immigration enforcement and border security. By finally enforcing our immigration laws, we will raise wages, help the unemployed, save billions and billions of dollars, and make our communities safer for everyone. We want all Americans to succeed, but that can't happen in an environment of lawless chaos. We must restore integrity and the rule of law at our borders.

For that reason, we will soon begin the construction of a great, great wall along our southern border. As we speak tonight, we are removing gang members, drug dealers, and criminals that threaten our communities and prey on our very innocent citizens. Bad ones are going out as I speak, and as I promised throughout the campaign.

To any in Congress who do not believe we should enforce our laws, I would ask you this one question: What would you say to the American family that loses their jobs, their income, or their loved one because America refused to uphold its laws and defend its borders?

Our obligation is to serve, protect, and defend the citizens of the United States. We are also taking strong measures to protect our nation from radical Islamic terrorism. According to data provided by the Department of Justice, the vast majority of individuals convicted of terrorism and terrorism-related offenses since 9/11 came here from outside of our country. We have seen the attacks at home—from Boston to San Bernardino to the Pentagon, and, yes, even the World Trade Center.

We have seen the attacks in France, in Belgium, in Germany, and all over the world. It is not compassionate, but reckless to allow uncontrolled entry from places where proper vetting cannot occur. Those given the high honor of admission to the United States should support this country and love its people and its values. We cannot allow a beachhead of terrorism to form inside America. We cannot allow our nation to become a sanctuary for extremists.

That is why my administration has been working on improved vetting procedures, and we will shortly take new steps to keep our nation safe and to keep out those who will do us harm.

As promised, I directed the Department of Defense to develop a plan to demolish and destroy ISIS—a network of lawless savages that have slaughtered Muslims and Christians, and men, and women, and children of all faiths and all beliefs. We will work with our allies, including our friends and allies in the Muslim world, to extinguish this vile enemy from our planet.

I have also imposed new sanctions on entities and individuals who support Iran's ballistic missile program, and reaffirmed our unbreakable alliance with the State of Israel.

Finally, I have kept my promise to appoint a justice to the United States Supreme Court, from my list of twenty judges, who will defend our Constitution.

I am greatly honored to have Maureen Scalia with us in the gallery tonight. Thank you, Maureen. Her late, great husband, Antonin Scalia, will forever be a symbol of American justice. To fill his seat, we have chosen Judge Neil Gorsuch, a man of incredible skill and deep devotion to the law. He was confirmed unanimously by the court of appeals, and I am asking the Senate to swiftly approve his nomination.

Tonight, as I outline the next steps we must take as a country, we must honestly acknowledge the circumstances we inherited. Ninety-four million Americans are out of the labor force. Over forty-three million people are now living in poverty, and over forty-three million Americans are on food stamps. More than one in five people in their prime working years are not working. We have the worst financial recovery in sixty-five years. In the last eight years, the past administration has put on more new debt than nearly all of the other presidents combined.

We've lost more than one-fourth of our manufacturing jobs since NAFTA was approved, and we've lost sixty thousand factories since China joined the World Trade Organization in 2001. Our trade deficit in goods with the world last year was nearly $800 billion. And overseas we have inherited a series of tragic foreign policy disasters.

Solving these and so many other pressing problems will require us to work past the differences of party. It will require us to tap into the American spirit that has overcome every challenge throughout our long and storied history. But to accomplish our goals at home and abroad, we must restart the engine of the American economy— making it easier for companies to do business in the United States, and much, much harder for companies to leave our country.

Right now, American companies are taxed at one of the highest rates anywhere in the world. My economic team is developing historic tax reform that will reduce the tax rate on our companies so they can compete and thrive anywhere and with anyone. It will be a big, big cut.

At the same time, we will provide massive tax relief for the middle class. We must create a level playing field for American companies and our workers. We have to do it. Currently, when we ship products out of America, many other countries make us pay very high tariffs and taxes. But when foreign companies ship their products into America, we charge them nothing, or almost nothing.

I just met with officials and workers from a great American company, Harley-Davidson. In fact, they proudly displayed five of their magnificent motorcycles, made in the USA, on the front lawn of the White House. And they wanted me to ride one and I said, "No, thank you."

At our meeting, I asked them, How are you doing, how is business? They said that it's good. I asked them further, How are you doing with other countries, mainly international sales? They told me—without even complaining, because they have been so mistreated for so long that they've become used to it—that it's very hard to do business with other countries because they tax our goods at such a high rate. They said that in the case of another country, they taxed their motorcycles at 100 percent. They weren't even asking for a change. But I am.

I believe strongly in free trade but it also has to be fair trade. It's been a long time since we had fair trade. The first Republican president, Abraham Lincoln, warned that the "abandonment of the protective policy by the American government . . . will produce want and ruin among our people." Lincoln was right—and it's time we heeded his advice and his words. I am not going to let America and its great companies and workers be taken advantage of any longer. They have taken advantage of our country. No longer.

I am going to bring back millions of jobs. Protecting our workers also means reforming our system of legal immigration. The current, outdated system depresses wages for our poorest workers, and puts great pressure on taxpayers. Nations around the world, like Canada, Australia, and many others, have a merit-based immigration system. It's a basic principle that those seeking to enter a country ought to be able to support themselves financially. Yet, in America, we do not enforce this rule, straining the very public resources that our poorest citizens rely upon. According to the National Academy of Sciences, our current immigration system costs American taxpayers many billions of dollars a year.

Switching away from this current system of lower-skilled immigration, and instead adopting a merit-based system, we will have so many more benefits. It will save countless dollars, raise workers' wages, and help struggling families—including immigrant families—enter the middle class. And they will do it quickly, and they will be very, very happy, indeed.

I believe that real and positive immigration reform is possible, as long as we focus on the following goals: to improve jobs and wages for Americans; to strengthen our nation's security; and to restore respect for our laws. If we are guided by the well-being of American citizens, then I believe Republicans and Democrats can work together to achieve an outcome that has eluded our country for decades.

Another Republican president, Dwight D. Eisenhower, initiated the last truly great national infrastructure program—the building of the Interstate Highway System. The time has come for a new *program of national rebuilding. America has spent approximately $6 trillion in the Middle East—all the while our infrastructure at home is crumbling. With this $6 trillion, we could have rebuilt our country twice, and maybe even three times if we had people who had the ability to negotiate.*

To launch our national rebuilding, I will be asking Congress to approve legislation that produces a $1 trillion investment in infrastructure of the United States—financed through both public and private capital—creating millions of new jobs. This effort will be guided by two core principles: buy American and hire American.

Tonight, I am also calling on this Congress to repeal and replace Obamacare with reforms that expand choice, increase access, lower costs, and, at the same time, provide better health care.

Mandating every American to buy government-approved health insurance was never the right solution for our country. The way to make health insurance available to everyone is to lower the cost of health insurance, and that is what we are going do.

Obamacare premiums nationwide have increased by double and triple digits. As an example, Arizona went up 116 percent last year alone. Governor Matt Bevin of Kentucky just said Obamacare is failing in his state—the state of Kentucky—and it's unsustainable and collapsing.

One-third of counties have only one insurer, and they are losing them fast. They are losing them so fast. They are leaving, and many Americans have no choice at all. There's no choice left. Remember when you were told that you could keep your doctor and keep your plan? We now know that all of those promises have been totally broken. Obamacare is collapsing, and we must act decisively to protect all Americans.

Action is not a choice, it is a necessity. So I am calling on all Democrats and Republicans in Congress to work with us to save Americans from this imploding Obamacare disaster.

Here are the principles that should guide Congress as we move to create a better health care system for all Americans:

First, we should ensure that Americans with preexisting conditions have access to coverage, and that we have a stable transition for Americans currently enrolled in the health care exchanges.

Secondly, we should help Americans purchase their own coverage through the use of tax credits and expanded health savings accounts—but it must be the plan they want, not the plan forced on them by our government.

Thirdly, we should give our great state governors the resources and flexibility they need with Medicaid to make sure no one is left out.

Fourth, we should implement legal reforms that protect patients and doctors from unnecessary costs that drive up the price of insurance, and work to bring down the artificially high price of drugs, and bring them down immediately.

And finally, the time has come to give Americans the freedom to purchase health insurance across state lines, which will create a truly competitive national marketplace that will bring costs way down and provide far better care. So important.

Everything that is broken in our country can be fixed. Every problem can be solved. And every hurting family can find healing and hope.

Our citizens deserve this, and so much more—so why not join forces and finally get the job done, and get it done right? On this and so many other things, Democrats and Republicans should get together and unite for the good of our country and for the good of the American people.

My administration wants to work with members of both parties to make childcare accessible and affordable, to help ensure new parents that they have paid family leave to invest in women's health, and to promote clean air and clean water, and to rebuild our military and our infrastructure.

True love for our people requires us to find common ground, to advance the common good, and to cooperate on behalf of every American child who deserves a much brighter future.

An incredible young woman is with us this evening, who should serve as an inspiration to us all. Today is Rare Disease Day, and joining us in the gallery is a rare disease survivor, Megan Crowley.

Megan was diagnosed with Pompe disease, a rare and serious illness, when she was fifteen months old. She was not expected to live past five. On receiving this news, Megan's dad, John, fought with everything he had to save the life of his precious child. He founded a company to look for a cure, and helped develop the drug that saved Megan's life. Today she is twenty years old and a sophomore at Notre Dame.

Megan's story is about the unbounded power of a father's love for a daughter. But our slow and burdensome approval process at the Food and Drug Administration keeps too many advances, like the one that saved Megan's life, from reaching those in need. If we slash the restraints, not just at the FDA but across our government, then we will be blessed with far more miracles just like Megan. In fact, our children will grow up in a nation of miracles.

But to achieve this future, we must enrich the mind and the souls of every American child. Education is the civil rights issue of our time. I am calling upon members of both parties to pass an education bill that funds school choice for disadvantaged youth, including millions of African American and Latino children. These families should be free to choose the public, private, charter, magnet, religious, or home school that is right for them.

Joining us tonight in the gallery is a remarkable woman, Denisha Merriweather. As a young girl, Denisha struggled in school and failed third grade twice. But then she was able to enroll in a private center for learning—a great learning center—with the help of a tax credit and a scholarship program.

Today, she is the first in her family to graduate, not just from high school, but from college. Later this year she will get her master's degree in social work. We want all children to be able to break the cycle of poverty just like Denisha.

But to break the cycle of poverty, we must also break the cycle of violence. The murder rate in 2015 experienced its largest single-year increase in nearly half a century. In Chicago, more than four thousand people were shot last year alone, and the murder rate so far this year has been even higher. This is not acceptable in our society.

Every American child should be able to grow up in a safe community, to attend a great school, and to have access to a high-paying job. But to create this future, we must work with, not against—not against—the men and women of law enforcement.

We must build bridges of cooperation and trust—not drive the wedge of disunity and, really, it's what it is, division. It's pure, unadulterated division. We have to unify.

Police and sheriffs are members of our community. They're friends and neighbors, they're mothers and fathers, sons and daughters—and they leave behind loved ones every day who worry about whether or not they'll come home safe and sound. We must support the incredible men and women of law enforcement.

And we must support the victims of crime. I have ordered the Department of Homeland Security to create an office to serve American victims. The office is called VOICE—Victims of Immigration Crime Engagement. We are providing a voice to those who have been ignored by our media and silenced by special interests. Joining us in the audience tonight are four very brave Americans whose government failed them. Their names are Jamiel Shaw, Susan Oliver, Jenna Oliver, and Jessica Davis.

Jamiel's seventeen-year-old son was viciously murdered by an illegal immigrant gang member who had just been released from prison. Jamiel Shaw Jr. was an incredible young man, with unlimited potential who was getting ready to go to college where he would have excelled as a great college quarterback. But he never got the chance. His father, who is in the audience tonight, has become a very good friend of mine. Jamiel, thank you. Thank you.

Also with us are Susan Oliver and Jessica Davis. Their husbands, Deputy Sheriff Danny Oliver and Detective Michael Davis, were slain in the line of duty in California. They were pillars of their community. These brave men were viciously gunned down by an illegal immigrant with a criminal record and two prior deportations. Should have never been in our country.

Sitting with Susan is her daughter, Jenna. Jenna, I want you to know that your father was a hero, and that tonight you have the love of an entire country supporting you and praying for you.

To Jamiel, Jenna, Susan, and Jessica, I want you to know that we will never stop fighting for justice. Your loved ones will never, ever be forgotten. We will always honor their memory.

Finally, to keep America safe, we must provide the men and women of the United States military with the tools they need to prevent war—if they must—they have to fight and they only have to win.

I am sending Congress a budget that rebuilds the military, eliminates the defense sequester, and calls for one of the largest increases in national defense spending in American history. My budget will also increase funding for our veterans. Our veterans have delivered for this nation, and now we must deliver for them.

The challenges we face as a nation are great, but our people are even greater. And none are greater or braver than those who fight for America in uniform.

We are blessed to be joined tonight by Carryn Owens, the widow of a US Navy special operator, Senior Chief William "Ryan" Owens. Ryan died as he lived: a warrior and a hero, battling against terrorism and securing our nation. I just spoke to our great General Mattis, just now, who reconfirmed that—and I quote—"Ryan was a part of a highly successful raid that generated large amounts of vital intelligence that will lead to many more victories in the future against our enemies." Ryan's legacy is etched into eternity. Thank you. And Ryan is looking down, right now—you know that—and he is very happy because I think he just broke a record.

For as the Bible teaches us, "There is no greater act of love than to lay down one's life for one's friends." Ryan laid down his life for his friends, for his country, and for our freedom. And we will never forget Ryan.

To those allies who wonder what kind of a friend America will be, look no further than the heroes who wear our uniform. Our foreign policy calls for a direct, robust, and meaningful engagement with the world. It is American leadership based on vital security interests that we share with our allies all across the globe.

We strongly support NATO, an alliance forged through the bonds of two world wars that dethroned fascism, and a Cold War, and defeated communism.

But our partners must meet their financial obligations. And now, based on our very strong and frank discussions, they are beginning to do just that. In fact, I can tell you, the money is pouring in. Very nice. We expect our partners—whether in NATO, the Middle East, or in the Pacific—to take a direct and meaningful role in both strategic and military operations, and pay their fair share of the cost. Have to do that.

We will respect historic institutions, but we will respect the foreign rights of all nations, and they have to respect our rights as a nation also. Free nations are the best vehicle for expressing the will of the people, and America respects the right of all nations to chart their own path. My job is not to represent the world. My job is to represent the United States of America.

But we know that America is better off when there is less conflict, not more. We must learn from the mistakes of the past. We have seen the war and the destruction that have ravaged and raged throughout the world—all across the world. The only long-term solution for these humanitarian disasters, in many cases, is to create the conditions where displaced persons can safely return home and begin the long, long process of rebuilding.

America is willing to find new friends, and to forge new partnerships, where shared interests align. We want harmony and stability, not war and conflict. We want peace, wherever peace can be found.

America is friends today with former enemies. Some of our closest allies, decades ago, fought on the opposite side of these terrible, terrible wars. This history should give us all faith in the possibilities for a better world. Hopefully, the 250th year for America will see a world that is more peaceful, more just, and more free.

On our 100th anniversary, in 1876, citizens from across our nation came to Philadelphia to celebrate America's centennial. At that celebration, the country's builders and artists and inventors showed off their wonderful creations. Alexander Graham Bell displayed his telephone for the first time. Remington unveiled the first typewriter. An early attempt was made at electric light. Thomas Edison showed an automatic telegraph and an electric pen. Imagine the wonders our country could know in America's 250th year.

Think of the marvels we can achieve if we simply set free the dreams of our people. Cures to the illnesses that have always plagued us are not too much to hope. American footprints on distant worlds are not too big a dream. Millions lifted from welfare to work is not too much to expect. And streets where mothers are safe from fear, schools where children learn in peace, and jobs where Americans prosper and grow are not too much to ask.

When we have all of this, we will have made America greater than ever before—for all Americans. This is our vision. This is our mission. But we can only get there together. We are one people, with one destiny. We all bleed the same blood. We all salute the same great American flag. And we all are made by the same God.

When we fulfill this vision, when we celebrate our 250 years of glorious freedom, we will look back on tonight as when this new chapter of American greatness began. The time for small thinking is over. The time for trivial fights is behind us. We just need the courage to share the dreams that fill our hearts, the bravery to express the hopes that stir our souls, and the confidence to turn those hopes and those dreams into action.

From now on, America will be empowered by our aspirations, not burdened by our fears; inspired by the future, not bound by the failures of the past; and guided by our vision, not blinded by our doubts.

I am asking all citizens to embrace this renewal of the American spirit. I am asking all members of Congress to join me in dreaming big, and bold, and daring things for our country. I am asking everyone watching tonight to seize this moment. Believe in yourselves, believe in your future, and believe, once more, in America.

Thank you, God bless you, and God bless the United States.

Trump's Charlotte Speech: "The New Deal for Black America"
October 26, 2016
As posted on RealClearPolitics by Tim Hains

It is great to be here in Charlotte to discuss an issue that means so much to me.

That is the issue of urban renewal, and the rebuilding of our inner cities.

Today I want to talk about how to grow the African-American middle class, and to provide a new deal for Black America. That deal is grounded in three promises: safe communities, great education, and high-paying jobs.

My vision rests on a principle that has defined this campaign: America First.

Every African-American citizen in this country is entitled to a government that puts their jobs, wages and security first.

I'm asking today for the honor of your vote, and the privilege to represent you as your President. Here is the promise I make to you: whether you vote for me or not, I will be your greatest champion. I have no special interest, I take no orders from donors or lobbyists—I work for you, and only you.

Our campaign is about change, optimism, and the future. I am asking people to break from the bitter failures of the past, and to imagine the amazing possibilities for our future.

Our opponent represents the rigged system and failed thinking of yesterday. Her campaign offers only the depressing pessimism that says this is as good as it gets, that nothing can ever really change.

Hillary has been there for 30 years and hasn't fixed anything— she's just made it worse.

American politics is caught in a time loop—we keep electing the same people, who keep making the same mistakes, and who keep offering the same excuses.

The fact that our corrupt Washington establishment has tried so hard to stop our movement is just more proof that we represent the kind of change that arrives only once in a lifetime.

Every day I'm out on the trail proposing fresh solutions and new thinking. And every day, the same people, getting rich off our broken system, tell us that we can't change and that we can't try anything new.

I have a message for all the doubters in Washington: America's future belongs to the dreamers, not the cynics.

And it's time to extend that dream to every African-American citizen in this country.

African-American citizens have sacrificed so much for this nation. They have fought and died in every war since the Revolution,

and from the pews and the picket lines they have lifted up the con-
science of our country in the long march for Civil Rights.

Yet, too many African-Americans have been left behind.

45% of African-American children under the age of 6 live in
poverty.

58% of African-American youth are not currently employed.

African-Americans comprise roughly 13 percent of the popula-
tion, yet make up 60% of murder victims under the age of 22.

In 2015, violent crime in Charlotte increased by 18 percent—
and it's expected to rise 24% in 2016.

In the city of Chicago, nearly 3,500 people have been shot since
January of this year.

The conditions in our inner cities today are unacceptable.

The Democrats have run our inner cities for fifty, sixty, seventy
years or more. They've run the school boards, the city councils, the
mayor's offices, and the congressional seats. Their policies have
failed, and they've failed miserably.

They've trapped children in failing government schools, and
opposed school choice at every turn.

The Clintons gave us NAFTA and China's entry into the World
Trade Organization, two deals that de-industrialized America,
uprooted our industry, and stripped bare towns like Detroit and
Baltimore and the inner cities of North Carolina. This state has
lost nearly half of its manufacturing jobs since Bill and Hillary's
NAFTA, decimating the African-American middle class.

Democratic policies have also given rise to crippling crime and
violence.

Then there is the issue of taxation and regulation. Massive
taxes, massive regulation of small business, and radical restrictions
on American energy, have driven jobs and opportunities out of
our inner cities. Hillary wants to raise taxes on successful small
businesses as high as 45 percent—which will only drive more jobs
out of your community, and into other countries.

One of the greatest betrayals has been the issue of immigration.
Illegal immigration violates the civil rights of African-Americans.
No group has been more economically harmed by decades of
illegal immigration than low-income African-American workers.

Hillary's pledge to enact "open borders,"—made in secret to a foreign bank—would destroy the African-American middle class.

At the center of my revitalization plan is the issue of trade. Massive, chronic trade deficits have emptied out our jobs. Just look at what has happened to Baltimore, Detroit, Pittsburgh, Cleveland, and right here in North Carolina. It's the greatest jobs theft in the history of the world.

If I'm President, and the executives at Ford Motor Company announce they are moving their plants and jobs to Mexico, I will pick up the phone and make a simple call. I will tell those executives that if they move their factories to Mexico, I will put a 35% tax on their product before they ship it back into the United States. We won't let your jobs be stolen from you anymore. When we stop the offshoring to low-wage countries, we raise wages at home— meaning rent and bills become instantly more affordable.

At the same time, my plan to lower the business tax from 35 percent to 15 percent will bring thousands of new companies onto our shores. It also includes a massive middle class tax cut, tax-free child-care savings accounts, and childcare tax deductions and credits.

I will also propose tax holidays for inner-city investment, and new tax incentives to get foreign companies to relocate in blighted American neighborhoods. I will further empower cities and states to seek a federal disaster designation for blighted communities in order to initiate the rebuilding of vital infrastructure, the demolition of abandoned properties, and the increased presence of law enforcement.

I will also pursue financial reforms to make it easier for young African-Americans to get credit to pursue their dreams in business and create jobs in their communities. Dodd-Frank has been a disaster, making it harder for small businesses to get the credit they need. The policies of the Clintons brought us the financial recession—through lifting Glass-Steagall, pushing subprime lending, and blocking reforms to Fannie and Freddie. It's time for a 21st century Glass-Steagall and, as part of that, a priority on helping African-American businesses get the credit they need.

We will also encourage small-business creation by allowing social welfare workers to convert poverty assistance into repayable but forgivable micro-loans.

Then there is the issue of public safety. Making our communities safe again will be a priority for the Trump Administration.

I have heard and have listened to the concerns raised by African-American citizens about our justice system, and I promise that under a Trump Administration the law will be applied fairly, equally and without prejudice. There will be only one set of rules— not a two-tiered system of justice. The best evidence of unequal justice is that Hillary Clinton could violate so many laws, bleach and delete 33,000 emails after a congressional subpoena, lie to Congress and the FBI—put our national security at grave risk— and not even face so much as a fine.

Equal justice also means the same rules for Wall Street. The Obama Administration never held Wall Street accountable.

We will also police our streets. I want every poor African-American child to be able to walk down the street in peace. Safety is a civil right. The problem is not the presence of police but the absence of police. I will invest in training and funding both local and federal law enforcement operations to remove the gang members, drug dealers, and criminal cartels from our neighborhoods. The reduction of crime is not merely a goal—but a necessity. We will get it done. The war on police urged on by my rival is reckless, and dangerous, and puts African-American lives at risk. We must work with our police, not against them.

On immigration, my policy is simple. I will restore the civil rights of African-Americans, Hispanic-Americans, and all Americans, by ending illegal immigration. I will reform visa rules to give American workers preference for jobs, and I will suspend reckless refugee admissions from terror-prone regions that cost taxpayers hundreds of billions of dollars. A portion of the money saved by enforcing our laws, and suspending refugees, will be re-invested in our inner cities. It is time to help the American citizens who have become refugees in their own country.

Infrastructure will be another major goal. My contract calls for 1 trillion dollars in infrastructure investment, of which the inner cities will be a major beneficiary.

I will also cancel all wasteful climate change spending from Obama-Clinton, including all global warming payments to the

United Nations. These steps will save 100 billion dollars over 8 years, and this money will be used to help rebuild the vital infrastructure, including water systems, in America's inner cities.

School choice is at the center of my plan. My proposal redirects education spending to allow every disadvantaged child in America to attend the public, private, charter, magnet, religious or home school of their choice. School choice is the great civil rights issue of our time, and I will be the nation's biggest cheerleader for school choice in all 50 states. I will also appoint a commission to investigate the school-to-prison pipeline and to shut it down and create a new pathway that leads from a great education to a great job. My plan will also ensure funding for Historically Black Colleges and Universities, more affordable 2- and 4-year colleges, and support for trade and vocational education.

Finally, today, my agenda includes the protection of religious liberty, the promotion of family, and support for the African-American church.

This is just the beginning. Because I will never, ever take the African-American community for granted. It will be my mission to prove to this country that yesterday does not have to be tomorrow. The cycle of poverty can be broken, and great new things can happen for our people.

But to achieve this future, we must reject the failed elites in Washington who've been wrong about virtually everything for decades.

The people opposing us promised that passing NAFTA, and opening our markets to China, would bring a new era of prosperity and job creation. Instead, they brought only poverty and heartache.

The people opposing us are the same people who've wasted 6 trillion dollars on wars in the Middle East that have produced only more terrorism, more death, and more suffering—imagine if that money had been spent at home.

My opponent unleashed ISIS on the world. She tried to build democracy in Libya, and failed. She tried to build democracy in Iraq, and failed. She tried regime change in Egypt, and failed. She pressed regime change in Syria, and failed. She tried a Russian reset that failed. She tried an Asia pivot that failed. Now, Hillary

Clinton wants to confront nuclear-armed Russia with a shooting war in Syria that could lead us into World War III.

Finally, our opponents passed a health care law, embraced by Hillary Clinton, over the furious objections of the American voter. Obamacare is now destroying our healthcare system—premiums are skyrocketing double-digits and are surging by more than 100% in the great state of Arizona. Doctors are quitting, insurers are leaving, and companies are fleeing. Every prediction they made about this law was a lie. If we don't repeal and replace this disastrous law, we will lose our healthcare system forever.

Now is the time to embrace a new direction.

I've been very lucky and have led a great life. Now I want to give back to the country which has been so good to me. I just left a hotel on Pennsylvania Avenue in Washington D.C., delivered under budget, and ahead of schedule, creating thousands of jobs, including construction. It will be one of the finest hotels anywhere in the world, and a great symbol for our country. I took two hours to fly into Washington, to cut the ribbon with my children, and then jump on the plane to be here with you. I wanted to be there for my children, who worked so hard on this hotel—parents must stick with, encourage, and support their children. They did a great job on the hotel, and I told them so. Likewise, the workers did a magnificent job—without them, it could never have been built so quickly and so beautifully. The rebuilding we did of the Old Post Office is the rebuilding I want to do for our country.

I want to go into the inner cities, the poor rural communities, and the failing schools, and I want to work on a national plan for revitalization. I'm tired of the excuses from our politicians. I'm tired of being told what can't be done. I'm tired of people asking Americans to defer their dreams to another day, but really another decade.

Enough waiting. The time is now. There is nothing we can't accomplish. There is no task or project too great. There is no dream outside our reach.

Everywhere I go in this country, all I see is untapped potential waiting to be set free. But we will never realize that potential if we continue putting our faith in a broken political system that has let us down time and again. We have to choose the more optimistic path—we have to choose to believe not in our politicians, but to believe in ourselves and in our country. If we do that, anything is possible.

I'm asking America to join me in dreaming big and bold things for our future. Let's close the history books on the failures in Washington, and let's open a new chapter of success and prosperity for everyone.

I am humbled beyond words to be the nominee for the party of Abraham Lincoln. And it is my highest and greatest hope that the Republican Party can be the home of the African-American vote once again.

Together, we will have a government of, by and for the people.

And we will make America great again for all Americans.

Trump's Gettysburg Speech: "The Contract with the American Voter"
October 22, 2016
As transcribed by CNN

Thank you, ladies and gentlemen. Thank you. Please sit down. Thank you. Thank you. It's my privilege to be here in Gettysburg's hallowed ground where so many lives were given in service to freedom. Amazing place.

President Lincoln served in a time of division like we have never seen before. It is my hope that we can look at his example to heal the divisions we are living through right now. We are a very divided nation.

I'm not a politician and have never wanted to be a politician. Believe me. But, when I saw the trouble our country was in, I knew I couldn't stand by and watch any longer. Our country has been so good to me. I love our country and I felt I had to act.

I have seen the system up close and personal for many years. I have been a major part of it. I know how the game works in Washington and on Wall Street. And I know how they have rigged the rules of the game against everyday Americans. The rules are rigged.

Nearly 1 in 4 Americans in their prime earning years isn't even working, 1 in 5 households have no one with a job, 45 million Americans are on food stamps and 47 million are living in poverty. We have failed our inner cities and in so doing have failed our African-American and Hispanic communities.

We have misguided military adventures overseas in wars that go on forever that just cannot be won by the people that are doing it now. They don't know how to win the wars. At home, we have our great veterans dying while waiting for medical care.

Change has to come from outside our very broken system. Our system is broken. The fact that Washington and the Washington establishment has tried so hard to stop our campaign is only more proof that our campaign represents the kind of change that only arrives once in a lifetime.

The system is totally rigged and broken. First, the issue of voter fraud. According to Pew, there are 24 million voter registrations in the United States that are either invalid or significantly inaccurate.

When I say that, there are such inaccuracies it's unbelievable, 1.8 million dead people are registered to vote and some of them are voting. I wonder how that happens, 2.8 million people are registered in more than one state. These are numbers, folks. These are numbers.

Fourteen percent of noncitizens are registered to vote. The system is also rigged because Hillary Clinton should have been precluded from running for the presidency of the United States.

But the FBI and the Justice Department covered up her crimes, which included lying to the FBI and Congress on numerous occasions and included saying I do not recall to the FBI on 39 separate times. She recalls everything else, but 39 separate times, she said, I do not recall. That's a lie, also.

Then there is the deletion of at least 33,000 e-mails after receiving a subpoena from the United States Congress. That's after receiving the subpoena. As an example, it was announced this week that the highly respected four-star general, James Cartwright, may be sentenced up to five years in prison with a massive fine for lying on one occasion to the FBI and he said he did that for national security reasons. Highly respected man. A four-star general.

This took place two days ago. How must he feel? A big part of the rigging of this election is the fact that Hillary is being allowed to run despite having broken so many laws on so many different occasions. Why is she allowed to run?

The dishonest mainstream media is also part and a major part of this corruption. They are corrupt. They lie and fabricate stories to make a candidate that is not their preferred choice look as bad and even dangerous as possible.

At my rallies, they never show or talk about the massive crowd size and try to diminish all of our events. On the other hand, they don't show the small size of Hillary's crowds, but, in fact, talk about how many people are there, very small crowds. You know it, they know it, and everybody knows it.

Over the last two days, three highly respected national polls said we are in first place. And one of those pollsters was the most accurate poll on the last two cycles, but the media refuses to even say it or put that word out.

They refuse to talk about it. They are trying desperately to suppress my vote and the voice of the American people as an example of the power structure I'm fighting, AT&T is buying Time Warner and thus CNN.

A deal we will not approve in my administration because it's too much concentration of power in the hands of too few. Likewise, Amazon, which through its ownership controls "The Washington Post," should be paying massive taxes, but it's not paying.

It's a very unfair playing field and you see what that's doing to department stores all over the country. Very, very unfair and you are talking about billions and billions of dollars they should be paying for taxes.

Additionally, Comcast's purchase of NBC concentrates far too much power in one massive entity that is trying to tell the voters what to think and what to do. Deals like this destroy democracy. We'll look at breaking that deal up and other deals like that.

This should never, ever have been approved in the first place. They've tried to poison the mind of the American voter. Every woman lied when they came forward to hurt my campaign. Total fabrication. The events never happened. Never. All of these liars will be sued after the election is over.

But a simple phone call placed to the biggest newspapers or television networks gets them wall-to-wall coverage with virtually no fact checking whatsoever. Here is why this is relevant to you. If they can fight somebody like me who has unlimited resources to fight back, just look at what they can do to you, your jobs, your security, your education, your health care, the violation of religious liberty, the theft of your second amendment, the loss of your factories, your homes and much more.

Look at what they have done to you with your jobs. It has just been learned, on video, that the violent protests at some of my rallies like in Chicago where police and others were seriously hurt, you saw that blood pouring down their face, were caused by paid DNC and Clinton campaign operatives.

We didn't know this. We didn't know this. This just came out two days ago on tape. We didn't know this. We were amazed at the level of violence. These were paid operatives, paid by the DNC and probably the Clinton campaign.

This is a criminal act. Policemen were badly hurt and so were many others. These people should be prosecuted, but—but because of the rigged system, they probably won't be. Just like we found out about these paid violent protesters, it was probably the DNC and the Clinton campaign that put forward these liars with their fabricated stories.

We'll find out about their involvement at a later date through litigation. I look so forward to doing that. The rigging of the system is designed for one reason, to keep the corrupt establishment and special interests in power at your expense, at everybody's expense. I have no special interests but you, the American voter.

I didn't have to do this, believe me. There's nothing easy about it, but, I had to do it. I love our country, I love the people of our country and I felt I had to do it. Thank you.

One thing we all know is that we will never solve our problems by relying on the same politicians who created these problems in the first place. Hillary Clinton is not running against me, she's running against change and she's running against all of the American people and all of the American voters.

We now find ourselves at that very special fork in the road. Do we repeat the mistakes of the past or do we choose to believe that a great future, yet unwritten, lies ahead for us and for our wonderful, beloved country?

I think it does. I know it does. My economic plan will deliver at least 25 million jobs in one decade. Now, our jobs have been taken away. They have gone to Mexico. They have gone to so many other countries.

It's a one-lane highway where they get the jobs, they get the factories, they get the money, and we get the drugs and we get the unemployment and it's going to change, believe me, it's going to change fast.

That goes for all countries. When you look at China, when you look at every country, every trade deal we have is horrible. We should be ashamed of the people and the people that let those seals happen.

They are defective and they knew they were defective. They were done for a reason and believe me, they will be unwound so fast and we will have trade. We will have great trade and it will be free trade. It will be fair trade and it will be real.

My security plan, so important. They have taken the jobs from us. My security plan will bring safety to our poorest communities. [My] ethics plan will end the corruption in our government. We will—corruption is massive. We will drain the swamp in Washington, D.C., and replace it with a new government of, by and for the people. Believe me.

That is why I have chosen Gettysburg to unveil this contract. I'm asking the American people to rise above the noise and the clutter of our broken politics and to embrace that great faith and optimism that has always been the central ingredient in the American character. There is nothing better or stronger than the American character.

I am asking the American people to dream big, once again. What follows is my 100-day action plan to make America great again. It's a contract between Donald J. Trump and the American voter and it begins with bringing honesty, accountability and change to Washington, D.C.

Therefore, on the first day of my term of office, my administration will immediately pursue the following six measures to clean up the corruption and special interest collusion in Washington.

First, a constitutional amendment to impose term limits on all members of Congress. Second, a hiring freeze on all federal employees to reduce federal work force through attrition, exempting military, public safety and public health.

Third, a requirement that for every new federal regulation, two existing regulations must be eliminated. Regulations are killing our country and our jobs.

Fourth, a five-year ban on White House and congressional officials becoming lobbyists after they leave government service. Making a fortune.

Fifth, a lifetime ban on White House officials lobbying on behalf of a foreign government. Very bad. Six, a complete ban on foreign lobbyists raising money for American elections. It's what's happening.

On the same day, I will begin taking and really taking strongly seven actions to protect American workers. Our American workers have been treated so badly by politicians that don't have their interests at heart.

And we are going to change that. We are going to change that very, very fast. First, I will announce my intention to totally re-negotiate NAFTA. One of the worst deals our country has ever made, signed by Bill Clinton. Withdrawal from the deal under Article 2205. Second, I will announce our withdrawal from the Transpacific Partnership, a potential disaster for our country. Third, I will direct my secretary of the treasury to label China a currency manipulator. China is a currency manipulator. What they have done to us by playing currency is very sad.

I don't blame them, they have been very smart. I blame our politicians for letting this take place. So easy to stop. So easy to stop. Fourth, I will direct the secretary of commerce and U.S. trade representative to identify all foreign trading abuses that unfairly impact American workers and direct them to use every tool under American and international law to end those abuses immediately.

Fifth, very importantly, I will lift the restrictions on the production of 50 trillion dollars' worth of job-producing American energy including shale, oil, natural gas, and clean coal. We will put our miners back to work.

Sixth, I will lift the Obama/Clinton roadblocks that allow for this vital energy infrastructure projects to go forward. We have roadblocks like you have never, ever seen, environmental blocks, structural blocks.

We are going to allow the Keystone pipeline and so many other things to move forward, tremendous numbers of jobs and good for our country.

We are going to cancel billions in payments to the United Nations climate change programs and use the money to fix America's water and environmental infrastructure. We are paying billions and billions and billions of dollars. We are going to fix our own environment.

Additionally, on the first day, I will take the following five actions to restore security and constitutional rule of law. We have to do that. Cancel every unconstitutional executive action, memorandum, and order issued by President Obama.

Second, begin the process of selecting a replacement for Justice Scalia. His wife has a Trump sign, his wife is a phenomenal woman. She has a Trump sign in her front yard. Isn't that nice?

I just found that out this morning. Isn't that nice? From one of the 20 judges of my list, you know we are going to make great decisions from 20 outstanding judges on a list we submitted who will uphold and defend the constitution of the United States.

Third, we will cancel all federal funding of sanctuary cities. Fourth, we will begin removing the more than 2 million criminal illegal immigrants from the country.

These are our drug dealers, gang heads, gang members. . . . And when Hillary Clinton was secretary of state, and they had someone who was bad, really bad.

And they brought them back to the country and the country wouldn't take them, she said bring them back. We won't force the country to take them. There won't be one such instance if I become president, believe me.

We are going to suspend immigration from terror-prone regions where vetting cannot safely occur. If you look at Syria, and the migration, we are taking in thousands and thousands of people into our country. We have no idea who they are, what their thought process is, where they come from.

And Hillary Clinton wants to increase the number of those thousands and thousands currently pouring in by 550 percent. Radical Islamic terror is right around the corner. We have to be so tough, so smart, so vigilant. We can't allow that to happen. We have enough problems.

All vetting of people coming into our country will be considered extreme vetting. We will be very careful. Next, I will work with Congress to introduce the following broader legislative measures and fight for their passage within the first 100 days of my administration.

Middle-class tax relief and simplification act, an economic plan designed to grow the economy 4 percent per year and create at least 25 million new jobs through massive tax reduction and simplification in combination with trade reform, regulatory relief, and lifting the restrictions on American energy.

Need that so badly, jobs, we need jobs. Our jobs have left us. Our good jobs have really left us. The largest tax reductions are for the middle-class who have been forgotten.

The forgotten man and woman, they have been forgotten. The middle-class with family, of two children, will get basically, approximately a 35 percent tax cut. That's what they can use. That money will go back into the economy.

The current number of brackets will be reduced from seven to three. And tax forms will likewise be greatly simplified.

The business rate will be lowered from 35 percent to 15 percent. And the trillions of dollars of American corporate money overseas can be brought back at a 10 percent rate. It stuck. We can't bring it back. 2.5 to 5 trillion dollars. Companies can't get it back into the country. Some companies are actually leaving not only because taxes are so high, but because they can't get their money and they are actually leaving to get their money. We are going to simplify that. We're going to have them bring the money back into our country and use the money and spend the money on building our country.

And the Offshoring Act, established tariffs to discourage companies from laying off their worker in order to relocate in other countries and ship their products back to the United States tax-free. They leave the United States, like Carrier, like Ford, like many others. *They leave the United States. They fire all of their employees. They go to Mexico or another country. They build a beautiful, brand-new plant. They hire other people. They then take their air conditioners, their cars, whatever they are making, they send a tax-free across what will be a very strong border, believe me. But they send it tax-free across the border. And what do we end up with? We have unemployment, tremendous losses. And we have none of the benefits. So, we will establish tariffs, that when they do that there will be consequences. We'll work with them. We'll be nice. We'll be fair. But there have to be consequences. And when they know there are consequences, our companies will stop leaving the United States and going to other countries.*

The American Infrastructure Act, leverages public/private partnerships and private investments through tax incentives to spur 1 trillion dollars in infrastructure investment over the next ten years. Our infrastructure is in such trouble. We've doubled our national debt to 20 trillion dollars under President Obama. In less than eight years, 10 trillion dollars has been added. Think of it. And we haven't fixed anything. We haven't fixed anything. What have we done? Our roads are broken, our bridges, our tunnels, our hospitals, our schools and we have 20 trillion dollars in debt, all-time high. That's true, our V.A. hospitals are in bad shape and our V.A. is in very, very bad shape. And we will fix that. We are going to work on fixing that because our veterans have not been treated properly. We have illegal immigrants that [are] treated far better in many instances than our veterans. And we're not going to have that.

School choice and Education Opportunity Act, redirects education dollars to give parents the right to send their kid, their children to public/private, charter, magnet, religious, or home schools of their choice.

And so importantly, we are going to end common core and bring education supervision to local communities. We do so badly on education. If you look at the lists and you see Sweden, Norway, Denmark, China, different countries at the top, you see us at the bottom. And yet, by far, per pupil, more money than anybody and it's not even close. We spend more money per pupil than anybody, not even close. We're at the bottom of the list. Other countries spending far less per pupil are at the top of the list. So obviously, our current system is not working. We will change it and we will make it good.

It expands vocational and technical education, which we've totally forgotten about in this country and make two- and four-year colleges more affordable. Have you ever gone to school and you've been with people that aren't good students but they can fix an engine or they can build a wall or they can do things that you wouldn't even think about because we can use some of the ones that build a wall. We're going to need them. We're going to need them. We're going to need them.

But, did you ever see that, how they are genius at fixing a car? They can do anything. But history, not so good. Physics, not so good. And we have to open vocational, again. Those are the people. These are great people.

The repeal and replace Obamacare act.

Fully repeal Obamacare and replace it with health savings accounts. And we can do that. The health savings accounts, it's one way, there are numerous ways. But this is one very good way. The ability to purchase health insurance across state lines, which we have to do because that's competition. The politicians won't let go of it because the insurance companies, they don't want competition. But we'll open it up. Believe me. We'll get rid of that. I've been saying it for years. And let states manage Medicaid funds. It will be so good.

Reforms will also include, cutting the red tape at the FDA. There are over 4,000 drugs awaiting approval. And we specially want to speed the approval of life-saving medications. I mean, they're looking at drugs that are looking very good and you have terminal patients that, it's over. These people, they're dying. They want to get the drug. They won't be living much longer. And we study it for years and years. At some point, they have to do what they have to do. They have to do it properly. But we have 4,000 different drugs and products waiting in line for approval and we can't get them approved. We're going to speed up that process very significantly.

Affordable Child Care and Elder Care Act allows Americans

to deduct child care and elder care from their taxes, incentivizes employers to provide on site, so important, child care services. And you see that with a couple of companies and it's such a great thing to see, and creates tax-free dependent care savings of cancer of both young and elderly dependents with matching contributions for low-income families. So good.

And Illegal Immigration Act. Fully funds the construction of a wall on our southern border. Don't worry about it. Remember, I said Mexico is paying for the wall, with the full understanding that the country of Mexico will be reimbursing the United States for the full cost of such a wall, OK? We're going to have the wall. Mexico is going to pay for the wall. Mexico's—by the way I met with the president of Mexico two and a half months ago, wonderful meeting, wonderful person. But I told him, it's a two-way highway, not a one-way highway. We have our people. We have to take care of our people. We have to protect our people. So it's got to be a two-way street, otherwise it's going to be a whole different deal.

But, it establishes a two-year mandatory minimum federal prison sentences if people come in illegally for illegally re-entering the United States after a previous deportation. And a five-year mandatory minimum for illegally re-entering for those with felony convictions, multiple misdemeanor convictions or two or more prior deportations. So, when somebody comes in, we send them out. They come back in, they go to prison for quite a while. If they come back, if they come back again, they go five years. Because what's happening is they're coming back ten times.

And I could go case after case, they come back. Look at what happened in San Francisco. Five times he came back. On the fifth time, he killed Kate, five times. But so many others, one ten times came back, killed somebody after ten times. When they get deported, they stay out. Otherwise, they have very serious prison terms. They will stay out. Once you do that, they will stay out. Right now, they have no consequence. They have no consequences.

Also, reforms on visa rules to enhance penalties for overstaying and to ensure open jobs are offered to American workers first. Number eight. Restoring Community Safety Act, reduces surge in crime, drugs and violence by creating a task force on violent crime, and increasing funding for programs that train and assist your local police. We're doing such a great job. Believe me.

The increase of resources for federal law enforcement agencies and federal prosecutors to dismantle criminal gangs. And put violent offenders behind bars or out of our country and into the country where they came from.

Restoring National Security Act which rebuilds our military, by eliminating the defense sequester, which has been very tough for our military and expanding military investment.

Now, at no time, practically, do we need a military like right now. We don't want to use it. But it's peace through strength. We need a strong military. Our military is so terribly depleted. It also provides our great veterans with the ability to receive public V.A. treatment or attend a private doctor of their choice. If they are waiting in line and I have the plan up. And we've gotten, as you know, tremendous support from veterans, from law enforcement, from veterans, from the military, tremendous support.

But if they are waiting in line and you see 22 suicides a day. People don't believe it, 22 a day. But if they're waiting in line for seven days, six days, nine days, they can't get to see a doctor. And a simple procedure or a simple prescription can solve their problem and they become very sick and they die. They die waiting in line. We're going to give them the power to go across the street, to a local doctor, a private doctor, a public hospital or private hospital, all looking to help and all looking to do business. And we'll pay the bill. So much cheaper, but much more importantly, the veterans will finally be taken care of properly. Because what they're going through now is unacceptable.

Also, we're going to protect our vital infrastructure from the new thing. It's called cyber-attack. It establishes new screen[ing] procedures for immigration to ensure those who are admitted to our country support our people and our values. We want people that love our country or can love our country and people that will love our citizens. We want people that can love us.

And there are ways, through talent, of determining that. And other countries do, but we don't. Just come on in, folks, come on in.

Clean up corruption in Washington, enact tough new ethic reforms to reduce the corrupting influence of special interests and donors on our politics.

On November 8th, Americans will be voting for this 100-day plan to restore prosperity to our country, secure our communities and honesty to our government.

This is my pledge to you. And if we follow these steps, we will once more have a government of, by and for the people. And importantly, we will make America great again. Believe me. Thank you. Thank you. Thank you very much. Thank you.

ENDNOTES

Chapter One: From Queens to the White House

1. www.nydailynews.com/news/politics/donald-trump-entering- 2016-presidential-race-article-1.2259706.
2. www.realclearpolitics.com/epolls/2016/president/us/2016_republican_presidential_nomination-3823.html#polls.
3. www.nytimes.com/2017/02/03/business/lockheed-lowers-price-on-f-35-fighters-after-prodding-by-trump.htm.

Chapter Two: The Four-Sided Table

1. www.people-press.org/2014/06/12/political-polarization-in-the-american-public.
2. www.washingtonpost.com/news/post-politics/wp/2017/01/28/trumps-lobbying-ban-is-both-tougher-and-weaker-than-obamas-rules.
3. http://time.com/3923128/donald-trump-announcement-speech.
4. www.reuters.com/video/2015/09/09/trump-we-are-led-by-very-very-stupid-peo?videoId=365547835.
5. www.raps.org/Regulatory-Focus/News/2017/02/02/26759/Trump-Signals-Support-for-Right-to-Try-Movement.

Chapter Three: Winning, Big League

1. www.military.com/daily-news/2016/11/02/survey-career-oriented-troops-favor-trump-over-clinton.html.

Chapter Four: The Rise of the IYI

1. www.washingtonpost.com/sf/local/2013/11/09/washington-a-world-apart.

Chapter Five: The Propaganda Media

1. www.people-press.org/files/legacy-pdf/427.pdf.
2. www.weeklystandard.com/four-year-honeymoon/article/693769.
3. www.politifact.com/punditfact/statements/2014/jan/10/jake-tapper/cnns-tapper-obama-has-used-espionage-act-more-all-.
4. www.nytimes.com/2016/05/15/us/politics/donald-trump-women.html.
5. www.politico.com/story/2016/05/ex-trump-girlfriend-new-york-times-223205.
6. www.nytimes.com/2014/06/09/us/for-illegal-immigrants-american-life-lived-in-shadows.html.
7. http://pbskids.org/itsmylife/family/immigration/article5.html.
8. www.pewinternet.org/2016/11/11/social-media-update-2016-methodology.
9. www.brandwatch.com/blog/96-amazing-social-media-statistics-and-facts-for-2016.

Chapter Six: Toxic Identity Politics

1. www.psychologytoday.com/blog/culturally-speaking/201112/colorblind-ideology-is-form-racism.
2. www.gallup.com/poll/1687/race-relations.aspx.
3. www.theatlantic.com/magazine/archive/2017/01my-president-was-black/508793.
4. Ibid.

5. www.nytimes.com/2015/10/11/magazine/the-year-we-obsessed-over-identity.html.
6. www.washingtonpost.com/news/in-theory/wp/2015/09/24/why-intersectionality-cant-wait.
7. Ibid.
8. www.nytimes.com/2017/01/09/us/womens-march-on-washington-opens-contentious-dialogues-about-race.html.
9. www.salon.com/2013/04/16/lets_hope_the_boston_marathon_bomber_is_a_white_american.
10. www.salon.com/2015/12/16/white_guys_are_killing_us_toxic_cowardly_masculinity_our_unhealable_national_illness
11. http://heatst.com/culture-wars/thought-catalog-publishes-an-enthusiastic-call-for-white-genocide.
12. www.salon.com/2015/12/22/white_men_must_be_stopped_the_very_future_of_the_planet_depends_on_it_partner/
13. www.salon.com/2015/07/07/the_plague_of_angry_white_men_how_racism_gun_culture_toxic_masculinity_are_poisoning_america_in_tandem.
14. www.buzzfeed.com/pedrofequiere/stop-white-ppl-2015.
15. www.drmartinlutherkingjr.com/wherewearegoing.htm.
16. www.vox.com/2016/4/21/11451378/smug-american-liberalism
17. www.washingtonpost.com/blogs/post-partisan/wp/2015/03/16/lesson-learned-from-the-shooting-of-michael-brown.
18. www.nationaljournal.com/s/32748/emerging-republican-advantage.
19. www.theatlantic.com/politics/archive/2016/07/with-diversity-on-the-left-the-white-working-class-moves-right/493286/
20. www.motherjones.com/politics/2016/11/rust-belt-democrats-saw-trump-wave-coming
21. www.nytimes.com/2016/11/20/opinion/sunday/the-end-of-identity-liberalism.html.
22. www.politico.com/story/2016/11/bernie-sanders-democrats-identity-politics-231710.
23. https://news.grabien.com/story-dnc-chair-candidates-bash-white-people-raciallycharged-foru.
24. www.theatlantic.com/politics/archive/2016/05/can-clinton-win-back-appalachia/480900.
25. http://reason.com/blog/2016/11/29/white-identity-politics-gave-us-trump-bu.

Chapter Seven: The Great Transition

1. https://data.bls.gov/cgi-bin/cpicalc.pl?cost1=12000&year1=1945&year2=2017.
2. http://data.worldbank.org/indicator/NY.GDP.PCAP.CD?locations=US&name_desc=false.
3. www.investopedia.com/articles/economics/08/north-american-free-trade-agreement.asp.
4. http://knowledge.wharton.upenn.edu/article/nafta-20-years-later-benefits-outweigh-costs.
5. www.investopedia.com/articles/economics/08/north-american-free-trade-agreement.asp.

Chapter Nine: The Permanent Opposition

1. https://learning.blogs.nytimes.com/2012/03/02/march-2-1877-rutherford-b-hayes-declared-winner-over-samuel-tilden-in-disputed-presidential-election.
2. www.civilwar.org/education/civil-war-casualties.html.
3. www.people-press.org/2014/06/12/political-polarization-in-the-american-public.
4. www.cnn.com/2017/01/19/politics/trump-inauguration-protests-womens-march.
5. www.kptv.com/story/34310810/bottles-flares-thrown-at-police-during-march-this-is-no-longer-a-peaceful-protest.
6. http://nytlive.nytimes.com/womenintheworld/2017/01/20/billionaire-george-soros-has-ties-to-more-than-50-partners-of-the-womens-march-on-washington.
7. www.aei.org/publication/margaret-thatcher-was-a-powerful-voice-for-free-enterprise-and-liberty.
8. http://thehill.com/homenews/campaign/302817-government-workers-shun-trump-give-big-money-to-clinton-campaign.
9. http://dailycaller.com/2017/01/28/warning-trumps-epa-secretary-will-have-16000-employees-working-against-him.
10. http://time.com/4067019/gallup-horse-race-polling.

Chapter Ten: The Safety Box

1. www.fbi.gov/news/pressrel/press-releases/fbi-releases-2015-crime-statistics.
2. www.fbi.gov/news/pressrel/press-releases/fbi-releases-preliminary-semiannual-crime-statistics-for-2016.
3. www.gallup.com/poll/190475/americans-concern-crime-climbs-year-high.aspx.
4. www.bbc.com/news/world-us-canada-32400497.
5. www.nyc.gov/html/nypd/html/home/poa_crime.shtml.
6. www.reuters.com/article/us-usa-drugs-poppies-idUSBRE96B01920130712.
7. www.latimes.com/nation/la-na-border-apprehensions-20170309-story.html.
8. http://ijr.com/2017/03/822619-i-had-dinner-with-the-afghanistan-ambassador-what-he-said-about-the-differences-between-trump-obama-is-stunning/
9. www.pewresearch.org/fact-tank/2016/10/18/most-americans-trust-the-military-and-scientists-to-act-in-the-publics-interest.

Chapter Eleven: The American Competitiveness Box

1. www.tradingeconomics.com/united-states/balance-of-trade.
2. https://taxfoundation.org/federal-capital-gains-tax-collections-1954-2009.
3. www.bls.gov/bls/news-release/empsit.htm#1997.
4. https://fred.stlouisfed.org/series/MEHOINUSA672N.
5. www.thebalance.com/dow-jones-closing-history-top-highs-and-lows-since-1929-3306174.
6. http://simplifygov.org/wp-content/uploads/2016/12/washingtonpost.com-Six-presidents-have-failed-to-cut-red-tape-Heres-how-Trump-could-succeed-2.pdf.
7. www.bls.gov/news.release/jolts.a.htm#jolts_tablea.f.p.
8. www.curbed.com/2017/2/1/14474716/construction-vocational-training-labor-shortage-homebuilding.
9. www.usatoday.com/story/news/nation/2014/09/30/job-economy-middle-skill-growth-wage-blue-collar/14797413.

Chapter Twelve: The Health Box

1. www.forbes.com/sites/johnlamattina/2015/12/04/
for-hepatitis-c-drugs-u-s-prices-are-cheaper-than-in-europe/#5cc2c0d564bb.
2. J. A. DiMasi, H. G. Grabowski, and R. A. Hansen, "Innovation in the
Pharmaceutical Industry: New Estimates of R&D Costs," *Journal of Health
Economics* 47 (2016): 20–33.
3. Alexander Tabarrok, Christopher-Paul Milne, and Joseph A. DiMasi, *An FDA
Report Card: Wide Variance in Performance Found Among Agency's Drug
Review*, (Manhattan Institute, 2014).
4. www.ncbi.nlm.nih.gov/pmc/articles/PMC5243120.

Chapter Thirteen: The Making-Government-Work Box

1. www.nextgov.com/cio-briefing/2016/09/report-federal-government-has-near-
monopoly-worst-customer-experience/131260.
2. www.people-press.org/2015/11/23/beyond-distrust-how-americans-view-
their-government.
3. www.washingtonpost.com/news/federal-eye/wp/2015/10/30/more-than-2500-
va-employees-were-on-paid-leave-last-year-the-va-hasnt-tracked-why.
4. www.usatoday.com/story/news/nation/2015/05/06/ousted-phoenix-va-chief-
lawsuit/70889960.
5. www.azcentral.com/story/news/arizona/investigations/2016/01/08/
suspended-va-bosses-return-phoenix-jobs-january-11/78517854; www.
azcentral.com/story/news/local/arizona-investigations/2016/06/08/
three-more-phoenix-va-officials-fired-after-wait-time-scandal/85614056.
6. www.federaltimes.com/story/government/management/oversight/2016/06/09/
va-fires-phoenix-execs-after-2-years-investigations/85643224.
7. https://www.reviewjournal.com/uncategorized/
nevada-rep-titus-calls-for-investigation-of-veterans-affairs-job-moves/.
8. http://pittsburgh.cbslocal.com/2014/10/03/va-wants-to-remove-pittsburgh-
hospitals-director.
9. http://www.thetowntalk.com/story/news/2017/02/22/va-employee-suspended-
years-after-death-patient/98259530/
10. http://dailycaller.com/2016/04/08/va-candy-man-may-keep-his-job-despite-
no-medical-license.
11. www.clarionledger.com/story/news/2016/02/13/taxpayers-pay-millions-
to-keep-questionable-va-doctors-on-leave/79659046.
12. Ibid.
13. https://oversight.house.gov/wp-content/uploads/2014/07/Sherk-Statement-IRS-
Abuses-7-30.pdf.
14. http://dailysignal.com/2016/06/16/government-rates-99-of-federal-employees-
fully-successful-or-higher.
15. www.fedview.opm.gov/2016FILES/2016_FEVS_Gwide_Final_Report.PDF.

ACKNOWLEDGMENTS

Understanding Trump has been a fascinating book to think through and write.

Without President Trump's generous willingness to talk about issues and policies, first as a candidate and then as president-elect and president, this book would have been implausible. As I listened to Trump and watched him make decisions, I really began to understand his principles and patterns. I'd like to thank President Trump for his leadership, and for the many enlightening conversations we've shared.

Similarly, I want to acknowledge and thank Don Jr., Ivanka, Eric, Tiffany, and Barron for their openness and willingness to be a part of their father's campaign and presidency. My understanding of what a strong and caring father Trump is came directly from his children. I also want to thank Melania for all she has personally done to bring beauty and grace to the White House. She is clearly in the Jackie Kennedy tradition and a first lady of whom we can all be proud.

Jared Kushner's openness in the campaign and since has been tremendously helpful. He is remarkably focused, practical, and committed to getting real work done.

On every occasion, Rhona Graff, Trump's remarkable senior vice president, has been extremely helpful. I would also like to thank Meredith McIver from the Trump Organization for her assistance.

There have been several close friends on both the campaign team and White House staff who have helped me better understand how the Trump system works. Corey Lewandowski was a real leader of the early campaign. He implemented Trump's design and got an amazing amount done. Paul Manafort was easy to work with and did a great job at the Republican convention. The team of Steve Bannon, Kellyanne Conway, and David Bossie provided extra punch and energy when it was desperately needed. Brad Parscale did a great job with data and social media and was one of the hidden strengths of the campaign.

Stephen Miller may have been the most heroic figure in the campaign other than Trump himself. Day after day, Stephen sat a few feet behind Trump on the airplane writing speech after speech. He is the philosopher-writer of the Trump team and continues in this role at the White House.

Despite the Trump campaign's heroic efforts, victory could not have been achieved without Reince Priebus's six years of hard work as the chairman of the Republican National Committee. With Mike Shields, Katie Walsh, and Sean Spicer, Reince built the largest party machine in Republican history. In October 2016 he had 8,500 paid staff providing organizational muscle to turn out voters on election day.

Joe Gaylord was my partner in our sixteen-year effort to grow the first House Republican majority in forty years. He applied these experiences to help me understand the Trump phenomenon.

Barry Casselman was the first to point out that real change was coming to the upper Midwest and that Iowa, Wisconsin, and Minnesota were in play. Salena Zito was similarly perceptive about the shift in western Pennsylvania.

Sean Hannity was both Trump's biggest booster and his most perceptive critic. Again and again he helped me understand what was happening in the campaign and what it meant.

Rayna Casey, a close friend and supporter, was the first person to bring the importance of Wollman Rink to my attention. As a businesswoman, she really understood Trump's skill as an entrepreneur in politics.

Vince Haley, then at Gingrich Productions and now writing in the White House, was the other person who very early on said, "This is a really smart guy who is doing something unique." Vince had lived through Dave Brat's stunning defeat of Eric Cantor and has a real sense of the underlying power of grassroots populism.

Vince, and his partner in writing, Ross Worthington, volunteered to work with Stephen Miller throughout the fall campaign and somehow never made it back to Gingrich Productions. They are energetically ensconced in the Eisenhower Executive Office Building, writing seven days a week.

Randy Evans, my adviser, friend, and supporter since 1976, was helpful throughout the two-year campaign. As Georgia Republican National Committeeman, he was intimately involved in the convention and in making sure that Trump won the majority of delegates. His strategic advice was remarkably helpful, and the concept of a book called *Understanding Trump* came from him.

My two daughters, Kathy Lubbers and Jackie Cushman, have grown up in politics and are very perceptive observers of the process. We had a running dialogue about the nomination and election process, and it has continued through the transition and the presidency.

Kate Hartson at Hachette has become a good friend and fellow enthusiast, and she is a great editor. This is our fifth book together, and it is a joy to work with her and the Hachette team.

Joe DeSantis and Louie Brogdon have been my primary collaborators in thinking through and writing *Understanding Trump*.

They started with my eight speeches on Trump at the Heritage Foundation and my speech on Trump at the National Defense University, and developed the first draft of the book. They have been great partners.

Ed Feulner, the founder of the Heritage Foundation, and Jim DeMint, its current leader, have both been helpful in allowing me to develop my thoughts in a series of lectures at Heritage.

Finally, all of this has been made possible through the support of our outstanding team at Gingrich Productions. Callista has driven the overall system as president. Her enthusiastic participation and encouragement have made this project fun and fulfilling. Bess Kelly has been our indispensable chief coordinator and implementer. Woody Hales has managed our very complex schedule. Christina Maruna has overseen our two million Twitter followers and 985,000 Facebook followers. John Hines has helped keep a variety of projects moving forward. Audrey Bird has executed our product marketing. And Taylor Swindle has reviewed and administered our contracts and finances. Together they have been a remarkable team.

ABOUT THE AUTHOR

NEWT GINGRICH is a former Speaker of the House and 2012 presidential candidate. He is a Fox News contributor and author of 35 books, including 15 *New York Times* bestsellers. Newt and his wife, Callista, host and produce documentary films. Recent films include *The First American* and *Nine Days That Changed the World*.